A *Golden Hands* PATTERN BOOK

KNITTING

A Golden Hands PATTERN BOOK

KNITTING

RANDOM HOUSE   NEW YORK

Library of Congress Cataloging in Publication Data
Knitting: a Golden hands pattern book.
Originally published under title: The Golden hands
book of knitting.
"The greater part of the material published in this book
was first published . . . in 'Golden hands.'"
1. Knitting—Patterns.   I. Golden hands.
TT820.G74   1973   746.4'3   72-11420
ISBN 0-394-48549-1

Manufactured in the United States of America
First American Edition

CONTENTS

About this book . . .

Here is a special collection of garments for every member of your family and a variety of colorful and original items to enhance your home.
There are layettes and playsuits for babies, fashionable sweaters and dresses for mothers and daughters, smart cardigans and ties for dads, and cheerful tablecloths, curtains and bedcovers for the house.
The collection is technically definitive, too. It should encourage the beginner and challenge the expert.
If you are a newcomer to the art of knitting, then turn to our Crash Course on page 121 which will lead you to that stage of confidence and skill in which you can tackle everything in the book. We suggest that you start with one of the simple items and then move on to the more complicated designs.
Knitting can be a totally absorbing and worthwhile hobby—even more so when it involves those nearest to you. Knitting can save you money, delight those who receive the finished articles and provide a satisfying creative outlet for your leisure time.

Photographs by Camera Press Femina Design, 29, 35, 36, 39. GMN, 18, 38, 45, 46, 57, 58, 59. Kamerabild, 27, 28, 32. Jan Ralf, 48. Lars Larsson, 50. Bo Appeltofft, 68. Svante Stostedt, 25. Stephen Hiett, 30, 31, 41. Sandra Lousada, 49. Jim Williams, 1. Simis Press, 14, 15, 16, 17, 19, 21, 23, 24, 26, 33, 37, 40, 44, 47, 52, 61, 66. Chris Lewis, 64, 65, 67, 70, 74, 72, 73. Peter Pugh Cook, 55. Mahoney, 20. Pingouin, 62, 63, 74, 75.

Diagrams by: Barbara Firth
              Paul Williams
              Trevor Laurence

YARNS AND GAUGES

Yarn colors and qualities vary from year to year. If you have a problem in obtaining a particular yarn, you should be able to use an alternative. However, you may find that the number of ounces, or balls, varies slightly.

The specially compiled chart on page 8 gives the gauges used for the yarns recommended in the patterns of this book. You may substitute one yarn for another within each group.

First, make sure that the yarn you plan to use for your garment knits to the right gauge. Knit a small gauge square— for example 4 inches by 4 inches—in the yarn of your choice. Check that you get the same number of stitches and rows to the inch (or 2 or 3 inches) as given in the pattern. The needle size is only a guide. You may need to use a needle size smaller or one larger than suggested, as some people knit loosely; others, tightly.

It's difficult to judge how to count, say, $3\frac{1}{2}$ stitches or $4\frac{1}{2}$ stitches to the inch. Therefore, it's always best to count stitches over 4 inches and then divide by 4. (For example, $3\frac{1}{2}$ sts $\times$ 4 over 1 in $=14$ sts over 4in.) If you're working with even half a stitch to the inch too few or too many, the finished garment will be too small or too large. Remember, always double check with a gauge square. In some cases, similar yarns knit to the same number of stitches to the inch, but the number of rows may be slightly different. You should be able to adjust garment lengths to your own requirements.

An extra tip: keep the dye lot number handy just in case you require more yarn to finish your work.

KNITTING NEEDLE SIZES

American	British	French
0	2	14
—	—	13
1	2.50	12
2	3.00	11
3	3.25	10
4	3.50	—
5	4.00	9
6	4.50	8
7	4.75	7
8	5.00	6
9	5.50	5
10	6.00	4
$10\frac{1}{2}$	7.00	3
11	8.00	2
13	9.25	1

Spinners' Addresses

In case of difficulty in obtaining any yarns featured in this book, please write directly to the following manufacturers to find out the location of your nearest retailer.

Bernat yarns by—
Emile Bernat & Sons Co.
Uxbridge, Massachusetts 01579

Bear Brand, Botany, Bucilla &
Fleisher yarns by—
Bernhard Ulmann Co.
Division of Indian Head
30-20 Thomson Avenue
Long Island City, New York 11101

Brunswick yarns by—
Brunswick Worsted Mills Inc.
Pickens, South Carolina 29671

Columbia-Minerva yarns by—
Columbia-Minerva Corp.
295 Fifth Avenue
New York, New York 10016

Dawn & **American Thread** yarns by—
American Thread
High Ridge Park
Stamford, Connecticut 06905

Reynolds yarns by—
Reynolds Yarns Inc.
215 Central Avenue
East Farmingdale, New York 11735

Spinnerin yarns by—
Spinnerin Yarn Co. Inc.
230 Fifth Avenue
New York, New York 10001

Unger yarns by—
William Unger & Co
230 Fifth Avenue
New York, New York 10001

GAUGE CHART

Gauge group 1

Gauge	Yarns
3½ sts on No.10½ needles	
4 sts on No.7 needles	Bear Brand or Fleisher — Four Seasons; Reynolds — Irish Fisherman
4 sts on No.10 needles	Unger — Regatta
4 sts on No.11 needles	Bernat — Jaegar Mohair-Spun
4½ sts on No.7 needles	Spinnerin — Wintuk Fingering
4½ sts on No.9 needles	Botany — Jiffy
5 sts on No.4 needles	Bernat — Venetian Highlights
5 sts on No.5 needles	Bernat — Les Bouquets; Unger — Les Bouquets
5 sts on No.6 needles	Bernat — Venetian; Reynolds — Gleneagles
5 sts on No.8 needles	Bernat — Berella Germantown
5½ sts on No.4 needles	Spinnerin — Wintuk Sport
5½ sts on No.5 needles	Reynolds — Danksyarn; Spinnerin — Mona; Unger — Les Bouquets
5¾ sts on No.5 needles	Unger — Les Coraux

Gauge group 2

Gauge	Yarns
6 sts on No.4 needles	Bernat — Nylo Sports; Botany — Winsome Souffle; Dawn — Wintuk Baby Yarn; Reynolds — Cascatelle Kermese; Spinnerin — Wintuk Fingering; Unger — Les Bouquets
6 sts on No.5 needles	Bear Brand or Fleisher; Botany — Twin-Pak Knitting Worsted; Columbia-Minerva — Featherweight Knitting Worsted, Wintuk Sports; Reynolds — Classique; Spinnerin — Wintuk Fingering
6½ sts on No.4 needles	Columbia-Minerva — Featherweight Knitting; Reynolds — Cashmere Lamb
6½ sts on No.5 needles	Columbia-Minerva — Featherweight Knitting Worsted
6½ sts to 2ins on No.9 needles	Coats of Clark's O.N.T. "Speed-Cro-Sheen"
7 sts on No.3 needles	Brunswick — Fairhaven Fingering Yarn; Coats and Clark's O.N.T. "Speed-Cro-Sheen"; Columbia-Minerva — Featherweight Knitting Worsted; Spinnerin — Mona
7 sts on No.4 needles	Botany — Win Sport; Columbia-Minerva — Nantuk Fingering Yarn; Unger — English Crepe

Gauge group 3

Gauge	Yarns (American Thread)
	American Thread — Puritan Bedspread Cotton
7½ sts on No.2 needles	
7½ sts on No.3 needles	Bear Brand or Fleisher — Ever-match Baby Zephyr, Win-Sport; Reynolds — Parfait
7½ sts to 3in on No.3 needles	Dawn — Wintuk Baby Yarn
7½ sts to 2in on No.9 needles	Unger — Regatta
8 sts on No.6 needles	Reynolds — Gleneagles
9 sts on No.5 needles	Spinnerin — Wintuk Featherlon
9 sts to 2in on No.6 needles	Bernat — Venetian; Reynolds — Irish Fisherman Yarn
9 sts to 2in on No.8 needles	Bear Brand or Fleisher; Botany — Shamrock
9 sts to 2in on No.10 needles	Bernat — Berella Germantown
10½ sts to 2in on No.6 needles	Bear Brand or Fleisher; Botany — Twin-Pak

75 designs for the family

1

Here is the most original and appealing baby set to appear for years—"patchwork" bell bottoms teamed with a pullover sporting striped epaulettes and armbands. The mock patchwork is most effective and yet quite simple to work.

Knit
Sizes : to fit 18 [20 : 22] inch chest.

2,3

Baby sacque in open-work pattern edged with garter stitch (above).

Knit
Size: to fit 18 [19] inch chest.

Arrowhead eyelet pattern gives a lively texture to this sacque (below).

Knit
Size: to fit 18 [19] inch chest.

4

Double seed stitch gives the pixie cap and jacket of this set a crisp texture. Leggings and mittens are in stockinette stitch.

Knit
Sizes: to fit 18 [20:22] inch chest.

5

Long-sleeved rompersuit with ridged bodice—
pants button at crotch.
Matching cardigan.

Knit
Sizes: to fit 18 [20:22:24]
inch chest.

6,7

Back buttoned cardigan (left) with lace trimmed neck edge.

Knit
Sizes: to fit 20 [22]
inch chest.

Garter stitch pullover (right) with lace edged yoke.

Knit
Sizes: to fit 17 [20:23]
inch chest.

8

Long-sleeved zippered
jumpsuit and
matching hat.

Knit
Sizes: to fit 18 [20:
22:24] inch chest.

9

A pretty dress, with a beautiful lacy stitch used for the short sleeves, skirt and center front It buttons up at the back.

Knit
Sizes: to fit 16|18 [20|22] inch chest.

10

Tinker-ball—a large knitted ball with a bell inside. Each of the six sections can be worked in 2 colors making 12 colors in all.

Knit
Diameter: 18 inches.

11

The brightest bathrobe in town for little boys and girls—made in a marvelous Fair Isle pattern with soft, knitting worsted weight yarn which comes in pretty pastel colors. (If you shorten the length it also makes a great cardigan.)

Knit
Sizes : to fit 20 [22:24] inch chest.

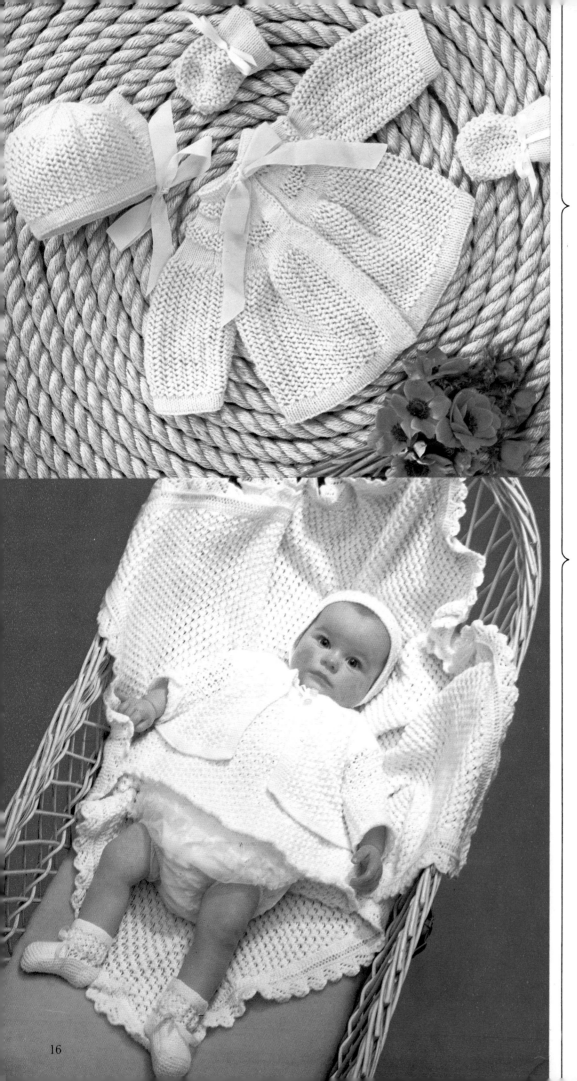

12

*Yoked sacque
worked in eyelet ridge
stitch, with matching
bonnet and mittens, all
trimmed with bows.*

*Knit
Sizes: to fit 18 [19]
inch chest.*

13

*This layette in bramble
stitch includes dress,
sacque, bonnet,
bootees and shawl.*

*Knit
Size: to fit 18 [20] inch
chest.
Shawl: 36 inches
square.*

Perfect for holidays this all-in-one shorts suit zippers up the front, and is edged with single crochet with contrasting color.

Knit
Sizes: to fit 22 [24:26] inch chest.

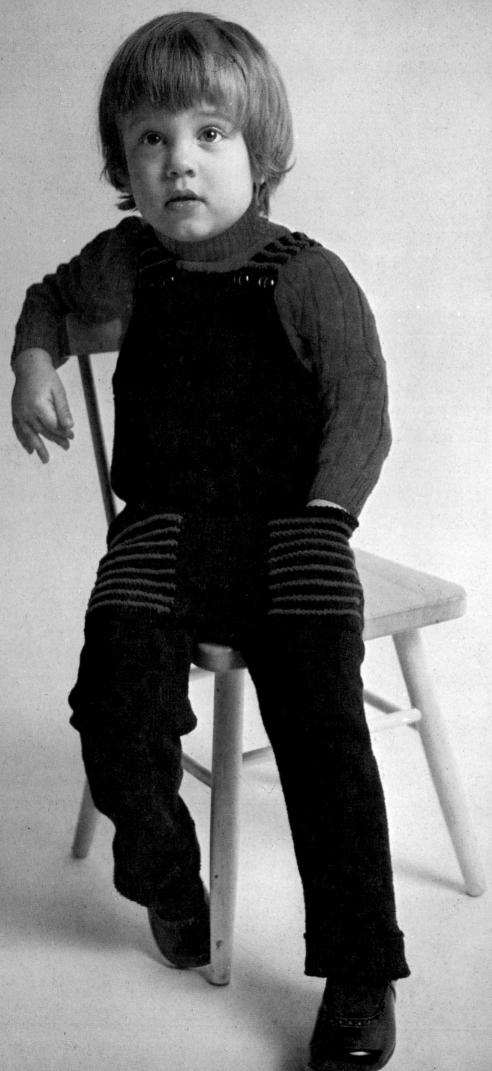

15

Practical and striking pullover and trousers with dungaree top and big striped pockets. The pullover is worked in wide rib and the dungarees in stockinette stitch.

Knit
Sizes: to fit 22 [24:26] inch chest.

16

*Fringed and braided
vest—warm and gay.
Knitted in stockinette
stitch and trimmed with
a crochet fringe and
picot edge. (Directions
for pullover not included.)*

Knit
*Sizes: to fit 24 [26:28]
inch chest.*

17

Crisp cotton knitted dress with narrow bands of contrasting color. The crocheted collar is trimmed with a tie bow.

Knit
Sizes: to fit 22 [24:26] inch chest.

18

Simple and delightful jumpsuit. The short sleeves are worked in wide two-color stripes and the two pockets have matching stripes.

Knit
Sizes: to fit 22 [24] inch chest.

19

Classic pullover in simple three-color Jacquard design, shown twice.

Knit
Sizes: to fit 26 [28:30:32] inch chest.

20

Hardy and warm Aran pullover with V or round neck and raglan sleeves. Worked in cables and lattice stitches.

Knit
Sizes: to fit 20 [22:24] inch chest.

21

A warm snow set. The pullover and hat have patterned inserts, the pants and warm mittens in solid color.

Knit
Sizes: to fit 24 [26:28:30] inch chest.

22

An eye-catching pullover with a 'Policeman' motif. Fun to make and wear. Or you can make this pullover in one color only —if you do, allow one extra ball of the main color.

Knit
Sizes: to fit 26 [28:30:32:34] inch chest.

23

A sport set of pullover, trousers, cap and mittens. The pullover, cap and mittens are worked in double seed stitch, the trousers in stockinette stitch.

Knit
Sizes : to fit 24 [26:28: 30] inch chest.

24

Bulky pullover, worked in broken basket stitch, with unusual raglan shaping and turned-down buttoned collar.

Knit
Sizes : to fit 24 [26:28: 30:32] inch chest.

25

Classic double-breasted pants suit. Worked in panels of single rib and stockinette stitch the jacket has a classic collar and the pants flare gently.

Knit
Sizes: to fit 28 [30:32:34] inch chest.

26

Casual pants suit for the fashion conscious. The long line pullover is worked in panels of mock cable stitch and the flared pants are in stockinette stitch.

Knit
Sizes: to fit 24 [26:28: 30:32:34] inch chest.

27

Teenage dress with a
bold two-color motif on
the center front of the
bodice. It has wide-
ribbed skirt and a round
neckline.

Knit
Sizes : to fit 32 [34:36]
inch chest.

28

Long-line cardigan with
a simple two-color
diamond motif on the
pockets and on the
matching hat.

Knit
Sizes : to fit 30 [32:34]
inch chest.

29

There's a wide range of
sizes in this
elegant lace-panelled
overblouse and matching,
cleverly shaped skirt.

Knit
Sizes 34-42 inch bust.

30

A jaunty beret
and scarf to cheer you
in even the very coldest
Winter wind.

Knit
Size Average head.

31

A skinny weskit
to make with or without
sleeves. The matching
hat completes the outfit.
Shown here in tweed
and solid colors.

Knit
Sizes 32-40 inch bust.
Average head.

32

Left : Simple to make—
great fun to wear. A gay
two-piece dress, with
contrasting striped yoke.

Knit
Sizes 34-38 inch bust.

33

Right : Striped maxi or
long, sleeveless
cardigan—wear it as you
will. Finish the edging
with a crochet border.

Knit
Sizes 32-40 inch bust.

*Colorful candy stripes,
a neat collar and ribbed
cuffs—all add up to a
bold, well-shaped shirt.*

Knit
Sizes 34-42 inch bust.

35

*Comfortably casual in
a plain pullover, topped
with a matching
striped cardigan. Gay in
bold contrasting colors;
chic in subtle colors
as shown here.*

Knit
Sizes 32-40 inch bust.

36

Just unfasten the laced front of this tunic before you put it on, and even the most elaborate hair-do will survive! The set-in sleeves are delightfully bell-shaped. All in all, the prettiest tunic yet.

*Knit
Sizes 32-40 inch bust.*

37

Far right Cable and rib panels for a casual, country look, with an interesting saddle-top shoulder. Add two stripes of color at the neck and cuffs, and you've a smart coordinate to match with either skirt or pants.

*Knit
Sizes 32-40 inch bust.*

38

Left Summer flattery in a delightful boat-neck. Cotton bouclé and a textured stockinette stitch go to make up this useful lightweight pullover.

*Knit
Sizes 32-42 inch bust.*

39

Right Applied smocking on bell sleeves is the outstanding feature of this eye-catching two-piece. The dress has a high ribbed collar, and the buttoned jacket is edged with single crochet.

*Knit
Sizes 32-38 inch bust.*

40

Superb styling for town or country. An overblouse suit with turtleneck, and a midi-skirt you can knit to any length.

*Knit
Sizes 34-40 inch bust.*

41

Traditional Aran stitches, a shaped waist, and slits front and back make this a tunic with a new look.

Knit
Sizes 34-42 inch bust.

Instructions for designs 1-41

"Patchwork" bell bottoms and epaulette pullover

Sizes
Pullover to fit 18[20:22]in chest
The figures in brackets [] refer to the 20 and 22in sizes respectively
Length at center back, 10½[11½:12½]in, adjustable
Sleeve seam, 7[8:9]in, adjustable
Bell bottoms length to back waist, 17[18:19]in
Inside leg length, 9[10:11]in
Gauge
7½sts and 9½ rows to 1 in over st st worked on No.3 needles
Materials
Reynolds Parfait 3[3:4] balls main color, A
1 ball each of contrast colors, B, C, D, E and F
No.3 knitting needles
No.2 knitting needles
4[4:5]in zipper
Waist length ¾in wide elastic
Stitch holder
Note
Separate balls of yarn are used for each color. Always twist yarns at back of work when changing colors.
Color sequence of each patch may be varied if desired.

Bell bottoms

Patchwork patt is worked over 24[27:30] sts.
1st patch (one color only)
1st row Using A, K to end.
2nd row Using A, P to end.
Rep these 2 rows 14[15:16] times more. 30[32:34] rows.
2nd patch
1st row K12[13:15]D, K12[14:15]E.
2nd row P12[14:15]E, P12[13:15]D.
Rep these 2 rows 6 times more.
15th row Using F, K to end.
16th row Using F, P to end.
Rep last 2 rows 0[1:2] times more.
Next row K12[13:15]A, K12[14:15]B.
Next row P12[14:15]B, P12[13:15]A.
Rep last 2 rows 6 times more. 30[32:34] rows.
3rd patch
1st row Using C, K to end.
2nd row Using C, P to end.
Rep these 2 rows 4 times more.
11th row K8[9:10]D, 8[9:10]E, 8[9:10]F.
12th row P8[9:10]F, 8[9:10]E, 8[9:10]D.
Rep these 2 rows 9[10:11] times more. 30[32:34] rows.
4th patch
1st row Using A, K to end.
2nd row Using A, P to end.
Rep these 2 rows 14[15:16] times more. 30[32:34] rows. Work subsequent patches using B, C, D, E and F.
5th patch
1st row K10[11:12]B, 4[5:6]C, 10[11:12]D.
2nd row P10[11:12]D, 4[5:6]C, 10[11:12]B.

Rep these 2 rows 5 times more.
13th row Using C, K to end.
14th row Using C, P to end.
Rep last 2 rows 2[3:4] times more.
Next row K10[11:12]E, 4[5:6]C, 10[11:12]F.
Next row P10[11:12]F, 4[5:6]C, 10[11:12]E.
Rep last 2 rows 5 times more. 30[32:34] rows.

Right leg front

Using No.3 needles and A, cast on 28[31:34] sts. Beg with a K row work 7 rows st st for hem.
Next row K all sts tbl to form hemline.
Work 1st, 2nd, 3rd, 4th and 5th patch patts, dec one st at beg of 9th and every foll 4th row 4 times in all. 24[27:30] sts.
Cont in patt without shaping until 60th[64th: 68th] row has been worked.
Keeping patt correct, inc one st at beg of next and every foll 4th row 6 times in all. 30[33:36] sts.
Cont in patt until 82nd[88th:94th] row has been worked, noting that extra sts are worked in first block of color.
Shape crotch
Keeping patt correct, bind off 2sts at beg of next row. Work 1 row.
Dec one st at beg of next row; then every other row 4 times in all. 24[27:30]sts.
Cont in patt without shaping until 142nd [152nd:162nd] row has been worked.
Using A, work 6 rows K1, P1 rib. Bind off loosely in rib.

Right leg side

Using No.3 needles and A, cast on 32[35:38] sts. Work hem as given for front.
Work 4th, 5th, 2nd, 1st and 3rd patch patts, shaping side on 9th row, as foll:
1st dec row K14[15:17] sts, K2 tog, K0[1:0], sl 1, K1, psso, K14[15:17] sts.
Work 3 rows patt without shaping.
2nd dec row K13[14:16] sts, K2 tog, K0[1:0], sl 1, K1, psso, K13[14:16] sts.
Work 3 rows patt without shaping.
3rd dec row K12[13:15] sts, K2 tog, K0[1:0], sl 1, K1, psso, K12[13:15] sts.
Work 3 rows patt without shaping.
4th dec row K11[12:14] sts, K2 tog, K0[1:0], sl 1, K1, psso, K11[12:14] sts. 24[27:30] sts.
Cont in patt without shaping until 143rd [153rd:163rd] row has been worked, ending with a K row.
Shape back (short rows)
** **Next row** Patt to last 8[9:10] sts, turn.
Next row Patt to end.
Next row Patt to last 16[18:20] sts, turn.
Next row Patt to end.
Next row Patt across all sts.
Using A, work 6 rows K1, P1 rib. Bind off loosely in rib.**

Right leg back

Cast on and work hem as given for front.
Work 3rd, 1st, 5th, 2nd and 4th patch patts, dec one st at end of 9th and every foll 4th row 4 times in all, noting that extra sts are worked in last block of color. 24[27:30] sts.
Cont in patt until 60th[64th:68th] row has been worked.
Keeping patt correct, inc one st at end of next and every other row 10 times in all. 34[37:40] sts.
Cont in patt until 83rd[89th:95th] row has been worked, noting that extra sts will be worked in last block of color, ending with a K row.

Shape crotch
Keeping patt correct, bind off 2sts at beg of next row. Work 1 row.
Dec one st at beg of next and every other row 8 times in all. 24[27:30] sts.
Cont in patt until 149th[159th:169th] row has been worked, ending with a K row.

Shape back
Work as given for side from ** to **, continuing 4th patch.

Left leg

Work as for Right leg front, right leg side and right leg back; reversing all shaping.

Finishing

Press each piece on WS under a damp cloth with a warm iron. Darn in ends. Join 3 Right leg sections tog, including hem and waist ribbing. Join Left leg in same way. Press seams. Join inner leg seams. Join backs and fronts from crotch to waist, including ribbing. Press seams. Turn hem to WS at hemline and sl st in place. Turn waist ribbing to WS and sl st in place. Run elastic through waistband and secure.

Pullover back

Using No.2 needles and A, cast on 72[80:88] sts.
Work 10[12:14] rows K1, P1 rib. Change to No.3 needles. Beg with a K row cont in st st until work measures 7[7¾:8½]in from beg, or desired length to underarm, ending with a P row.

Shape armholes
Bind off 3[4:5] sts at beg of next 2 rows.

Divide for back opening
Next row K2 tog, K31[34:37] sts, turn.
Complete right shoulder first.
Dec one st at armhole edge on every other row until 28[30:32] sts rem.
Cont without shaping until armhole measures 3½[3¾:4]in from beg, ending at armhole edge.

Shape shoulder
Next row Bind off 16[17:18] sts, work to end.
Slip sts on holder for back neck.
With RS of work facing, attach yarn to rem sts and complete to correspond to first side, reversing shaping.

Pullover front

Work as given for back, omitting back opening, until front measures 6 rows less than back to shoulder, ending with a P row.

Shape neck
Next row K22[23:24] sts, turn. Complete left shoulder first.
Bind off 3sts at neck edge every other row twice.
Work until front measures same as back to shoulder, ending at armhole edge.

Shape shoulder
Next row Bind off 16[17:18] sts. Fasten off.
With RS of work facing, sl next 12[14:16] sts onto holder and leave for center neck. Attach yarn to rem sts and complete to correspond to first side, reversing shaping.

Sleeves

Using No.2 needles and A, cast on 38[40:42] sts.
Work 10[12:14] rows K1, P1 rib. Change to No.3 needles.
Work 30[32:34] rows patt as given for 1st patch, then cont in st st using A only, inc one st at each end of 7th and every foll 8th row until there are 46[50:54] sts. Cont without shaping until sleeve measures 7[8:9]in from beg, or desired length to underarm, ending with a P row.

Shape cap
Bind off 3[4:5] sts at beg of next 2 rows. Dec one st at each end of next and every other row until 32sts rem. Work 1 row. Dec one st each end of every row until 10sts rem. Work 2¼[2½:2¾]in patt as given for 1st patch on these 10sts. Bind off.

Neckband

Press each piece as given for Bell bottoms. Sew sleeves into armholes, joining saddle top of sleeves to back and front shoulders. Using No.2 needles and A and with RS neck facing, K across 12[13:14]sts for left back neck, pick up and K 8sts across left sleeve top, pick up and K 10sts down left side of neck, K across 12[14:16]sts on center front holder, pick up and K 10sts up right side of neck, pick up and K 8sts across right sleeve top and K12[13:14]sts from right back neck holder. 72[76:80]sts. Work 1½[1¾:2]in K1, P1 rib. Bind off loosely in rib.

Finishing

Join side and sleeve seams. Press seams. Fold neckband in half to WS and sl st in place. Sew in zipper to back neck to top of neckband.

2 *Baby sacque patterned in openwork stitch*

Sizes
To fit 18[19]in chest
The figures in brackets [] refer to the 19in size
Length to center back, 9½[10¼]in
Sleeve seam, 5¾[6½]in

Gauge
7½sts and 9½ rows to 1in over patt worked on No.3 needles;
7sts and 10 rows to 1in over lace patt worked on No.3 knitting needles

Materials
Bear Brand Ever-Match Baby Zephyr
3[4] balls
No.3 knitting needles
No.1 knitting needles
Three small buttons

Sacque back

Using No.3 needles cast on 123[135] sts.
K 9 rows garter st (g st). Commence patt.
1st row (RS) K to end.
2nd row P to end.
3rd row K7, *ytf, K2 tog tbl, K10, rep from * to last 8sts, ytf, K2 tog tbl, K6.
4th row P to end.
5th row K5, *K2 tog, ytf, K1, ytf, K2 tog tbl, K7, rep from * to last 10sts, K2 tog, ytf, K1, ytf, K2 tog tbl, K5.
6th row P to end.
7th row K to end.
8th row P to end.
9th row K13, *ytf, K2 tog tbl, K10, rep from * to last 2 sts, K2.
10th row P to end.
11th row K11, *K2 tog, ytf, K1, ytf, K2 tog tbl, K7, rep from * to last 4 sts, K4.
12th row P to end.
These 12 rows form patt. Cont in patt until work measures 5½[6]in from beg, ending with a WS row.
Next row K5[1] sts, *K2 tog, rep from * 55[63] times more, K6[6] sts. 67[71] sts.
K 3 rows g st.

Shape armholes
Next row Bind off 3[4] sts, K to end.
Next row Bind off 3[4] sts, P to end.
Next row K2 tog, K10[11], *ytf, K2 tog tbl, K10, rep from * to last 13[14] sts, ytf, K2 tog tbl, K9[10], K2 tog.
Next row P to end.
Next row K2 tog, K7[8], *K2 tog, ytf, K1, ytf, K2 tog tbl, K7, rep from * to last 14[15] sts, K2 tog, ytf, K1, ytf, K2 tog tbl, K7[8], K2 tog.
Next row P to end.
Next row K2 tog, K to last 2 sts, K2 tog.
Next row P to end.
Next row K3[4], *ytf, K2 tog tbl, K10, rep from * to last 4[5] sts, ytf, K2 tog tbl, K2[3].
Next row P to end.
Next row K1[2], *K2 tog, ytf, K1, ytf, K2 tog tbl, K7, rep from * to last 6[7] sts, K2 tog, ytf, K1, ytf, K2 tog tbl, K1[2].
Next row P to end.
Keeping patt correct, cont without shaping until armholes measure 3¼[3½]in from beg, ending with a WS row.

Shape shoulders
Bind off 5[5] sts at beg of next 4 rows and 6 [6] sts at beg of next 2 rows. Bind off rem 23 [25] sts.

Left front

Using No.3 needles cast on 69[69] sts. K9 rows g st. Commence patt.
1st row (RS) K to end.
2nd row K6, P to end.
3rd row K7, * ytf, K2 tog tbl, K10, rep from * to last 14 sts, ytf, K2 tog tbl, K12.
4th row K6, P to end.
5th row K5, *K2 tog, ytf, K1, ytf, K2 tog tbl, K7, rep from * to last 16 sts, K2 tog, ytf, K1, ytf, K2 tog tbl, K11.
6th row K6, P to end.
7th row K to end.
8th row K6, P to end.
9th row K13, *ytf, K2 tog tbl, K10, rep from * to last 8 sts, K8.
10th row K6, P to end.
11th row K11, *K2 tog, ytf, K1, ytf, K2 tog tbl, K7, rep from * to last 10 sts, K10.
12th row K6, P to end.
Keeping patt correct cont until work measures 5½[6]in from beg, ending with a WS row.
Next row *K2 tog, rep from * to last 5[9] sts, K5[9] sts. 37[39] sts.
K3 rows g st.

Shape armhole
Next row Bind off 3[4] sts, K to end.
Next row K6, P to end.
Next row K2 tog, K10[11], ytf, K2 tog tbl, K10, ytf, K2 tog tbl, K8.
Next row K6, P to end.
Next row K2 tog, K7[8], K2 tog, ytf, K1, ytf, K2 tog tbl, K7, K2 tog, ytf, K1, ytf, K2 tog tbl, K7.
Next row K6, P to end.

Next row K2 tog, K to end.
Next row K6, P to end.
Next row K3[4], ytf, K2 tog tbl, K10, ytf, K2 tog tbl, K14.
Next row K6, P to end.
Next row K1[2], K2 tog, ytf, K1, ytf, K2 tog tbl, K7, K2 tog, ytf, K1, ytf, K2 tog tbl, K13.
Next row K6, P to end.
Cont in patt until armhole measures 2¼[2½]in from beg, ending at front edge.
Shape neck
Next row Bind off 10[11] sts, patt to end.
Dec one st at neck edge on next 5 rows. Cont without shaping until armhole measures same as back to shoulder, ending at armhole edge.
Shape shoulder
Bind off 5[5] sts every other row twice.
Work 1 row. Bind off rem 6[6] sts.

Right front

Using No.3 needles cast on 69[69] sts. K 9 rows g st. Commence patt.
1st row K to end.
2nd row P to last 6 sts, K6.
3rd row K13, *ytf, K2 tog tbl, K10, rep from * to last 8 sts, ytf, K2 tog tbl, K6.
4th row P to last 6 sts, K6.
5th row K11, *K2 tog, ytf, K1, ytf, K2 tog tbl, K7, rep from * to last 10 sts, K2 tog, ytf, K1, ytf, K2 tog tbl, K5.
6th row P to last 6 sts, K6.
7th row K to end.
8th row P to last 6 sts, K6.
9th row K19, *ytf, K2 tog tbl, K10, rep from * to last 2 sts, K2.
10th row P to last 6 sts, K6.
11th row K17, *K2 tog, ytf, K1, ytf, K2 tog tbl, K7, rep from * to last 4 sts, K4.
12th row P to last 6 sts, K6.
Cont in patt until work measures 5½[6]in from beg, ending with a WS row.
Next row K5[9] sts, *K2 tog, rep from * to end. 37[39] sts.
Next row K to end.
Next row (buttonhole row) K2, bind off 2, K to end.
Next row K to end, casting on 2 sts above those bound off on previous row.
Shape armhole
Next row K to end.
Next row Bind off 3[4] sts, P to last 6 sts, K6.
Next row K9, ytf, K2 tog tbl, K10, ytf, K2 tog tbl, K9[10], K2 tog.
Next row P to last 6 sts, K6.
Next row K7, K2 tog, ytf, K1, ytf, K2 tog tbl, K7, K2 tog, ytf, K1, ytf, K2 tog tbl, K7[8], K2 tog.
Next row P to last 6 sts, K6.
Next row K to last 2 sts, K2 tog.
Next row P to last 6 sts, K6.
Next row K2, bind off 2, K11, ytf, K2 tog tbl, K10, ytf, K2 tog tbl, K2[3].
Next row P to last 4 sts, K2, cast on 2, K2.
Next row K13, K2 tog, ytf, K1, ytf, K2 tog tbl, K7, K2 tog, ytf, K1, ytf, K2 tog tbl, K1[2].
Next row P to last 6 sts, K6.
Complete to correspond to left front, reversing all shapings and working a 3rd buttonhole on 9th row from previous one.

Sleeves

Using No.1 needles cast on 38[38] sts. Work 1in K1, P1 rib, inc one st at end of last row. 39[39] sts. Change to No.3 needles and work in patt as given for back, inc one st at each end of 7th and every foll 6th[5th] row until there are 49[53] sts and working extra sts into patt. Cont without shaping until sleeve measures 5¾

[6½] in from beg, ending with a WS row.
Shape cap
Bind off 3[4] sts at beg of next 2 rows. Dec one st at each end of next and every other row until 29[31] sts rem. Dec one st at each end of every row until 7[9] sts rem. Bind off.

Collar

Using No.3 needles cast on 75[77] sts. K9 rows g st. Commence patt.
1st row K to end.
2nd and every other row K6, P to last 6 sts, K6.
3rd row K13[14], *ytf, K2 tog tbl, K10, rep from * to last 14[15] sts, ytf, K2 tog tbl, K12[13].
5th row K11[12], *K2 tog, ytf, K1, ytf, K2 tog tbl, K7, rep from * to last 16[17] sts, K2 tog, ytf, K1, ytf, K2 tog tbl, K11[12].
7th row K to end.
8th row As 2nd.
Change to No.1 needles.
9th row K19[20], *ytf, K2 tog tbl, K10, rep from * to last 8[9] sts, K8[9].
11th row K17[18], *K2 tog, ytf, K1, ytf, K2 tog tbl, K7, rep from * to last 10[11] sts, K10[11].
12th row As 2nd.
Bind off.

Finishing

Press each piece under a dry cloth with a cool iron for synthetics or a damp cloth with a warm iron for wool. Join shoulder, side and sleeve seams. Sew in sleeves. Sew collar into position, placing bound-off edge to neck, beg and ending at center of front borders Buttonhole-st around buttonholes and sew on buttons.

Baby sacque in arrowhead eyelet pattern

Sizes, gauge, and materials
Same as for design No. 2.

Back

Using No.3 needles cast on 111[121] sts. K9 rows g st.
Commence patt.
1st row K1, *ytf, sl 1, K1, psso, K5, K2 tog, ytf, K1, rep from * to end.
2nd and every other row P to end.
3rd row K2, *ytf, sl 1, K1, psso, K3, K2 tog, ytf, K3, rep from * to last 9 sts, ytf, sl 1, K1, psso, K3, K2 tog, ytf, K2.
5th row K3, *ytf, sl 1, K1, psso, K1, K2 tog, ytf, K5, rep from * to last 8 sts, ytf, sl 1, K1, psso, K1, K2 tog, ytf, K3.
7th row K4, *ytf, sl 1, K2 tog, psso, ytf, K7, rep from * to last 7 sts, ytf, sl 1, K2 tog, psso, ytf, K4.
8th row P to end.
These 8 rows form a patt. Cont in patt until 6[7] complete patts have been worked.
Next row K11[10] sts, *K2 tog, rep from * 43[49] times more, K12 [11] sts. 67[71] sts. K3 rows g st. Beg with a K row cont in st st.
Shape armholes
Bind off 3 sts at beg of next 2 rows. Dec one st at each end of next and every other row until 53[55] sts rem. Cont without shaping until armholes measure 3¼[3½]in from beg, ending with a P row.
Shape shoulders
Bind off 5 sts at beg of next 6 rows. Bind off rem 23[25] sts.

Left front

Using No.3 needles cast on 57[67] sts. K 9 rows g st. Commence patt.
1st row K1, *ytf, sl 1, K1, psso, K5, K2 tog, ytf, K1, rep from * to last 6 sts, K6.
2nd and every other row K6, P to end.
3rd row K2, *ytf, sl 1, K1, psso, K3, K2 tog, ytf, K3, rep from * to last 5 sts, K5.
5th row K3, *ytf, sl 1, K1, psso, K1, K2 tog, ytf, K5, rep from * to last 4 sts, K4.
7th row K4, *ytf, sl 1, K2 tog, psso, ytf, K7, rep from * to last 3 sts, K3.
8th row K6, P to end.
Cont in patt keeping 6 g st border correct until 6[7] complete patts have been worked.
Next row K8[5] sts, *K2 tog, rep from * 19[27] times more, K9[6] sts. 37[39] sts.
K 3 rows g st. Beg with a K row cont in st st keeping g st border correct.
Shape armhole
Bind off 3 sts at beg of next row. Dec one st at armhole edge every other row until 30[31] sts rem. Cont without shaping until armhole measures 2¼[2½]in from beg, ending at front edge.
Shape neck
Next row Bind off 10[11] sts, P to end.
Dec one st at neck edge on next 5 rows. Cont without shaping until armhole measures same as back to shoulder, ending at armhole edge.
Shape shoulder At arm edge bind off 5 sts every other row 3 times.

Right front

Using No.3 needles cast on 57[67] sts. K 9 rows g st. Commence patt.
1st row K7, *ytf, sl 1, K1, psso, K5, K2 tog, ytf, K1, rep from * to end.
2nd and every other row P to last 6 sts, K6.
3rd row K8, *ytf, sl 1, K1, psso, K3, K2 tog, ytf, K3, rep from * to last 9 sts, ytf, sl 1, K1, psso, K3, K2 tog, ytf, K2.
5th row K9, *ytf, sl 1, K1, psso, K1, K2 tog, ytf, K5, rep from * to last 8 sts, ytf, sl 1, K1, psso, K1, K2 tog, ytf, K3.
7th row K10, *ytf, sl 1, K2 tog, psso, ytf, K7, rep from * to last 7 sts, ytf, sl 1, K2 tog, psso, ytf, K4.
8th row P to last 6 sts, K6.
Cont in patt keeping 6 g st border correct until 6[7] complete patts have been worked.
Next row K9[6] sts, *K2 tog, rep from * 19[27] times more, K8[5] sts. 37[39] sts.
Next row K to end.
Next row (buttonhole row) K2 sts, bind off 2 sts, K to end.
Next row K to end casting on 2 sts above those bound off on previous row.
Complete to correspond to left front, reversing all shapings and working 2 more buttonholes at intervals of 1in measured from base of previous buttonhole.

Sleeves

Using No.1 needles cast on 36[38] sts. Work 1in K1, P1 rib, ending with a RS row.
Next row Rib 6[8], *pick up loop that lies between st just worked and next st on left-hand needle and K tbl, rib 6[10], rep from * to end. 41[41] sts.
Change to No.3 needles and work in patt as given for back, inc one st at each end of 11th and every foll 12th[10th] row until there are 47[49] sts. Cont without shaping until 6[7] complete patts have been worked.
Shape cap
Keeping patt correct, bind off 3 sts at beg of next 2 rows. Dec one st at each end of next and every other row until 25[27] sts rem.

Dec one st at each end of every row until 7[9] sts rem. Bind off.

Collar

Using No.3 needles cast on 74[76] sts. K9 rows g st.
Next row K to end.
Next row K6, P to last 6 sts, K6.
Rep last 2 rows until work measures 1¾in from beg. Change to No.1 needles and work for ½in more. Bind off.

Finishing

Finish as for design No. 2.

4 *Set with pixie cap and double seed stitch yoke and sleeves*

Sizes
To fit an 18[20:22]in chest
The figures in brackets [] refer to the 20 and 22in sizes respectively
Coat length at center back, 11[12:13]in
Sleeve seam, 6[7½:9]in
Gauge
5½ sts and 7½ rows to 1in over st st worked on No.4 needles
Materials
Bucilla Multi
Coat 2[3:3] balls
Leggings 2[2:3] balls
Cap and mittens 1[1:2] balls
Hood(not shown) and mittens 1[1:2] balls
One pair No.4 needles
One pair No.2 needles
Stitch holder
Three buttons for coat
One button for cap or hood
Waist length of elastic for leggings
1½ yds of ribbon for mittens

Coat back

Using No.4 needles cast on 89[95:101] sts.
Commence seed st patt.
1st row K1, *P1, K1, rep from * to end.
2nd row P1, *K1, P1, rep from * to end.
3rd row As 2nd row.
4th row As 1st row.
Beg with a K row change to st st until work measures 6[6½:7]in from beg, ending with a K row. **
Next row P5[8:11] sts, *P2 tog, rep from * 39 times more, P to end. 49[55:61] sts.
Work 4 rows seed st patt.
Shape raglan sleeves
Keeping patt correct dec one st at each end of next and every other row until 15[17:19] sts rem. Work 1 row. Bind off.

Coat left front

Using No.4 needles cast on 45[49:53] sts and work as given for back to **.
Next row P2[4:6] sts, *P2 tog, rep from * 19 times more, P to end.
Work 4 rows seed st patt.
Shape raglan sleeve
Keeping patt correct dec one st at beg of next and every other row until all sts are worked, *at the same time* shape neck when work measures 9½[10½:11]in from beg, ending at center front edge.
Shape neck
Bind off 3[4:5] sts at beg of next row, then dec one st at neck edge on every row 4[5:6] times in all.

Coat right front

Work as given for left front, reversing shaping.

Sleeves

Using No. 2 needles cast on 33 [35:37] sts. Work 6 rows K1, P1 rib. Change to No.4 needles and seed st patt as given for back. Keeping patt correct, inc one st at each end of every 4th row until there are 43[47:51] sts. Cont without shaping until sleeve measures 6[7½:9]in from beg, ending with a WS row.
Shape raglan cap
Work as given for back until 9 sts rem. Work 1 row. Bind off.

Front borders

Using No.2 needles cast on 7 sts. Work 6[6½:7] in K1, P1 rib.
Next row (buttonhole row) Rib 2 sts, bind off 3 sts, rib to end.
Next row Rib to end casting on 3 sts above those bound-off on previous row.
Cont in rib working 2 more buttonholes in same way at intervals of 1½[1¾:1¾]in from center of previous buttonhole. Cont in rib until border measures 9½[10½:11]in from beg. Bind off in rib. Work other border in same way, omitting buttonholes.

Finishing

Do not press. Join raglan, side and sleeve seams. Oversew borders to center front edges, having buttonhole band on right front for a girl and left front for a boy.
Collar Using No.2 needles pick up and K 61[65:73] sts evenly around neck, beg and ending 3 sts from center front edges. Work 18[20:22] rows K1, P1 rib.
Bind off loosely in rib. Sew on buttons.

Leggings left leg

Using No.2 needles cast on 56[62:68] sts. Work 4 rows K1, P1 rib.
Next row Rib 1 st, *yrn, rib 2 tog, rep from * to last st, rib 1 st.
Work 5 more rows K1, P1 rib.
Change to No.4 needles and beg with a K row work in st st.
Shape back: short rows
1st row K13[15:17] sts, turn.
2nd row P.
3rd row K26[30:34] sts, turn.
4th row P.
5th row K39[45:51] sts, turn.
6th row P.
Beg with a K row cont in st st across all sts, inc one st at each end of 9th[11th:13th] and every foll 6th row until there are 70[76:82] sts.
Dec one st at each end of 7th[9th:11th] and every other row until 60[66:72] sts rem and then every foll 4th row until 38[44:50] sts rem.
Cont without shaping for a further 1[1½:2]in, ending with a P row.
Next row K1, *ytf, K2 tog, rep from * to last st, K1.
Next row P to end.
Shape foot
Next row K34[38:42] sts, turn and P12 [14:16] sts. Work 20[22:24] rows st st on these sts.
Next row pick up and K11[12:13] sts along side of foot, K4 [6:8] sts.
Next row P27[32:37] sts, pick up and P11[12:13] sts along side of foot, P22[24:26] sts.
60[68:76] sts. Beg with a K row work 6 rows st st.
Next row K32[34:36] sts, K2 tog tbl, K10 [14:18] sts, K2 tog, K14[16:18] sts.
Next row P to end.
Cont dec in this way above dec on previous row every K row twice. Bind off.

Leggings right leg

Work as given for left leg, reversing all shaping.

Finishing

Do not press. Join back, front and leg seams. Join foot seams. Run elastic through eyelets at waist and ribbon through eyelets at ankles.

Cap

Using No.2 needles cast on 67[73:79] sts. Work 6 rows seed st patt as given for coat back. Beg with a K row work 6 rows st st. Work 6 more rows seed st patt. Change to No.4 needles. ***
Beg with a P row to reverse work cont in st st for a further 4½[5:5½]in, ending with a P row.
Shape back
Next row Bind off 22[24:26] sts, K to end.
Next row Bind off 22[24:26] sts, P to end.
Cont in st st on center 23[25:27] sts for a further 4[4¼:4½]in, ending with a P row.
Next row K2[1:0] sts, *K3 tog, rep from * to end. Bind off rem sts.
Neck edging
Using No.2 needles cast on 4 sts. Work 10[12:14]in g st.
Next row K1, ytf, K2 tog, K1.
Next row K to end.
Next row K2 tog twice.
Next row K2 tog. Fasten off.

Finishing

Do not press. Join bound-off sts to side edges of back. Turn back brim. Oversew neck edging to lower edge of bonnet, stretching to fit and leaving 2[2½:3]in free at shaped end. Sew on button.

Hood (not shown)

Work as given for bonnet to ***. Beg with a K row cont in st st until work measures 6½[7¼:8]in

from beg, ending with a P row. Bind off.
Neck edging
Work as given for neck edging of bonnet.

Finishing

Do not press. Fold bound-off edge in half and join tog to form back. Sew on neck edging as given for cap.

Mittens

Using No.2 needles cast on 33[37:41] sts. Work 4 rows seed st patt. Change to No.4 needles.
Beg with a K row work 6 rows st st.
Next row K1, *K2 tog, ytf, K2, rep from * to end.
Beg with a P row cont in st st until work measures 2½[3:3½]in from beg, ending with a P row.
Shape tip
Next row K1, *K2 tog, rep from * to end.
Next row P to end.
Next row K1, *K2 tog, rep from * to end.
Thread yarn through rem sts, draw up and fasten off.

Finishing

Do not press. Join side seams. Run ribbon through eyelets at wrist.

5 *Long sleeved romper-suit and cardigan in ridged stitch*

Sizes
To fit an 18[20:22:24]in chest
The figures in brackets [] refer to the 20, 22 and 24 in sizes respectively
Cardigan length down center back, 10[11:12½:14] in down Sleeve seam, 6[7:8:10]in
Rompers length at center back, 15½[16½:18½:19½]in
Sleeve seam, 6[7:8:10]in
Gauge
5 sts and 9 rows to 1in over patt worked on No.5 needles
Materials
3[4:4.4] Ungers Les Bouquets for cardigan
4[5:6:6] balls of Ungers Les Bouquets for rompers
One pair of No.5 knitting needles
One pair No.3 knitting needles
Stitch holder
4 buttons for cardigan
5 buttons for rompers
No.H crochet hook

Cardigan back

Using No.3 needles cast on 51[55:59:63] sts. Work 12 rows K1, P1 rib. Change to No.5 needles.
1st row K to end.
2nd row P to end.
3rd row K to end.
4th row *P1, K into st below next st and sl st off needles — called K1B —, rep from * to last st, P1.
5th, 6th and 7th rows As 1st, 2nd and 3rd rows.
8th row P2, *K1B, P1, rep from * to last st, P1.
These 8 rows form patt and are rep throughout.
Cont in patt until work measures 5½[6:7:8]in from beg, ending with a 4th or 8th patt row.
Shape raglan armholes
Next row K2 tog, work to last 2 sts, K2 tog.
Work 3 rows without shaping. Rep these 4 rows 3[4:5:6] times more, then dec at each end of every other row until 17[19:21:23] sts rem. Work 1 row.
Bind off.

Cardigan left front

Using No.3 needles cast on 25[27:29:31] sts. Work as given for back until front measures same as back to armhole, ending at armhole edge.
Shape raglan armhole
Next row K2 tog, work to end.
Work 3 rows without shaping. Rep these 4 rows 3[4:5:6] times more, then dec at each end of every other row until all sts are worked off, *at the same time* when work measures 6½[7:8:9]in from beg, shape neck, ending at center front edge.
Shape neck
Dec one st at beg of next and every 4th row 7[8:9:10] times in all.

Cardigan right front

Work as given for left front, reversing all shaping.

Sleeves

Using No.3 needles cast on 37[39:41:43] sts. Work 1½in K1, P1 rib. Change to No.5 needles. Work in patt as given for back, inc one st at each end of every 12th row until there are 41[43:45:47] sts. Cont without shaping until sleeve measures 6[7:8:10]in from beg, ending with a 4th or 8th patt row.
Shape raglan cap
Work as given for back raglan shaping until 7 sts rem.
Work 1 row.
Bind off.

Front border

Using No.3 needles cast on 7 sts. Work ½in K1, P1 rib.
Next row (buttonhole row) Rib 3 sts, bind off 1 st, rib 3 sts.
Next row Rib 3 sts, cast on 1 st, rib 3 sts.
Cont in K1, P1 rib, working 3 more buttonholes in same way at intervals of 2[2:2¼:2¾]in from center of previous buttonhole, then cont until border is long enough to fit up center fronts, edges and around neck. Bind off in rib.

Finishing

Press lightly. Join raglan, side and sleeve seams. Oversew front border to cardigan fronts and around neck, having buttonholes on right front for a girl and left front for a boy. Sew on buttons.

Romper back

Using No.5 needles cast on 15[15:17:17] sts. Beg with a K row work in st st, inc one at each end of every row until there are 49[55:61:67] sts. Cast on 6 sts at beg of next 2 rows.
**Dec one st at each end of every foll 6th row until 51[57:63:69] sts rem. Cont without shaping until work measures 7[7½:8½:9]in from beg, ending with a P row.
Waist ribbing
Work 4 rows K1, P1 rib.
Next row Rib 1 st, *yrn, rib 2 tog, rep from * to end.
Work 2 more rows K1, P1 rib.
Next row Rib 3[3:3:1] sts, *rib 2 tog, rib 7[5:4:4] sts, rep from * 4[6:8:10] times more, rib 2 tog, rib to end. 45[49:53:57] sts.
Cont in patt as given for cardigan back, inc one st at each end of every 10th row until there are 51[55:59:63] sts. Cont without shaping until work measures 11[11½:13:13½]in from beg ending with a 4th or 8th patt row. **
Shape raglan
Work as given for cardigan back until 17[19:21:23] sts rem. Work 1 row. Bind off.

Romper front

Using No.5 needles cast on 15[15:17:17] sts.
Beg with a K row work 3[4:6:7] rows st st.
Cast on 3 sts at beg of next 12[14:14:16] rows and 5[5:7:7] sts at beg of foll 2 rows. Work as given from ** to ** for romper back.
Shape raglan armhole and divide for front opening
Next row K2 tog, work 21[23:25:27] sts, turn.
Slip rem sts on holder. Work 3 rows without shaping then dec one st at armhole edge on next row. Dec one st at armhole edge on every foll 4th row 2[3:4:5] times more, then on every other row until all sts are worked, *at the same time* shape neck when center front opening measures 2½[2½:3:3]in from beg.
Shape neck
Dec one st at neck on every row 5[6:7:8] times.
Attach yarn to center edge of sts left on holder, bind off first 5 sts, work to end. Complete to correspond to first side, reversing shaping.

Sleeves

Work as given for sleeves of cardigan.

Front borders

Using No.3 needles cast on 7 sts. Work 1¼[1¼:1¾:1¾]in K1, P1 rib. Work buttonhole rows as given for cardigan front border. Cont until work measures 2½[2½:3:3] in from beg. Bind off in rib. Work another border in same way, omitting buttonhole.

Finishing

Press lightly. Join raglan, side and sleeve seams. Fold cuffs in half to WS and sl st down.
Oversew borders into center front opening, having buttonhole on right front for a girl and left front for a boy. Sew down at bottom.
Neckband Using No.3 needles pick up and K 67[73:75:81] sts evenly around neck, including borders. Work 6 rows K1, P1 rib working buttonhole as before on 3rd and 4th rows. Bind off in rib.
Legbands Using No.3 needles pick up and K 56[61:65:71] sts evenly around each leg. Work 12 rows K1, P1 rib. Bind off loosely in rib. Fold legbands in half to WS and sl st down.
With RS work facing work 2 rows sc between legs on front. Work 2 rows sc between legs on back, forming 3 buttonholes on 2nd row by working ch2 and skipping 2sc.
Using 2 strands of yarn make a crochet chain, run through eyelets at waist. Sew on buttons.

6 *Back buttoned cardigan with lace-trimmed neck edge*

Sizes
To fit 17[20:23]in chest
The figures in brackets [] refer to the 20 and 23in sizes respectively
Length down center back, 9½[11:12½]in
Sleeve seam, 5½[6½:8]in
Gauge
5½ sts and 8 rows to 1in over patt worked on

No.5 needles; 5 sts and 10 rows to 1in over
garter st worked on No.5 needles
Materials
3[4:4] balls Ungers Les Bouquets
No.5 knitting needles
No.3 knitting needles
Stitch holder
Six buttons
Lace for neck trimming

Front

Using No.3 needles cast on 50[58:66] sts. Work
3[3½:4]in K1, P1 rib. Change to No.5 needles.
Commence patt.
1st row K2, *P2, K2, rep from * to end.
2nd row P2, *K2, P2, rep from * to end.
3rd row K to end.
4th row As 1st row.
5th row As 2nd row.
6th row P to end.
These 6 rows form patt and are rep throughout.
Cont in patt until work measures 5[6:7]in from
beg, ending with a WS row.
Shape raglan armholes
Next row K1, K2 tog, patt to last 3 sts, K2 tog
tbl, K1.
Next row K1, patt to last st, K1.
Rep last 2 rows until 28[34:40] sts rem. Work
1 row.
Shape neck
Next row K1, K2 tog, patt 9[10:11] sts, slip
rem sts on holder.
Dec one st at neck edge on every row 4 times,
at the same time cont to work raglan shaping
until 2 sts rem. K2 tog. Fasten off.
With RS of work facing, attach yarn to rem sts,
bind off first 4[8:12] sts, then work on rem sts
to correspond to other side, reversing shaping.

Right back

Using No.3 needles cast on 22[26:30] sts.
Work as given for front until work measures
same as front to armhole, ending with a WS row.
Shape raglan armhole
Next row K1, K2 tog, patt to end.
Next row Patt to last st, K1.
Rep last 2 rows until 4[6:8] sts rem. Work 1
row. Bind off.

Left back

Work as given for right back, noting that first
raglan shaping row will read: Patt to last 2 sts,
K2 tog tbl, K1.

Sleeves

Using No.3 needles cast on 30[34:34] sts.
Work 1½in K1, P1 rib. Change to No.5 needles.
Work in patt as given for front, inc one st at
each end of every 4th row until there are
42[46:50] sts. Cont without shaping until sleeve
measures 5½[6½:8]in from beg, ending with a
WS row.
Shape cap
Work raglan shaping as given for front until
6 sts rem. Work 1 row. Bind off.

Borders

Using No.3 needles cast on 5 sts. Work in garter
st (g st) throughout. Work ¼[½:¾]in.
Next row (buttonhole row) K2, bind off one, K2.
Next row K2, cast on one, K2.
Work 4 more buttonholes in same way at
intervals of 1¾[2:2¼]in from center of previous
buttonhole. Cont until border measures 9[10½:12]
in from beg. Bind off. Work other border in
same way, omitting buttonholes.

Finishing

Press lightly. Join raglan seams. Join side and
sleeve seams. Oversew borders to center back
edges, stretching slightly.
Neck edge Using No.3 needles and with RS
of work facing, pick up and K 53[61:69] sts
evenly around neck. Work 4 rows K1, P1 rib,
working a buttonhole as given for border on
1st row. Bind off in rib. Sew on buttons. Sew lace
to beg of neck ribbing.

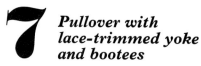

7 Pullover with lace-trimmed yoke and bootees

Sizes
To fit 17[20:23]in chest
The figures in brackets [] refer to the 20 and
23in sizes respectively
Pullover length at center back, 9[10:11]in
Sleeve seam, 4½[5:7]in
Bootees to fit the 17 and 20 in chest sizes
Gauge
Same as for design 8
Materials
Ungers Les Bouquets
Pullover 3 balls
Bootees 1[1:1] ball
or Ungers Les Coraux
Pullover 1[2:2] balls
Bootees 1[1:1] ball
No.5 knitting needles, No.3 knitting needles
Stitch holder. Lace for trimming
Three buttons for pullover
Ribbon for bootees and bow

Pullover backs and front

Using No.5 needles cast on 106[122:138] sts.
Work 3 complete patt as given for cardigan
front design No.8. Change to garter st (g st).
Cont until 4½[5:5½]in from beg, ending with
a WS row.
Divide for armholes
Next row K24[28:32] sts, K2 tog, turn and
slip rem sts on holder. Complete left back on
these sts. Work 1 row. Dec one st at inside
edge on next and every other row 7[9:11] times
more. K 1 row. Slip sts on holder.
Break yarn and attach to next 54 [62:70] sts for
front, work to end.
Next row K2 tog, K to last 2 sts, K2 tog.
Cont dec in this way on every other row 7[9:11]
times more. K 1 row. Slip sts on holder.
Break yarn and attach to rem 26[30:34] sts for
right back and complete as given for left back,
reversing shaping.

Sleeves

Using No.3 needles cast on 30[32:34] sts. Work
K1, P1 rib, for 1 in; inc along last row to 36[40:44]
sts, as folls:
Next row (inc row) Rib 2, *rib twice into next
st, rib 4[3:2], rep from * 4[6:8] times more,
rib twice into next st, rib to end.
Change to No.5 needles. Work in g st. Cont
until sleeve measures 4½[5:7]in from beg.
Shape top
Dec one st at each end of next and every other
row until 20 sts rem. Slip sts on holder.

Yoke

Using No.5 needles and with WS of work facing,
sl sts from right back holder, sleeve, front,
sleeve and left back onto one needle.
114[122:130] sts.

Next row (RS) K2[2:6], *K2 tog, K10[11:11],
rep from * 8 times more, K2 tog, K to end.
Next row P to end.
Next row P to end.
Next row K to end.
Next row P to end.
Next row K to end.
Next row K 1[1:5], *K2 tog, K9[10:10], rep
from * 8 times more, K2 tog, K to end.
Next row P to end.
Change to No.3 needles. Work 11 rows patt
as for bottom of pullover.
Next row P8[3:7], *P2 tog, P2[3:3], rep from
* 18 times more, P2 tog, P to end.
Next row P to end.
Next row K to end.
Next row P3[7:11], *P2 tog, P1, rep from *
21 times more, P2 tog, P to end.
Work 5 rows K1, P1 rib. Bind off in rib.

Finishing

Press lightly. Beg at lower edge join backs tog
for 6in. Join sleeve seams. Sew in sleeves. Work
2 rows sc along each side of back opening,
working 3 button loops on last row by working
ch2 and skipping 2sc. Sew on buttons. Sew lace
around beg of yoke. Trim front with ribbon bow.

Bootees

Using No.5 needles cast on 30 sts. Work 3
complete patt as given for cardigan front.
Next row K1, ytf, K2 tog, rep from * to last
st, K1.
Next row P to end.
Next row K19 sts. Turn and K8 sts.
Work 18 rows g st on these 8 sts.
Next row K8 sts, pick up and K 12 sts along
side of foot, K rem 11 sts.
Next row P31 sts, pick up and P 12 sts along
other side of foot, P rem 11 sts.
Work 8 rows in patt as given for cardigan front.
Next row K2 tog, K23 sts, K2 tog tbl, K2 tog,
K23 sts, K2 tog tbl.
Next row K to end.
Rep these 2 rows once more, working the dec
above previous ones. Bind off.

Finishing

Press lightly. Join seam along bottom of foot
and back of leg. Run ribbon through eyelets
at ankles. Sew lace around top of bootees.

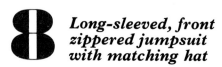

8 Long-sleeved, front zippered jumpsuit with matching hat

Sizes
To fit 18[20:22:24]in chest
The figures in brackets [] refer to the 20,22 and
24in sizes respectively
Length from center back to toe, 27½[30:32½:35]in
Sleeve seam, 7[8:9:10]in
Gauge
6 sts and 8 rows to 1in over st st worked on
No.5 needles
Materials
Unger Les Coraux 5[5:6:6]
balls for Jumpsuit
1[1:1:2:2] balls for Hat
or Ungers Les Bouquets
5[5:6:6] balls for Jumpsuit
1[1:1:1] balls for Hat
No.5 knitting needles, No.3 knitting needles
One 10in zipper

46

Jumpsuit right side

Using No.5 needles, beg at toe and cast on 14[18:24:30] sts. Beg with a K row work in st st. Work 2 rows
Next row K twice into first st, K5[7:10:13] sts, K twice into each of next 2 sts, K to last 2sts, K twice into next st, K1.
Beg with a P row work 3 rows st st.
Next row K twice into first st, K7[9:12:15] sts, K twice into each of next 2 sts, K to last 2 sts, K twice into next st, K1.
Beg with a P row work 3 rows st st.
Next row K twice into first st, K9[11:14:17] sts, K twice into each of next 2 sts, K to last 2 sts, K twice into next st, K1.
Beg with a P row cont in st st without shaping until work measures 3[4:4½:5]in from beg, ending with a P row.
Next row K3[3:6:9] sts, *K twice into next st, K1, rep from * 9[11:11:11] times more, K twice into next st, K to end. 37[43:49:55] sts.
Change to No.3 needles. Work 13 rows K1, P1 rib. Change to No.5 needles.
Commence patt.
1st row (RS) P1, *K5, P1, rep from * to end.
2nd row P to end.
These 2 rows form patt and are rep throughout.
Cont in patt until work measures 1½[2:2½:3]in from beg of patt. Keeping patt correct, inc one st at each end of next and every foll 4th row 10 times in all, then each end of every foll 3rd row 9 times in all. Dec one st at each end of every foll 3rd row 3 times in all. Cont in patt without shaping for a further 1½[2:2½:3]in, ending with a 2nd row.**
Shape center front
Next row Patt 14 sts, K2 tog tbl, P1, K2 tog, patt to end.
Next row P to end. Keeping patt correct, work 6 rows without shaping.
Next row Patt 13 sts, K2 tog tbl, P1, K2 tog, patt to end. Keeping patt correct, work 7 rows without shaping.
Next row Patt 14 sts, K up 1, P1, K up 1, patt to end.
Keeping patt correct, work 7 rows without shaping.
Rep last 8 rows once more.
Cont in patt without shaping until work measures 16½[17½:19:20½]in from beg of patt, ending with a 2nd row.
Divide for raglan armhole
Next row Patt 34[37:40:43] sts, bind off one st, patt to end.
Next row Patt 34[37:40:43] sts, turn and slip rem sts on holder for front.
Next row K1, K2 tog, patt to end.
Next row Patt to last st, K1.
Rep last 2 rows until 13[14:15:16] sts rem. Work 1 row. Bind off.
Attach yarn at inside edge of rem sts on holder.
Next row K1, patt to end.
Next row Patt to last 3 sts, K2 tog tbl, K1.
Rep last 2 rows until 19[22:25:26] sts rem. Work 1 row.
Shape neck
Bind off 7 sts at beg of next row, then dec one st at neck edge on every row 5[6:7:8] times in all, *at the same time* cont to dec at raglan edge as before until 2 sts rem. K2 tog. Fasten off.

Jumpsuit left side

Work as given for right side to **.
Shape center front
Next row Patt to last 19 sts, K2 tog tbl, P1, K2 tog, patt 14 sts. Rep the dec and inc as given for right side as now established, then cont without shaping until work measures 16½[17½:19:20½]in from beg of patt, ending with a 2nd row.

Divide for raglan armhole
Next row Patt 34[37:40:43] sts, bind off one st, patt to end.
Next row Patt 34[37:40:43] sts, turn and slip rem sts on holder for back.
Next row K1, K2 tog, patt to end.
Next row Patt to last st, K1.
Cont with raglan shaping and shape neck as given for right side, reversing shaping.
Attach yarn at inside edge of rem sts on holder.
Next row K1, patt to end.
Next row Patt to last 3 sts, K2 tog tbl, K1.
Complete as given for back of right side.

Sleeves

Using No.3 needles cast on 38[40:42:44] sts. Work 2in K1, P1 rib.
Change to No.5 needles. Beg with a K row work in st st, inc one st at each end of 5th and every foll 5th row until there are 50[54:58:62] sts.
Cont without shaping until sleeve measures 7[8:9:10]in from beg, ending with a P row.
Shape raglan cap
Next row K1, K2 tog, K to last 3 sts, K2 tog tbl, K1.
Next row K1, P to last st, K1.
Rep last 2 rows until 8 sts rem. Work 1 row. Bind off.

Finishing

Press lightly. Join foot and leg seams. Join center backs tog then join center fronts, leaving 10in open for zipper fastener. Join sleeve seams. Sew in sleeves.
Collar Using No.3 needles and with WS of work facing, pick up and K 61[67:73:75] sts evenly around neck, beg and ending 3 sts from center front edges. Work 20[20:24:24] rows K1, P1 rib. Break off yarn. Pick up and rib 14[14:18:18] sts along side of collar, rib across sts on needle and pick up and rib 14[14:18:18] sts along other side of collar. Work 1 row K1, P1 rib. Bind off in rib. Sew in zipper.

Hat

Using No.3 needles cast on 103[103:109:109] sts. Work 17 rows K1, P1 rib. Change to No.5 needles. Work in patt as given for Jumpsuit until work measures 6[6:6½:6½]in from beg, end with a 2nd row. Change to No.3 needles.
Shape top
Next row K2[2:5:5] sts, *K3 tog, K5, rep from * 11 times more, K3 tog, K to end.
K 5 rows g st without shaping.
Next row K1[1:4:4] sts, *K3 tog, K3, rep from * 11 times more, K3 tog, K to end. K5 rows g st without shaping.
Next row K1[1:3:3] sts, *K2 tog, rep from * to end. K 1 row.
Next row *K2 tog, rep from * to end.
Thread yarn through rem sts, draw up and fasten off.
Join side edges of hat tog.

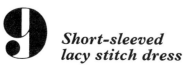

Short-sleeved lacy stitch dress

Sizes
To fit 16/18[20/22]in chest

Figures in brackets [] refer to the 20/22in size
Length to center back, 14[15]in
Sleeve seam, 1½in
Gauge
7sts and 9 rows to 1in over st st worked on No.4 needles
Materials
Botany Win-Sport, 3[4] 2-oz skeins
No.4 knitting needles
Three small buttons

Back

Using No.4 needles cast on 121[141] sts.
Work 4 rows garter st (g st). Commence patt.
1st row K2 tog, *K3, ytf, K1, ytf, K3, sl 1, K2 tog, psso, rep from * ending last rep K2 tog instead of sl 1, K2 tog, psso.
2nd and every other row P to end.
3rd row As 1st.
5th row As 1st.
7th row P to end.
8th row P to end.
These 8 rows form patt. Cont in patt until work measures 10[10½]in from beg, ending with a WS row. **
Next row (dec row) K3[7] sts, *K2 tog, rep from * to last 2[6] sts, K to end. 63[77] sts.
Next row P to end.
Beg with a K row, cont in st st.
Shape armhole and divide for back opening
Next row Bind off 2[2] sts, K31[38] sts, turn. Complete right shoulder on these sts.
Next row K3 sts, P to end.
Keeping 3 sts in g st for border at back opening, dec one st at armhole edge on every row until 27[32] sts rem. Cont without shaping until work measures 1½[1¾]in from beg of back opening, ending with a WS row.
Next row (buttonhole row) K to last 3 sts, ytf, K2 tog, K1.
Work another buttonhole in this way when work measures 1½[1¾]in from previous buttonhole, then cont until work measures 14[15]in from beg, ending with a WS row.
Shape shoulders
Bind off 8[9] sts at beg of next 2 rows.
Bind off rem 11[14] sts. Attach yarn to rem sts and with RS of work facing cast on 3 sts for underlap. Keeping these 3 sts in g st, complete to correspond to other shoulder, reversing shapings and omitting buttonholes.

Front

Work as given for back to **.
16/18in size only
Next row K2, (K3 tog, K2 tog) 9 times, K3 tog, patt 21 sts, (K3 tog, K2 tog) 9 times, K3 tog, K2. 63 sts.
20/22in size only
Next row (K2 tog) 24 times, (K3 tog) 4 times, patt 21 sts, (K3 tog) 4 times, (K2 tog) 24 times. 77 sts.
Both sizes
Next row P to end.
Keeping patt correct on center 21 sts, cont in st st on rem sts.
Shape armholes
Bind off 2 sts at beg of next 2 rows. Dec one st at each end of every row until 51[61] sts rem. Cont without shaping until work measures 13[14]in from beg, ending with a WS row.
Shape neck
Next row K20[23] sts, bind off 11[15] sts, K to end.
Cont on these sts for right shoulder, dec one st at neck edge on every row until 16[18] sts rem. Cont without shaping until front measures same as back to shoulder, ending at armhole edge.
Shape shoulder

Bind off 8[9] sts every other row twice.
Attach yarn to rem sts and work to correspond to first side, reversing shapings.

Sleeves

Using No.4 needles cast on 37[46] sts. Work 4 rows g st.
Next row K4[1] sts, *inc in next st, K1[2] sts rep from * to last 5[0] sts, K5[0]. 51[61] sts.
Next row K to end.
Work 8 patt rows as given for back.
Shape cap
Keeping patt correct bind off 2 sts at beg of next 2 rows. Dec one st at each end of next and every other row until 23[25] sts rem.
Next row P1, (P2 tog) to end. Bind off.

Neckband

Join shoulder seams. Using No.4 needles and with RS of work facing, pick up and K 59[63] sts around neck edge. K3 rows g st working 3rd buttonhole on 2nd row as before.
Bind off.

Finishing

Press under a dry cloth with a cool iron. Sew in sleeves. Join side and sleeve seams. Press seams. Sew on buttons.

10 *Knitted 6-section tinker-ball with bell*

Materials
Oddments of Sports yarn in 12 or less colors, or a total of 2oz
No.5 knitting needles
Cotton for stuffing, small bell
Ball measures 18in circumference
First section
Using No.5 needles and 1st color cast on 2 sts. K1 row. Work in garter st, inc one st each end of next, then following 3rd row twice, then following 4th row twice, then following 6th row twice and following 7th row twice. 20 sts. Work 10 rows without shaping. Break off 1st color and attach 2nd color. Work 10 rows without shaping. Dec one st at each end of next, then following 7th row twice, then following 6th row twice, then following 4th row twice and following 3rd row twice, 2sts. K1 row. Bind off. Work 5 more sections in the same way using colors as desired.
Finishing
With RS facing join side seams of each section leaving about 2in of last seam open. Stuff with cotton, inserting bell in middle of cotton. Oversew rem seam.

11 *Fair Isle bathrobe with tie belt*

Sizes
To fit 20[22:24]in chest
The figures in brackets [] refer to the 22 and 24in sizes respectively
Length at center back, 22[24:26]in adjustable
Sleeve seam, 6½[8:9½]in adjustable
Gauge
6½ sts and 6½ rows to 1in over Fair Isle patt worked on No.5 needles
Materials
Columbia-Minerva Featherweight Knitting Worsted
3[3:4] skeins main color, A
1[1:1] skeins each of contrast colors B, C, D and E
No.5 knitting needles
No.3 knitting needles
Stitch holders. Eight small buttons
Note
Weave yarns not in use across back of work

Back and fronts

Using No.5 needles and A, cast on 150[162:174] sts. Beg with a K row work 7 rows st st.
Next row K all sts tbl to form hemline.
Commence Fair Isle patt.
1st row (RS) *K1 A, 1B, rep from * to end.
2nd row *P1 A, 1B, rep from * to end.
3rd row As 1st.
4th row As 2nd. Break off B.
5th row K3 A, *5A, 2C, 5A, rep from * to last 3sts, K3 A.
6th row P3 A, *4A, 1C, 2A, 1C, 4A, rep from * to last 3 sts, P3 A.
7th row K3 A, *3A, 1C, 1A, 2C, 1A, 1C, 3A, rep from * to last 3 sts, K3 A.
8th row P1 C, 2A, *2A, 1C, 6A, 1C, 2A, rep from * to last 3 sts, P2 A, 1C.
9th row K1 A, 1C, 1A, *1A, 1C, (2A, 1C) 3 times, 1A, rep from * to last 3 sts, K1 A, 1C, 1A.
10th row P1 B, 1C, 1B, *1B, 1C, 1B, 2C, 2B, 2C, 1B, 1C, 1B, rep from * to last 3 sts, P1 B, 1C, 1B.
11th row K as 10th row. Break off B.
12th row P as 9th row.
13th row K as 8th row.
14th row P as 7th row.
15th row K as 6th row.
16th row P as 5th row. Break off C.
17th row *K1 A, 1E, rep from * to end.
18th row *P1 A, 1E, rep from * to end.
19th row As 17th.
20th row As 18th.
21st row K1 D, 2A, *1A, 1D, (3 A, 1D) twice, 2A, rep from * to last 3 sts, K1 A, 1D, 1A.
22nd row P1 D, 1A, 1D, *(1A, 1D) twice, (2A, 1D) twice, 1A, 1D, rep from * to last 3 sts, P1 A, 1D, 1A.
23rd row As 21st.
24th row P3 A, *6A, 1D, 5A, rep from * to last 3 sts, P3 A.
25th row K3 E, *4E, 1D, 1E, 1D, 5E, rep from * to last 3 sts, K3 E.
26th row P3 D, *1E, 4D, 1E, 1D, 1E, 4D, rep from * to last 3 sts, P1 E, 2D.
27th row K2 D, 1E, *4D, 1E, 1D, 1E, 4D, 1E. rep from * to last 3 sts, K3 D.
28th row P3 E, *5E, 1D, 1E, 1D, 4E, rep from * to last 3 sts, P3 E. Break off E.
29th row K3 A, *5A, 1D, 6A, rep from * to last 3 sts, K3 A.
30th row P1 A, 1D, 1A, *2A, 1D, (3A, 1D) twice, 1A, rep from * to last 3 sts, P2 A, 1D.
31st row K1 A, 1D, 1A, *1D, 1A, 1D, (2A, 1D) twice, 1A, 1D, 1A, rep from * to last 3 sts, K1 D,1A,1D.
32nd row As 30th. Break off D.
These 32 rows form patt and are rep throughout, noting that in next rep rows 1-4 will be worked with A and C, rows 5-16 will read B for C and C for B, rows 17-20 will be worked with A and D and rows 21-32 will read E for D and D for E. Cont in patt until work measures 12½[13¼:14]in from hemline, or desired length to underarm less 4½[5½:6½]in. Mark beg of next row noting that this row will commence sleeve patt. Cont in patt until work measures 17[18¾-20½]in from hem line, or desired length to underarm ending with a RS row.
Divide for armholes
Next row Keeping patt correct, patt 35[37:39] sts, bind off 4[6:8] sts, patt across 72[76:80] sts, bind off 4[6:8] sts, patt across 35[37:39] sts. Complete right front first. Dec one st at armhole edge on every row 5[6:7] times in all. Cont without shaping until armhole measures 3½[3¾:4]in from beg, ending at front edge.
Shape neck
Bind off 5 sts at beg of next row. Dec one st at neck edge on next 5[6:7] rows. Cont without shaping until armhole measures 4½[4¾:5]in from beg, ending at armhole edge.
Shape shoulder
Bind off 10 sts at beg of next and foll alt row.
With RS of work facing attach yarn to center 72[76:80] sts and complete back. Keeping patt correct, dec one st at each end of every row 5[6:7] times in all. Cont without shaping until armholes measure same as front to shoulder, ending with a WS row.
Shape shoulder
Bind off 10 sts at beg of next 4 rows. Bind off rem 22[24:26] sts.
With RS of work facing attach yarn to rem sts and complete left front to correspond to right front, reversing shapings.

Sleeves

Using No.3 needles and A, cast on 46[50:56] sts. Work 2[2¼:3]in K1, P1 rib, inc 8[4:10]sts evenly across last row. 54[54:66] sts. Adjust length here. Change to No.5 needles.
Work in patt as given for back and fronts, beg with same patt row as marked, until sleeve measures 6½[8:9½]in from beg, ending with same patt row as back and fronts at underarm.
Shape cap
Keeping patt correct, bind off 2[3:4] sts at beg of next 2 rows. Dec one st at each end of next and every other row until 30[32:34] sts rem. Work 1 row. Bind off 3 sts at beg of next 6 rows. Bind off rem 12[14:16] sts.

Front borders

Mark positions for 8 buttons on left front for a girl or right front for a boy, top one to come in neckband with 7 more spaced at 2[2¼:2½]in intervals. Using No.3 needles and A cast on 8 sts. Work in K1, P1 rib until border is long enough to fit from hemline to neck shaping when slightly stretched, making buttonholes as markers are reached as foll:
Next row (buttonhole row) Rib 3 sts, bind off 2 sts, rib to end.
Next row Rib to end, casting on 2 sts above those bound-off in previous row.
Slip sts on holder. Make button border in same way, omitting buttonholes.

Neckband

Join shoulder seams. Using No.3 needles, A and with RS of work facing, work in rib across sts on one front border, pick up and K20[21:22] sts up front neck, pick up and K22[24:26] sts across back neck, pick up and K20[21:22] sts down front neck and work in rib across sts for other front border. 78[82:86] sts. Work 7 rows K1, P1 rib, making buttonhole as before on 3rd and 4th rows. Bind off loosely in rib.

Belt

Using No.3 needles and A cast on 8 sts. Work 36in K1, P1 rib, or desired length. Bind off in rib.

Finishing

Press each piece on WS under a damp cloth with a warm iron. Join sleeve seams. Sew in sleeves. Turn hem to WS at hemline and sl st down. Sew on front borders. Press seams. Sew on buttons.

12 Yoked sacque set worked in eyelet ridge stitch

Sizes

To fit 18[19]in chest
The figures in brackets [] refer to the 19in size
Length at center back, 10[10½]in
Sleeve seam, 5¼[5¾]in

Gauge

6 sts and 10½ rows to 1in over patt worked on No.4 needles

Materials

Dawn Wintuk Baby Yarn; 1-oz skeins
Sacque 4[4] balls
Bonnet and mittens 1[1] ball each
No. 3 knitting needles
No.4 knitting needles
No.6 knitting needles
No.3 long knitting needles for yoke
¾yd 1in ribbon for sacque
1yd 1in ribbon for bonnet
¾yd baby ribbon for mittens

Sacque back

Using No.6 needles cast on 72[76] sts. Beg with a K row work 5 rows st st.
Next row (hemline) K all sts.
Beg with a K row work 6 rows st st. Change to No.4 needles. Commence patt.
1st row (RS) K1, *yrn, P2 tog, rep from * to last st, K1.
This row forms patt. Cont in patt until work measures 5¼[5¾]in from hemline. Mark each end of last row with colored thread. Cont in patt for 1 inch more, ending with WS row. Slip sts on holder.

Sacque left front

Using No.6 needles cast on 35[37] sts. Beg with a K row work 5 rows st st.
Next row (hemline) K all sts.
Next row K to end, cast on 11sts. 46[48] sts.
Next row P to end.
Next row K to last 6 sts, sl 1 p-wise, K5.
Next row P to end.
Rep last 2 rows once more. Change to No.4 needles. Commence patt.
1st row K1, *yrn, P2 tog, rep from * to last 11 sts, K5, sl 1 p-wise, K5.
2nd row P11 sts, *yrn, P2 tog rep from * to last st, K1.
These 2 rows form patt. Cont in patt until work measures 5¼[5¾]in from hemline. Mark side edge of last row with colored thread. Cont in patt for 1 inch more, ending with a WS row. Slip sts on holder.

Sacque right front

Using No.6 needles cast on 35[37] sts. Beg with a K row work 5 rows st st.
Next row (hemline) K all sts.
Next row Cast on 11 sts, K across these 11 sts, K to end.
46[48] sts.
Next row P to end.
Next row K5, sl 1 p-wise, K to end.
Next row P to end.
Rep last 2 rows once more. Change to No.4 needles. Commence patt.
1st row K5, sl 1 p-wise, K5, *yrn, P2 tog, rep from * to last st, K1.
2nd row K1, *yrn, P2 tog, rep from * to last 11 sts, P11.
Finish to correspond to left front.

Sleeves

Using No.3 needles cast on 42[44] sts. Beg with a K row work 5 rows st st.
Next row (hemline) K all sts.
Beg with a K row work 6 rows st st. Change to No. 4 needles. Cont in patt as given for back until sleeve measures 5¼[5¾]in from hemline. Mark each end of last row with colored thread. Cont in patt for 1 inch more, ending with WS row. Slip sts on holder.

Yoke

Using long No.3 needles, with RS of work facing, beg at right front, K5, sl 1 p-wise, K6, (K2 tog) 17[18] times, K across 42[44] sts of first sleeve, across back K2, (K2 tog) 34[36] times, K2, K across 42[44] sts of 2nd sleeve, across left front (K2 tog) 17[18] times, K6, sl 1 p-wise, K5. 180[188] sts.
Next row P to end.
Next row K5, sl 1 p-wise, K to last 6 sts, sl 1 p-wise, K5.
Next row P to end.
Next row K5, sl 1 p-wise, K17[21], *sl 1, K1, psso, K2 tog, K9, rep from * to last 27[31] sts, sl 1, K1, psso, K2 tog, K17[21], sl 1 p-wise, K5. 158[166] sts.
Next row P to end.
Next row K5, sl 1 p-wise, K to last 6 sts, sl 1 p-wise, K5.
Next row P to end.
Rep last 2 rows once more.
Next row K5, sl 1 p-wise, K16[20], *sl 1, K1, psso, K2 tog, K7, rep from * to last 26[30] sts, sl 1, K1, psso, K2 tog, K16[20], sl 1 p-wise, K5. 136[144] sts.
Next row P to end.
Next row K5, sl 1 p-wise, K5, *yrn, P2 tog, rep from * to last 11 sts, K5, sl 1 p-wise, K5.
Next row P11, *yrn, P2 tog, rep from * to last 11 sts, P11.
Rep last 2 rows twice more.
Next row K5, sl 1 p-wise, K to last 6 sts, sl 1 p-wise, K5.
Next row P to end.
Next row K5, sl 1 p-wise, K15[19], *sl 1, K1, psso, K2 tog, K5, rep from * to last 25[29] sts, sl 1, K1, psso, K2 tog, K15[19], sl 1 p-wise, K5. 114[122] sts.
Next row P to end.
Next row K5, sl 1 p-wise, K to last 6 sts, sl 1 p-wise, K5.
Next row P to end.
Rep last 2 rows once more.
Next row K5, sl 1 p-wise, K14[18], *sl 1, K1, psso, K2 tog, K3, rep from * to last 24[28] sts, sl 1, K1, psso, K2 tog, K14[18], sl 1 p-wise, K5. 92[100] sts.
Next row P to end.
Next row K5, sl 1 p-wise, K6, *yrn, P2 tog, rep from * to last 11 sts, K5, sl 1 p-wise, K5.
Next row P11, *yrn, P2 tog, rep from * to last 11 sts, P11.
Rep last 2 rows twice more.
Next row K5, sl 1 p-wise, K13[13], *K2 tog, K2, rep from * to last 21[21] sts, K2 tog, K13[13] sl 1 p-wise, K5. 78[84] sts.
Next row P to end.
Next row K5, sl 1 p-wise, K5, ytf, K2 tog to form eyelet hole, K to last 13 sts, K2 tog, ytf, K5, sl 1 p-wise, K5.
Next row P to end.
Next row Bind off 11 sts, K to last 6 sts, sl 1 p-wise, K5.
Next row Bind off 11 sts, K to end to mark fold line.
Beg with a K row work 4 rows st st. Bind off loosely.

Finishing

Press pieces under a damp cloth with a warm iron for wool or dry cloth with a cool iron for synthetics. Join side and sleeve seams as far as colored threads. Join rem section of sleeve to rem section of armhole. Fold hem, cuffs, front and neck edging to WS at hemline and sl st down.
Run ribbon through neck, bringing ribbon out at eyelet holes.

Bonnet

Using No.3 needles cast on 90[94] sts. Work hem as given for sacque back. Change to No.4 needles. Work in patt as given for sacque back until work measures 4[4¼]in from hemline, ending with a WS row.
2nd size only
Next row K12 sts, *K2 tog, K21 sts, rep from * to last 13 sts, K2 tog, K11 sts. 90 sts.
Next row P to end.
Both sizes
Shape back
1st row *K7, K2 tog, rep from * to end. 80 sts.
2nd and every other row P to end.
3rd row *K6, K2 tog, rep from * to end. 70 sts.
5th row *K5, K2 tog, rep from * to end. 60 sts.
7th row *K4, K2 tog, rep from * to end. 50 sts.
9th row *K3, K2 tog, rep from * to end. 40 sts.
11th row *K2, K2 tog, rep from * to end. 30 sts.
13th row *K1, K2 tog, rep from * to end. 20 sts.
14th row *P2 tog, rep from * to end. 10 sts.
Break yarn, thread through rem sts, draw up and fasten off.

Finishing

Press as given for coat. Join back seam as far as shaping. Fold face edging to WS at hemline and sl st down.
Neck edging Using No.3 needles and with RS of work facing, pick up and K 70[74] sts evenly along base of bonnet. Beg with a P row work 4 rows st st.
Next row (hemline) K all sts.
Beg with a K row work 4 rows st st. Bind off loosely.
Fold neck edging to WS at hemline and sl st down.
Run ribbon through neck hem.

Mittens

Using No.3 needles cast on 40 sts. Beg with a K row work 11 rows st st.
Next row (hemline) K all sts.
Beg with a K row work 12 rows st st.
Make eyelet holes
Next row *K2, ytf, K2 tog, rep from * to end.
Next row P to end.
Change to No.4 needles. Cont in patt as given for sacque back until work measures 3¾[4]in from hemline.
End with a WS row.
Shape tip
1st row *K2, K2 tog, rep from * to end. 30 sts.
2nd row K to end.
3rd row *K1, K2 tog, rep from * to end. 20 sts.
4th row *K2 tog, rep from * to end. 10 sts.
Break yarn, thread through rem sts, draw up and fasten off.

Finishing

Press as given for sacque. Join side seam. Fold cuff to WS at hemline and sl st down. Run ribbon through eyelet holes at wrist.

Bramble stitch layette with shawl

Sizes

To fit an 18[20]in chest
The figures in brackets [] refer to the 20in size
Dress length to center back, 12[14]in
Sleeve seam, 1½in
Sacque length to center back, 10[11]in
Sleeve seam, 5½[6]in
Shawl 36 by 36in

Gauge

7 sts and 10 rows to 1in over patt worked on No.3 needles

Materials

Brunswick Fairhaven Fingering Yarn
Dress 4[5] balls
Sacque 3[4] balls
Bonnet and Bootees 1 ball each
Shawl 10 balls
No.1 knitting needles, No.3 knitting needles, No.5 knitting needles
Two buttons for dress
Three buttons for sacque
¾yd ribbon for bootees. ½yd ribbon for bonnet.

Dress back

Using No.3 needles cast on 127[139] sts.
1st row (RS) *K1, ytf, sl 1, K1, psso, K1, K2 tog, ytf, rep from * to last st, K1.
2nd row *P2, yrn, P3 tog, yrn, P1, rep from * to last st, P1.
3rd row *K1, K2 tog, ytf, K1, ytf, sl 1, K1, psso, rep from * to last st, K1.
4th row P2 tog, *yrn, P3, yrn, P3 tog, rep from * to last 5 sts, yrn, P3, yrn, P2 tog.
These 4 rows form patt. Cont in patt until work measures 8½[10]in from beg, ending with a 4th patt row.
Shape raglan
Next row Bind off 6 sts, K to end.
Next row Bind off 6 sts, P3 tog, *P2 tog, rep from * to last st, P1. 58[64] sts.
Beg with a K row cont in st st, dec one st at each end of next four rows.**
Divide for back opening
Next row K2 tog, K23[26] sts. Turn. Slip rem sts on holder.
Next row K3, P to end.
*** Keeping 3 sts at inner edge in garter st (g st), dec one st at raglan edge on every RS row only until 12[13] sts rem, ending with a P row. Bind off. Attach yarn to rem sts at inner edge, K to last 2 sts, K2 tog.
Next row P to last 3 sts, K3.
Complete to correspond to first side, working from ***.

Dress front

Work as given for back to **. Dec one st at each end of every RS row until 36[40] sts rem, ending with a P row.
Shape neck
Next row K2 tog, K11[13] sts and slip on holder, bind off next 10 sts, K to last 2 sts, K2 tog.
Cont dec at raglan edge as before, *at the same time* dec one st at neck edge on next 2 rows, then on every RS row until 3 sts rem. Dec at raglan edge only on next row. K2 tog. Fasten off. Attach yarn to rem sts at inner edge and complete to correspond to first side.

Sleeves

Using No.3 needles cast on 49[55] sts. Work 4 patt rows as given for back 4 times in all.

Shape raglan

Beg with a K row cont in st st, binding off 6 sts at beg of next 2 rows. Dec one st at each end of every RS row until 7[9] sts rem, ending with a P row. Bind off.

Neck edging

Join raglan seams. Using No.1 needles and with RS of work facing, pick up and K 68[72] sts evenly around neck edge. Bind off tightly.

Finishing

Press each piece lightly on WS under a dry cloth using a cool iron. Join side and sleeve seams. Make 2 button loops at back opening. Press seams. Sew on buttons.

Sacque

Using No.1 needles cast on 187[205] sts and work in one piece to armholes. Work 8 rows g st. Change to No.3 needles. Keeping 6 sts at each end in g st, cont in patt as given for dress until work measures 6½[7]in from beg, ending with a 4th patt row.
Divide for armholes
Next row K34[48] sts, bind off 10 sts, K81[89] sts, bind off 10 sts, K to end.
Complete left front on these sts.
Next row K6, P1, *P2 tog, P2, rep from * to last 4[5] sts, P to end. 35[39] sts.
** Beg with a K row cont in st st, dec one st at raglan edge on next 6[8] rows, then on every RS row until 23[25] sts rem, ending at center front edge.
Shape neck
Next row K6 sts and slip on holder, bind off next 3 sts, work to end.
Cont dec at raglan edge as before, *at the same time* dec one st at neck edge on the next 4 rows, then every other row until 3 sts rem. Dec at raglan edge only on next row. K2 tog. Fasten off.
With WS of work facing attach yarn to center sts and complete back.
Next row P1, *P2 tog, P2, rep from * to end. 61[67] sts.
Beg with a K row cont in st st, dec one st at each end of next 6[8] rows, then on every RS row until 25[27] sts rem, ending with a P row. Bind off.
With WS of work facing attach yarn to rem sts and complete right front on these sts.
Next row P6[7] sts, *P2 tog, P2, rep from * to last 9 sts, P2 tog, P1, K6.
Next row (buttonhole row) K3 sts, ytf, K2 tog, K to end.
Complete to correspond to left front working from ** and working 2nd buttonhole on 10th[12th] row from previous one.

Sleeves

Using No.3 needles cast on 49[55] sts. Work 4 patt rows as given for dress until sleeve measures 5½[6]in from beg, ending with a 4th patt row.
Shape raglan
Work as given for dress sleeve.

Neckband

Join raglan seams. Using No.1 needles and with RS of work facing, K across sts on holder at right front, pick up and K60[64] sts evenly all around neck edge to left front band, K across sts on holder. 72[76] sts. Work 8 rows g st making 3rd buttonhole as before on 4th row. Bind off.

Finishing

Press as given for dress. Join sleeve seams. Press seams. Sew on buttons.

Bonnet

Using No.1 needles cast on 85[91] sts. Work 8 rows g st. Change to No.3 needles and cont in patt as given for dress until work measures 3½[3¾]in from beg, ending with a 4th patt row.
Shape back
1st row K5[1] sts, *K2 tog, K8 sts, rep from * to end.
2nd and every other row P to end..
3rd row K5[1] sts, *K2 tog, K7 sts, rep from * to end.
5th row K5[1] sts, *K2 tog, K6 sts, rep from * to end.
Cont dec in this way on every other row until 21[19] sts rem, ending with a K row.
Next row P1, * P2 tog, rep from * to end. Break yarn, thread through rem sts, draw up and fasten off. Join back seam for approx 2½in.

Neck edging

Using No.1 needles and with RS of work facing, pick up and K66[70] sts evenly around lower edge of bonnet. Bind off firmly.

Finishing

Press seam as given for dress. Sew on ribbon at either side to tie under chin.

Bootees

Using No.1 needles cast on 43 sts. Work 8 rows g st. Work 4 patt rows as given for dress 4 times in all.
Divide for instep
Next row K28 sts, turn, K13 sts, turn.
Work 22 rows g st on these 13 sts. Break yarn, With RS of work facing, attach yarn at side of instep and pick up and K12 sts evenly from side of instep, K across instep sts, pick up and K12 sts from other side of instep, K to end of row. 67 sts. Work 15 rows g st across all sts.
Shape sole
1st row K5 sts, K2 tog, K20 sts, K2 tog, K9 sts, K2 tog, K20 sts, K2 tog, K5 sts.
2nd row K4 sts, K2 tog, K20 sts, K2 tog, K7 sts, K2 tog, K20 sts, K2 tog, K4 sts.
3rd row K3 sts, K2 tog, K20 sts, K2 tog, K5 sts, K2 tog, K20 sts, K2 tog, K3 sts.
4th row K2 sts, K2 tog, K20 sts, K2 tog, K3 sts, K2 tog, K20 sts, K2 tog, K2 sts.
5th row K1 st, K2 tog, K20 sts, K2 tog, K1 st, K2 tog, K20 sts, K2 tog, K1 st. Bind off.

Finishing

Join leg and foot seams. Press seams. Run ribbon through last row of patt holes at ankles.

Shawl center piece

Using No.5 needles cast on 217 sts. Work in patt as given for dress until work measures 32 in from beg, ending with a 4th patt row. Bind off.

Shawl border

Using No.3 needles cast on 12 sts.
1st row K5 sts, yrn, P2 tog, K1, (yrn, P2 tog) twice.
2nd row Ytf, K7 sts, yrn, P2 tog, K2 sts, sl1.
3rd row K5 sts, yrn, P2 tog, K2 sts, yrn, P2 tog, ytf, K2 sts.
4th row Yrn, P2 tog, K7 sts, yrn, P2 tog, K2 sts, sl 1.

5th row K5 sts, yrn, P2 tog, K3 sts, yrn, P2 tog, ytf, K2 sts.
6th row Yrn, P2 tog, K8 sts, yrn, P2 tog, K2 sts, sl 1.
7th row K5 sts, yrn, P2 tog, K4 sts, yrn, P2 tog, ytf, K2 sts.
8th row Yrn, P2 tog, K9 sts, yrn, P2 tog, K2 sts, sl 1.
9th row K5 sts, yrn, P2 tog, K9 sts.
10th row K5 sts, pass 1st, 2nd, 3rd and 4th sts over 5th st, K6 sts, yrn, P2 tog, K2 sts, sl 1.
These 10 rows form patt. Cont in patt until border fits along cast on edge of center piece, work 1½in more to allow for easing around corner, cont and work the same length 3 times more, ending with a 10th patt row. Bind off.

Finishing

Join short edges of border. Pin border to center piece, placing marker at each corner and seam to last corner. Join border to center piece using a flat seam and easing in fullness at corners. Press seam and edges.

All-in-one shorts suit, with crochet edging

Sizes
To fit 22 [24:26]in chest
The figures in brackets [] refer to the 24 and 26in sizes respectively.
Length to shoulder, 17 [18½:20]in
Sleeve seam, 1 [1¼:1½]in
Gauge
5 sts and 6 rows to 1in over st st worked on No.6 needles
Materials
7[8:9] skeins Bernat Venetian in main color, A
1 ball of contrast color, B
No.4 knitting needles
No.6 knitting needles
No.E crochet hook
10 [12:14]in zipper

Right half
Using No.4 needles and A, cast on 78[83:88] sts. Beg with a K row work 5 rows st st.
Next row K all sts tbl to form hemline. Change to No.6 needles. Beg with a K row cont in st st until work measures 1½ [2:2½] in from hemline, ending with a P row.
Shape gusset
Bind off at beg of next and every row 5 sts once, 3 sts once and 2 sts twice. Dec one st at each end every other row 3 times. Cont without shaping until work measures 4 [4½:5]in from hemline, ending with a P row. Bind off 3 sts at beg of next row. 57[62:67] sts. Cont without shaping until work measures 13 [14:15]in from hemline, ending with a P row.
Divide for armhole
Next row K23[25:27] sts, bind off 6 sts, K to end.
Complete this side first.
Next row P to end.
Bind off 2 sts at beg of next row, then dec one st at this edge every other row twice. 24[27:30] sts. Cont without shaping until armhole measures 4 [4½:5]in from beg, ending with a P row.
Shape shoulder and neck
Next row Bind off 4[4:6] sts, K to end.
Next row Bind off 8[9:10] sts, P to end.
Next row Bind off 4[6:6] sts, K to end.
New row Bind off 2 sts, P to end.
Bind off rem 6 sts.
With WS of work facing, attach yarn to rem sts,

bind off 2 sts, P to end. Dec one st at armhole edge every other row twice. Cont without shaping until armhole measures 2 [2½:3]in from beg, ending with a P row.
Shape neck
Bind off 2 sts at beg of next row. Dec one st at neck edge every other row 3 times. 14[16:18] sts. Cont without shaping until armhole measures same as back to shoulder, ending with a K row.
Shape shoulder
At arm edge, bind off 4[4:6] sts once, 4[6:6] sts once and 6 sts once.

Left half
Work as given for right half, reversing all shapings.

Sleeves
Using No.4 needles and A, cast on 42[44:46] sts. Work hem as given for right half. Change to No.6 needles. Beg with a K row cont in st st, inc one st at each end of 3rd [5th:5th] row. Cont without shaping until sleeve measures 1 [1¼:1½]in from hemline, ending with a P row.
Shape cap
Bind off 4 sts at beg of next 2 rows and 2 sts at beg of next 2 rows. Dec one st at each end every other row 7[8:9] times, ending with a P row. Bind off 2 sts at beg of next 4 rows. Bind off rem 10 sts.

Pocket
Using No.4 needles and A, cast on 16 sts. Beg with a K row work 2in st st, ending with a K row.
Next row K all sts tbl to mark fold line.
Beg with a K row work 3 rows st st. Bind off.

Finishing
Press each piece lightly under a damp cloth with a warm iron. Join shoulder seams. Sew in sleeves. Join sleeve and back seams. Join lower part of front seam leaving 9 [11:13]in open for zipper. Turn all hems to WS and sl st down. Using No.E crochet hook and A, with RS of work facing, work in sc along front opening, around neck and down other side of front opening. Break off A. Attach B and start again at beg of row, work one ss into each st all around, then work across lower edge of opening. Break off B. Attach A and start again at beg of row, work one sc into each st, working behind the row of B into the loops of first row of A, working 3 sc into each front corner of neck edge. turn and work a 2nd row of sc. Break off A. With RS of work facing and A, beg at corner of neck and work a row of sc around neck to other corner, turn and work a 2nd row of sc. Fasten off. Sew in zipper to front opening. Turn hem at top of pocket to WS and sl st down. Make a crochet ch using B and sew onto pocket in the shape of an initial. Sew on pocket. Press all seams.

Practical dungaree and pullover set with big striped pockets

Sizes
To fit 22 [24:26]in chest
The figures in brackets [] refer to the 24 and 26in sizes respectively
Pullover length to shoulder, 12½[14½:16½]in
Sleeve seam 8 [9½:11]in
Trousers inside leg, 12½ [14½:17]in
Gauge
7 sts and 9 rows to 1in over st st worked on No.4 needles

Materials
Columbia Minerva Nantuk Fingering Yarn
Pullover 4[5:6] skeins in main color, A
Trousers 6[8:9] skeins of contrast color, B
1 skein of main color, A
No.2 knitting needles; No.4 knitting needles
Set of 4 No.2 double-pointed needles
4 buttons

Pullover back
Using No.2 needles and A, cast on 79[85:93] sts.
1st row K1, *P1, K1, rep from * to end.
2nd row P1, *K1, P1, rep from * to end.
Rep these 2 rows for 1½in, ending with a 2nd row and inc one st at end of last row on 24in size only. 79[86:93] sts. Change to No.4 needles.
1st row *P2, K5, rep from * to last 2 sts, P2.
2nd row *K2, P5, rep from * to last 2 sts, K2. These 2 rows form patt. Cont in patt until work measures 8 [9½:11]in from beg, ending with a WS row.
Shape armholes
Bind off 5 sts at beg of next 2 rows. 69[76:83] sts. Dec one st at each end every other row until 27[30:33] sts rem, ending with a WS row. Slip sts on holder.

Pullover front
Work as given for back until 45[48:51] sts rem after beg armhole shaping, ending with a WS row.
Shape neck
Next row Dec one st, rib 15 sts, turn and slip rem sts on holder.
Next row Rib to end.
Next row Dec one st, rib to last 2 sts, dec one st. Rep last 2 rows 5 times more, then cont to dec at raglan edge only every other row twice, ending with a RS row.
Next row P2 tog. Fasten off.
With RS of work facing, sl first 11[14:17] sts on holder and leave for center neck, attach yarn to rem sts, rib to last 2 sts, dec one st. Complete to correspond to first side, reverse shaping.

Sleeves
Using No.2 needles and A, cast on 39[43:47] sts. Work in K1, P1 rib as given for back for 1½in, ending with a 2nd row. Change to No.4 needles.
1st row K1[3:5] sts, *P2, K5, rep from * to last 3[5:7] sts, P2, K1[3:5] sts.
2nd row P1[3:5] sts, *K2, P5, rep from * to last 3[5:7] sts, K2, P1[3:5] sts.
Cont in rib as established, inc one st at each end of 5th and every foll 4th[6th:6th] row until there are 59[63:67] sts, and working extra sts into patt when possible. Cont without shaping until sleeve measures 8 [9½:11]in from beg, ending with a WS row.

Shape raglan cap
Bind off 5 sts at beg of next 2 rows. Dec one st at each end every other row until 7 sts rem, ending with a WS row. Slip sts on holder.

Neckband
Join raglan seams. Using set of 4 No.2 needles, A and with RS of work facing, K across sts of back neck and left sleeve, K2 tog at seam, pick up and K16 sts down side of neck, K across center front neck sts, pick up and K16 sts up other side of neck, then K across sts of right sleeve, K last st tog with first st of back neck. 82[88:94] sts. Join. Work in rounds of K1, P1 rib for 3½ [4:4½]in. Bind off loosely in rib.

Finishing
Press each piece under a damp cloth with a

A B C D E F
G H I J K L
M N O P Q R
S T U V W X
Y Z

warm iron. Join side and sleeve seams. Sew in sleeves. Press seams.

Trousers right half
Using No.2 needles and B, cast on 70[75:80] sts. Beg with a K row work 10 rows st st. P 1 row to mark hemline. Beg with a P row work 11 rows st st. P 1 row to mark 2nd fold line. Beg with a P row work 6 rows st st. Change to No. 4 needles. Beg with a K row to reverse work, cont in st st, inc one st at each end of every 14th [14th:16th] row until there are 82[89:96] sts. Cont without shaping until work measures 11½ [13½:16]in from 2nd fold line, ending with a P row. Inc one st at each end of every other row 5 times, ending with a P row. 92[99:106] sts.
Shape gusset
Bind off 4 sts at beg of next row; then 2 sts every other row 3 times. Dec one st at each end of every other row twice; then every 4th row twice, ending with a P row. 74[81:88] sts. Slip sts on holder to be worked later.

Trousers left half
Work as given for right half, reversing shaping of gusset and ending with a P row.

Trousers body
Next row K first 73[80:87] sts of left half, K next st tog with first st of right half, K to end. 147[161:175] sts.
Cont in st st until work measures 5½ [6:6½]in from beg of body, ending with a P row.
Shape back
Next row K16[20:24] sts, turn and P to end.
Next row K12[15:18] sts, turn and P to end.
Next row K8[10:12] sts, turn and P to end.
Next row K4[5:6] sts, turn and P to end.
K 1 row across all sts, then shape other side to correspond to first side, reading K for P and P for K.
Next row P to end.
Next row K110[120:121] sts, turn and slip rem 37[41:44] sts on holder.
Next row P73[79:87] sts, turn and slip rem 37[41:44] sts on holder.
Cont in st st until work measures 11 [12:13½]in from gusset, ending with a K row.
Next row K11[12:13] sts, P to last 11[12:13] sts, K to end.
Next row K to end.
Next row Bind off 11[12:13] sts K-wise, P to last 11[12:13] sts, bind off rem sts K-wise. Break off yarn. Attach yarn to rem sts and cont in st st, dec one st at each end every other row until 33[37:41] sts rem, ending with a P row. Change to No.4 needles. K 2 rows garter st.
Next row K3 sts, bind off 2 sts, K4 sts, bind off 2 sts, K to last 11 sts, bind off 2 sts, K4 sts, bind off 2 sts, K to end.
Next row K to end, casting on 2 sts above those bound-off on previous row.
K3 more rows garter st. Bind off K-wise.
With RS of work facing, attach yarn to rem sts on holder, K across all sts, K2 tog in center. 73[81:87] sts. Complete to correspond to first side, omitting buttonholes.

Pockets (make 2)
Using No.2 needles and B, cast on 26[28:30] sts. K 2 rows. Attach A. **K2 rows A, then work 4 rows st st using B. Rep from ** until work measures 4½ [4¾:5]in from beg, ending with K 2 rows A. K3 rows B. Bind off K-wise using B.

Straps (make 2)
Using No.2 needles and B, cast on 16 sts. P 1 row.
2nd row Using B, K to end.
3rd row Using B, K2, ytf, sl 1 P-wise, P10, sl 1 P-wise, ytb, K2.
4th and 5th rows As 2nd and 3rd rows.
6th and 7th rows Using A, K to end.
Rep rows 2-7 for 8 [8½:9]in. Bind off.

Finishing
Press as given for pullover.
Join back seam. Join leg seams and gusset. Join side seams. Turn in hem at first fold line to RS and sl st down, then turn up hem to RS again on 2nd fold line and press to form turn up.
Using No.2 needles, B and with RS of work facing, pick up and K 66[70:74] sts around armhole. K 6 rows. Bind off K-wise. Turn in edges of straps at sl st line and st down. Sew straps to back, then sew on 2 buttons to other end of each strap to fasten. Sew on pockets. Press all seams.

16 *Fringed and braided vest*

Sizes
To fit 24 [26:28]in chest
The figures in brackets [] refer to the 26 and 28in sizes respectively
Length to shoulder, 11 [12¼:13½]in
Gauge
4½ sts and 6 rows to 1in over st st worked on No.7 needles, using yarn double throughout
Materials
5[7:8] skeins Spinner Wintuk Fingering in main color, A
1 skein each of contrast colors, B and C
No.7 knitting needles
One No.E crochet hook

Back
Using No.7 needles and A double throughout, cast on 59[64:69] sts. Beg with a K row work 6½ [7¼:8]in st st, ending with a P row.
Shape armholes
Bind off 4 sts at beg of next 2 rows; then 2 sts at beg of next 2 rows. Dec one st at each end, every other row 4[5:6] times, then at each end of every 4th row twice. 35[38:41] sts. Cont without shaping until work measures 11 [12¼:13½]in from beg, ending with a K row.
Shape neck and shoulders
Next row P12[13:14] sts, bind off 11[12:13] sts, P to end.
Complete this side first.
Next row Bind off 5 sts, K to last 2 sts, K2 tog.
Next row P to end.
Bind off rem 6[7:8] sts.
With RS of work facing, attach yarn to rem 12[13:14] sts and complete to correspond to first side, reversing shaping.

Right front
Using No.7 needles and A double throughout, cast on 23[26:29] sts. Beg with a K row work in st st, inc one st at beg of 3rd row. Inc 1st at front edge every other row twice, then every 4th row twice. 28[31:34] sts. Cont without shaping until work measures same as back to underarm, ending with a K row.
Shape armhole
At arm edge, bind off 4 sts; then 2 sts once. Dec one st at armhole edge every other row 4[5:6] times; then on every 4th row twice, *at the same time* shape front edge when work measures 9 [9¾:10½]in from beg, ending with a P row.
Shape front edge
Dec one st at front edge every other row 10[11:12] times rows. Cont without shaping until work measures same as back to shoulder, ending with a K row. Bind off.

Left front
Work as given for right front, reversing all shapings.

Finishing
Press each piece under a damp cloth with a warm iron.
Join shoulder and side seams.
Fringe Using No.E crochet hook and A single, make a ch long enough to fit around outer edge of vest, turn and work 1 row sc along ch. Fasten off. Cut a strip of cardboard about 1½in wide. Commence at beg of sc row, attach yarn and ch1, *loop around cardboard, insert hook into next st and draw up a loop, yrh and draw through 2 loops, ch1, rep from * all along row, taking cardboard out of loops at intervals. Fasten off. Make 2 more pieces for armholes.
Picot edging Using No.E crochet hook and B, make a ch long enough to fit around outer edge of vest about ½in inside the edge.
Next row Into 2nd ch from hook work 1sc, *work 3sc into next ch, rep from * to end. Fasten off.
Sew fringe to edges of vest with WS of sc row facing outwards. Sew picot edging ½in inside edge with picots facing towards outer edge.
Using No.E crochet hook and C, with RS of work facing, work a ch all around about ½in inside picot edging, making loops at each lower corner, also at center back neck and center of lower edge of back.
Press all seams.

17 *Dress with narrow contrasting bands*

Sizes
To fit 22 [24:26]in chest
The figures in brackets [] refer to the 24 and 26in sizes respectively
Length to shoulder, 15½ [17:18½]in
Sleeve seam, 1½ [2:2½]in
Gauge
7½ sts and 10 rows to 1in over st st worked on No.2 needles
Materials
6[7:8] balls American Thread Puritan Bedspread Cotton in main color, A. 1 ball of contrast color, B
No.1 knitting needles; No.2 knitting needles
One No.B crochet hook
3 buttons

Back
Using No.1 needles and A, cast on 134[142:150] sts. Beg with a K row work 7 rows st st.
Next row K all sts tbl to form hemline.
Change to No.2 needles. Beg with a K row work 12 rows st st. Attach B. (K 2 rows B then work 6 rows st st with A) twice, K 2 rows B. Break off B and cont in st st with A only.
Shape darts
Next row K1, K2 tog, K27[29:31] sts, sl 1, K1, psso, K27[29:31] sts, K2 tog, K12 sts, sl 1, K1, psso, K27[29:31] sts, K2 tog, K27[29:31] sts, sl 1, K1, psso, K1. 128[136:144] sts.
Beg with a P row work 7[9:11] rows st st.
Next row K1, K2 tog, K26[28:30] sts, sl 1, K1, psso, K25[27:29] sts, K2 tog, K12 sts, sl 1, K1, psso, K25[27:29] sts, K2 tog, K26[28:30] sts, sl 1, K1, psso, K1. 122[130:138] sts.
Cont dec in this way on every foll 8th [10th:12th] row until 86[94:102] sts rem. Cont without shaping until work measures 11½ [12½:13½]in from hemline, ending with a P row.

Shape armholes

Bind off 5 sts at beg of next 2 rows; then 2 sts at beg of next 2 rows. Dec one st at each end of every other row 3[4:5] times; ending with a P row. 66[72:78] sts.

Divide for opening

Next row K31[34:37] sts, turn and cast on 4 sts, slip rem sts on holder.

Next row K4 sts, P to end.

Keeping 4 sts at inside edge in garter st, cont without shaping until armhole measures 4 [4½: 5]in from beg, ending with a WS row.

Shape shoulder and neck

Next row Bind off 5[5:6] sts, K to end.

Next row Bind off 11[12:13] sts, P to end.

Next row Bind off 5[5:6] sts, K to end.

Next row Bind off 3 sts, P to end.

Next row Bind off 5[5:6] sts. K to last 2 sts. K2 tog.

Next row P to end.

Bind off rem 5[7:6] sts.

Mark positions for 3 buttons on this side, first to come on 7th row above beg of opening, and last to come 2 rows below neck shaping with one more evenly spaced between.

With RS of work facing, attach yarn to rem sts, K to end.

Next row P to last 4 sts, K4.

Rep last 2 rows twice more.

Next row (buttonhole row) K2 sts, bind off 2 sts, K to end.

Next row Patt to end, casting on 2 sts above those bound-off on previous row.

Complete to correspond to first side, making buttonholes as before as markers are reached, and reversing all shapings.

Front

Work as given for back until armhole shaping is completed. Cont without shaping until armholes measure 2½ [3:3½]in from beg, ending with a P row.

Shape neck

Next row K28[30:32] sts, turn and slip rem sts on holder.

At neck edge, bind off 2 sts every other row twice, then dec one st at neck edge every other row until 20[22:24] sts rem. Cont without shaping until armhole measures same as back to shoulder, ending at armhole edge.

Shape shoulder

At neck edge, bind off 5[5:6] sts every other row 3 times and 5[7:6] sts once.

With RS of work facing, sl first 10[12:14] sts onto holder, attach yarn to rem sts and K to end. Complete to correspond to first side, reversing shaping.

Sleeves

Using No.1 needles and A, cast on 54[58:62] sts. Beg with a K row work 7 rows st st.

Next row K all sts tbl to form hemline.

Change to No.2 needles. Beg with a K row cont in st st, inc one st at each end of 7th and foll 4th row. Cont without shaping until sleeve measures 1½ [2:2½]in from hemline, ending with a P row.

Shape cap

Bind off 5 sts at beg of next 2 rows. Dec one st at each end every other row 10[12:14] times. Bind off 2 sts at beg of next 6 rows; then 3 sts at beg of next 2 rows. Bind off rem 10 sts.

Collar

Using No.2 needles and A, cast on 49[51:53] sts.

1st row P1, *K1, P1, rep from * to end.

2nd row K1, *P1, K1, rep from * to end.

Rep these 2 rows twice more.

Next row Rib 5 sts, K to last 5 sts, rib 5.

Next row Rib 5 sts, P to last 5 sts, rib 5.

Rep last 2 rows once more.

Next row Rib 5 sts, K1, K2 tog, K to last 8 sts, sl 1, K1, psso, K1, rib 5.

Cont dec in this way on every 4th row 4 times more. Cont without shaping until work measures 2 [2¼:2½]in from beg, ending with a WS row. Bind off 12[13:14] sts once; then 5 sts every other row 4 times. Bind off rem sts. Work second piece in same manner, reversing shaping.

Edging

Using No.B crochet hook, B and with RS of collar facing, crochet a ch along the 3rd st from edge, (the P st), down side of collar along 2nd row of lower edge, then along 3rd st in from other side. Rep along 5th st and 4th row from lower edge. Fasten off.

Finishing

Press each piece under a damp cloth with a warm iron. Join shoulder seams. Sew in sleeves. Join side and sleeve seams. Turn hems to WS and sl st down. Sew on 2 pieces of collar. Sew down underflap on back opening. Press seams. Sew on buttons. Using 2 strands each of A and B, make a ch 24 [26:28]in long. Tie into a bow and sew to front neck edge under collar.

Jumpsuit with short striped sleeves and zippered front closing

Sizes

To fit 22 [24]in chest

The figures in brackets [] refer to the 24in size only

Length to shoulder, 26½ [30½]in

Sleeve seam, 4½ [5]in

Gauge

6 sts and 8 rows to 1in over rib patt worked on No.4 needles

Materials

6[7] balls Bear Brand or Fleisher or Botany Soufflé in main color, A

2[2] balls of contrast color, B

No.2 knitting needles; No.4 knitting needles

4in contrasting color zipper.

Right half

Using No.2 needles and A, cast on 86[91] sts.

1st row P1, *K4, P1, rep from * to end.

2nd row K1, *P4, K1, rep from * to end.

These 2 rows form patt. Cont in patt until work measures 1¼in from beg, ending with a 1st row.

Next row K all sts tbl to form hemline.

Change to No.4 needles. Beg with a 1st row, cont in rib until work measures 12 [15]in from hemline, ending with a WS row.

Shape crotch

Bind off 3 sts at beg of next 2 rows, 2 sts at beg of next 2 rows. Dec one st at each end of next and every foll 4th 3 times more. 68[73] sts. Cont without shaping until work measures 22 [25½]in from hemline, ending with a WS row.

Divide for armhole

Next row Rib 31[33] sts, bind off 6[7] sts, rib to end.

Cont on last 31[33] sts for back. Dec one st at armhole edge every other row 3 times. Cont without shaping until armhole measures 3½ [4]in from beg, ending with a WS row.

Shape shoulder

At arm edge, bind off 5 sts every other row twice and 4[5] sts once. Slip rem 14[15] sts on holder.

With WS of work facing, attach yarn to rem sts

and rib to end. Dec one st at end of every other row 3 times. Cont without shaping until armhole measures 2½ [3]in from beg, ending with a RS row.

Shape neck

Next row Rib to last 10[11] sts, turn and slip these 10[11] sts on holder.

Dec one st at neck edge every other row 4 times. Cont without shaping until armhole measures same as back to shoulder, ending with a RS row.

Shape shoulder

At arm, bind off 5 sts twice and 4[5] sts once.

Left half

Work as given for right half, reversing all shapings.

Sleeves

Using No.2 needles and A, cast on 50[54] sts. Work 1½in K2, P2 rib, ending with a WS row. Change to No.4 needles.

Next row K2[4] sts, *P1, K4, rep from * to last 3[5] sts, P1, K2[4] sts.

Next row P2[4] sts, *K1, P4, rep from * to last 3[5] sts, K1, P2[4] sts.

Rep last 2 rows once more. Attach B, Cont in rib as established, working 4 rows B and 4 rows A throughout and K each first row at change of color, *at the same time* inc one st at each end of next and every foll 6th row until there are 56[60] sts. Cont without shaping until sleeve measures 4½ [5]in from beg, ending with a WS row.

Shape cap

Bind off 2 sts at beg of every row until 20 sts rem. Cont on these 20 sts for length of shoulder, ending with a WS row. Slip sts on holder.

Neckband

Sew saddle caps of sleeves to front and back shoulders. Join center back seam. Using No.2 needles, A and with RS of work facing, K across front neck sts, pick up and K8 sts up side of neck, K across sts of right sleeve, back neck and left sleeve, K2 tog at each seam and centre back seam, pick up and K8 sts down other side of neck, then K across front neck sts. 101[105] sts.

Next row K2[4] sts, (P2, K2 tog, K1, P2, K2) 11 times, K0[2] sts. 90[94] sts.

Next row K4[2] sts, (P2, K2) 20[22] times, P2, K4[2] sts.

Next row K2[4] sts, (P2, K2) 21[21] times, P2, K2[4] sts.

Rep last 2 rows for 1½in, ending with a RS row. Bind off in rib.

Pockets (make 2)

Using No.2 needles and A, cast on 18 sts. Beg first row with K2, work 4 rows K2, P2 rib. Change to No.4 neeedles. Attach B. K 1 row.

Next row K2 sts, *P4, K1, rep from * twice more, K1.

Next row K1, P1, *K4, P1, rep from * twice more, K1.

Rib 1 more row, then work 4 rows A, 4 rows B, 4 rows A, always K first row at change of color.

Next row Using B, K2 sts, K2 tog, rib to last 4 sts, K2 tog tbl, K2 sts.

Next row K2 sts, P3, K1, P4, K1, P3, K2.

Next row K1, P1, K2 tog, rib to last 4 sts, K2 tog tbl, P1, K1.

Keeping striped patt correct, cont dec in this way at each end of every other row until 8 sts rem. Bind off.

Finishing

Press each piece under a dry cloth with a cool iron. Join center front seam, leaving top 4in open for zipper. Sew in zipper. Sew in sleeves.

Join sleeve seams. Join leg seams. Turn hems to WS and sl st down. Sew on pockets. Press seams.

Pullover with three-color Jacquard design

Sizes
To fit 26 [28:30:32]in chest
The figures in brackets [] refer to the 28, 30 and 32in sizes respectively
Length to shoulder, 16 [18:20:22]in
Sleeve seam, 11 [12½:14:16]in

Gauge
7½ sts and 10 rows to 1in over st st worked on No.3 needles.

Materials
5[5:6:7] skeins Dawn Wintuk Baby Yarn in main color, A
2 skeins each of contrast colors, B and C
No.2 knitting needles; No.3 knitting needles
Set of 4 No.2 double-pointed needles

Back
Using No.2 needles and A, cast on 101[109: 117:125] sts.
1st row K1, *P1, K1, rep from * to end.
2nd row P1, *K1, P1, rep from * to end.
Rep these 2 rows for 1½in, ending with a 2nd row and inc one st at end of last row. 102[110: 118:126] sts. Change to No.3 needles. Commence patt.
1st row Using A, K to end.
2nd row Using A, P to end.
Rep last 2 rows once more.
5th row Using B, K1, *K3 sts, sl 1 keeping the yarn on WS of work, rep from * to last st, K1.
6th row Using B, P1, *sl 1 keeping yarn at front of work, P3, rep from * to last st, P1.
7th row Using A, K1, *sl 1, K3, rep from * to last st, K1.
8th row Using A, P1, *P3, sl 1, rep from * to last st, P1.
9th row Using B, K2, *sl 1, K3, rep from * to end.
10th row Using B, *P3, sl 1, rep from * to last 2 sts, P2.
11th-14th rows Using A, work in st st.
15th and 16th rows Using C, as 5th and 6th rows.
17th and 18th rows As 7th and 8th rows.
19th and 20th rows Using C, as 9th and 10th rows.
These 20 rows form patt. Cont in patt until work measures 11 [12½:14:15½]in from beg, ending with a WS row.

Shape armholes
Keeping patt correct, bind off 3 sts at beg of next 2 rows. Dec one st at each end every other row 5[6:7:8] times. 86[92:98:104] sts. Cont without shaping until armholes measure 5 [5½: 6:6½]in from beg, ending with a WS row.

Shape shoulders
Bind off 5 sts at beg of next 6[6:10:10] rows and 6[7:6:8] sts at beg of next 4[4:2:2] rows. Slip rem 32[34:36:38] sts on holder.

Front
Work as given for back until armholes measure 3 [3½:4:4½]in from beg, ending with a WS row.

Shape neck
Keeping patt correct, patt 33[35:37:39] sts, turn and slip rem sts on holder. Bind off 2 sts at neck edge on next row, then dec one st at neck edge every other row until 27[29:31:33] sts rem. Cont without shaping until armhole measures same as back to shoulder, ending with a WS row.

Shape shoulder
At arm edge, bind off 5 sts every other row 3[3:5:5] times and 6[7:6:8] sts every other row 2[2:1:1] times. With RS of work facing, sl first 20[22:24:26] sts on holder and leave for center neck, attach yarn to rem sts and patt to end. Complete to correspond to first side, reversing all shapings.

Sleeves
Using No.2 needles and A, cast on 53[57:61: 65] sts. Work 2½in rib as given for back, ending with a 2nd row and inc one st at end of last row on all sizes. 54[58:62:66] sts. Change to No.3 needles. Beg with a K row cont in patt as given for back, inc one st at each end of 5th and every foll 6th row until there are 80[86:92:98] sts. Cont without shaping until sleeve measures 11 [12½:14:16]in from beg, ending with a WS row.

Shape cap
Keeping patt correct bind off 3 sts at beg of next 2 rows. Dec one st at each end of next and every other row until 62[64:70:72] sts rem, ending with a WS row. Bind off 2 sts at beg of next 10[10:12:12] rows; 3 sts at beg of next 6 rows; and 4 sts at beg of next 4 rows; bind off rem 8[10:12:14] sts.

Neckband
Join shoulder seams. Using set of 4 No.2 double-pointed needles and A, with RS of work facing, K across back neck sts on holder, pick up and K 22 sts down side of neck, K across center front neck sts and pick up and K 22 sts up other side of neck. Join. Work in rounds of K1, P1 rib for 2 [2:3:3]in. Bind off loosely in rib.

Finishing
Press each piece under a damp cloth with a warm iron. Sew in sleeves. Join side and sleeve seams. Fold neckband in half to WS and sl st in place. Press seams.

Aran pullovers with V or round necklines

Sizes
To fit 20 [22:24]in chest
The figures in brackets [] refer to the 22 and 24in sizes respectively
Length to shoulder, 12 [13½:15]in
Sleeve seam, 8½ [10:11½]in

Gauge
9 sts and 12 rows to 2in over st st worked on No.6 needles

Materials
6[7:8] balls Reynolds Irish Fisherman Yarn
No.6 knitting needles; No.4 knitting needles
One cable needle
Set of 4 No.4 double-pointed needles for V-neck pullover
One button for round neck pullover

Note
For V-neck pullover it is essential to finish with the 4th row of patt st, and length to underarm can only be adjusted by adding or subtracting 8 rows.
For round neck pullover, length to underarm can be adjusted as required without interfering with the patt.

Round neck pullover back
Using No.4 needles cast on 48[54:58] sts.
Work 9 rows K1, P1 rib.
Next row Rib 4[4:6] sts, *inc in next st, rib 2 sts, rep from * to last 5[5:7] sts, inc in next st,
rib to end. 62[70:74] sts.
Change to No.6 needles. Commence patt.
1st row (K1, P1) 1[3:4] times, K into back of next st – called KB1 –, P2, sl next 2 sts on cable needle and hold at front of work, P2 sts, then K2 sts from cable needle – called T4F –, P3, sl next 2 sts onto cable needle and hold at front of work, K2 sts, then K2 sts from cable needle – called C4F –, P4, (K into front of 2nd st on left-hand needle, then P first st and sl both sts off needle tog – called T2R –, P into back of 2nd st on left-hand needle, then K first st and sl both sts off needle tog – called T2L –, P2) 4 times, P2, sl next 2 sts on cable needle and hold at back of work, K2 sts, then K2 sts from cable needle – called C4B –, P3, sl next 2 sts on cable needle and hold at back of work, K2 sts, then P2 sts from cable needle – called T4B –, P2 KB1, (P1, K1) 1[3:4] times.
2nd row (P1, K1) 1[3:4] times, P1, K4, P2, K3, P4, K4, (P1, K2) 8 times, K2, P4, K3, P2, K4, P1, (K1, P1) 1[3:4] times.
3rd row (P1, K1) 1[3:4] times, KB1, P2, T4B, P1, T4B, T4F, P1, (T2R, P2, T2L) 4 times, P1, T4B, T4F, P1, T4F, P2, KB1, (K1, P1) 1[3:4] times.
4th row (K1, P1) 1[3:4] times, P1, K2, P2, K3, P2, K4, P2, K1, P1, (K4, P 2nd st on left-hand needle then P first st and sl both sts off needle tog – called cross 2P) 3 times, K4, P1, K1, P2, K4, P2, K3, P2, K2, P1, (P1, K1) 1[3:4] times.
5th row (K1, P1) 1[3:4] times, KB1, P1, sl next st onto cable needle and hold at back of work, K2, then P st from cable needle – called T3B –, P3, K2, P4, K2, P1, (T2L, P2, T2R) 4 times, P1, K2, P4, K2, P3, sl next 2 sts on cable needle and hold at front of work, P1 st, then K2 sts from cable needle – called T3F –, P1, KB1, (P1, K1) 1[3:4] times.
6th row (P1, K1) 2[4:5] times, (P2, K4) twice P2, (K2, P1) 8 times, K2, (P2, K4) twice, P2, (K1, P1) 2[4:5] times.
7th row (P1, K1) 1[3:4] times, KB1, P1, T3F, P3, T4F T4B, (P2, T2L, T2R) 4 times, P2, T4F, T4B, P3, T3B, P1, KB1, (K1, P1) 1[3:4] times.
8th row (K1, P1) 1[3:4] times, P1, K2, P2, K5, P4, K5, (cross 2P, K4) 3 times, cross 2P, K5, P4, K5, P2, K2, P1, (P1, K1) 1[3:4] times.
These 8 rows form patt. Cont in patt until work measures 7 [7¾:8½]in from beg, or desired length to underarm ending with a 4th patt row.

Shape raglan armholes
** Bind off 1[2:2] sts at beg of next 2 rows.
3rd row K1, sl 1, K1, psso, patt to last 3 sts, K2 tog, K1.
4th row P2 sts, patt to last 2 sts, P2. **
Rep last 2 rows until 34[36:36] sts rem, ***, ending with a WS row.
Next row K1, sl 1, K2 tog, psso, patt to last 4 sts, K3 tog, K1.
Next row As 4th raglan armhole row.
Rep last 2 rows until 22[24:24] sts rem, ending with a RS row.
Next row P2[3:3] sts, (P2 tog, P2) 4 times, P2 tog, P2[3:3] sts.
Sl rem 17[19:19] sts on holder.

Round neck pullover front
Work as given for back to ***, ending with a RS row.

Shape neck
Next row Patt 12[13:13] sts, (P2 tog, P2) twice, P2 tog, P1[2:2] sts, sl the last 9[11:11] sts just worked onto a holder for center neck and patt to end on rem 11 sts.
Complete this side first.
Next row K1, sl 1, K2 tog, psso, patt to last 2 sts, work 2 tog.
Next row Work 2 tog, patt to last 2 sts, P2.

Rep last 2 rows once more. Dec one st at neck edge only on next row. Bind off.
With RS of work facing, attach yarn to rem sts and work to correspond to first side, reversing all shapings.

Sleeves
Using No.4 needles cast on 28[30:32] sts.
Work 9 rows K1, P1 rib.
Next row Rib 5[4:3] sts, *inc in next st, rib 1, rep from * to last 7[6:5] sts, inc in next st, rib to end. 37[41:45] sts.
Change to No.6 needles. Commence patt.
1st row (K1, P1) 1[2:3] times, KB1, P2, T4F, P3, C4F, P5, C4B, P3, T4B, P2, KB1, (P1, K1) 1[2:3] times.
2nd row (P1, K1) 1[2:3] times, P1, K4, P2, K3, P4, K5, P4, K3, P2, K4, P1, (K1, P1) 1[2:3] times.
3rd row (P1, K1) 1[2:3] times, KB1, P2, T4B, P1, T4B, T4F, P1, T4B, T4F, P1, T4F, P2 KB1, (K1, P1) 1[2:3] times.
4th row (K1, P1) 1[2:3] times, P1, K2, P2, K3, P2, K4, P2, K1, P2, K4, P2, K3, P2, K2, P1, (P1, K1) 1[2:3] times.
5th row (K1, P1) 1[2:3] times, KB1, P2, T3B, P3, K2, P4, K2, P1, K2, P4, K2, P3, T3F, P1, KB1, (P1, K1) 1[2:3] times.
6th row (P1, K1) 2[3:4] times, P2, (K4, P2) twice, K1, (P2, K4) twice, P2, (K1, P1) 2[3:4] times.
7th row (P1, K1) 1[2:3] times, KB1, P1, T3F, P3, T4F, T4B, P1, T4F T4B P3, T3B, P1, KB1, (K1, P1) 1[2:3] times.
8th row (K1, P1) 1[2:3] times P1, K2, P2, (K5, P4) twice, K5, P2, K2, P1, (P1, K1) 1[2:3] times.
Cont in patt, inc one st at each end of next and every foll 8th[10th:12th] rows, and working increased sts in double seed st, until there are 47[51:55] sts. Cont without shaping until sleeve measures 8½ [10:11½]in from beg, or desired length to underarm ending with a WS row.
Shape cap
Work as given for back from ** to **. Rep last 2 rows until 19[15:15] sts rem, ending with a WS row.
Next row K1, sl 1, K2 tog, psso, patt to last 4 sts, K3 tog, K1.
Next row P2 sts, patt to last 2 sts, P2,
Rep last 2 rows 2[1:1] times more. Sl rem 7 sts on holder.

Neckband
Join raglan seams leaving left back seam open. Using No.4 needles cast on 3 sts, then with RS of work facing K across sts of left sleeve top, pick up and K6 sts down left side of neck, K across front neck sts, pick up and K6 sts up right side of neck, K across sts of right sleeve top and back neck.
1st row *K1, P1, rep from * to last 3 sts, K3.
2nd row K4 sts, *P1, K1, rep from * to last st, P1. Keeping garter st and rib correct, work 1 more row.
Next row (buttonhole row) Patt 2 sts, bind off 2 sts, patt to end.
Next row Patt to end, casting on 2 sts above those bound off on previous row.
Work 2 more rows.
Next row Bind off 3 sts, patt to end.
Work 8 more rows. Sl sts on to holder.
Finishing
Press each piece lightly on WS under a damp cloth with a warm iron. Join rem raglan seam, leaving top 1½in open. Sew in sleeves. Fold neckband in half to WS and sl st down catching every st. Join side and sleeve seams. Press seams. Sew on button.
V-neck pullover back
Work as given for round neck pullover, binding off sts at end.

V-neck pullover front
Work as given for back to beg of raglan armhole shaping.
Shape raglan armholes and divide for neck
Next row Bind off 1[2:2] sts, patt 28[31:33] sts, K into front of 2nd st on left-hand needle then K first st and sl both sts off needle tog, turn and sl rem 31[35:37] sts on holder.
Next row P2 sts, patt to last 2 sts, P2.
Next row K1, sl 1, K1, psso, patt to last 3 sts, K2 tog, K1.
Rep last 2 rows until 16[19:25] sts rem. Cont to dec one st at raglan edge every other row, *at the same time* dec one st at neck edge on every foll 4th row until 7 sts rem, ending with a WS row.
Next row K1, sl 1, K2 tog, psso, patt one st, K2.
Next row P2 sts, patt one st, P2.
Next row K1, K3 tog, K1.
Next row P3 sts.
Next row K2 tog, K1. Bind off.
With RS of work facing, attach yarn to rem sts.
1st row K into back of 2nd st on left-hand needle, then K first st, work in patt to end.
2nd row Bind off 1[2:2] sts, patt to last 2 sts, P2.
3rd row K1, sl 1, K1, psso, patt to last 3 sts, K2 tog, K1.
Complete to correspond to first side, reversing all shapings.

Sleeves
Work as given for round neck pullover.

Neckband
Join raglan seams. Using set of 4 No.4 needles and with RS of work facing, pick up and K 17[19:19] sts across back neck, pick up and K 6 sts across sleeve top, pick up and K34[38:42] sts down left side of neck, make one st at center neck by lifting loop between 2 center sts and Ktbl, pick up and K34[38:42] sts up right side of neck and pick up and K6 sts across other sleeve cap.
1st round P1, *K1, P1, rep from * to 2 sts before made st at center front, sl 1, K1, psso, K1, K2 tog, **P1, K1, rep from ** to end.
Keeping rib correct, cont to dec one st at each side of center K st on next 6 rounds. Bind off in rib, still dec at center front.

Finishing
Press as given for crew neck pullover. Sew in sleeves. Join side and sleeve seams. Press seams.

 Snow suit of pullover, pants, hat and mittens

Sizes
To fit 24 [26:28:30]in chest
The figures in brackets [] refer to the 26, 28 and 30in sizes respectively
Sweater length to shoulder, 13½ [15½:17½:19½]in
Sleeve seam, 10 [11½:13:14½]in
Pants inside leg, 12 [14:17:21]in
Gauge
7½ sts and 10 rows to 2in over st st worked on No.9 needles
Materials
10[10:12:12] balls Unger's Regatta in main color, A, for complete set
1 ball each of contrast color, B and C
5[6:6:7] balls of A for pullover and hat only
5[6:6:7] balls of A for pants and mittens only
No.7 knitting needles
No.9 knitting needles
Waist length of elastic

Pullover back
Using No.7 needles and A, cast on 49[53:57:61] sts.
1st row K1, *P1, K1, rep from * to end.
2nd row P1, *K1, P1, rep from * to end.
Rep these 2 rows once more, then first of them again. Change to No.9 needles. P 1 row. Commence patt.
1st row K0[0:0:2] C, 0[0:1:1] A, 0[0:1:1] C, 0[1:1:1] A, 5[6:6:6] C, *1A, 1C, 1A, 6C, rep from * 3 times more, 1A, 1C, 1A, 5[6:6:6] C, 0[1:1:1] A, 0[0:1:1] C, 0[0:1:1] A, 0[0:0:2] C.
2nd row P0[0:0:2] A, 0[1:3:3] B, 5[6:6:6] A, *3B, 6A, rep from * 3 times more, 3B, 5[6:6:6] A, 0[1:3:3] B, 0[0:0:2] A.
Cont in this way working in patt from chart on next page, until 20 rows have been completed. Cont in st st using A only until work measures 7½ [9:10½:12]in from beg, ending with a P row.
Shape armholes
Bind off 2 sts at beg of next 2 rows.
Next row K3 sts, K2 tog, K to last 5 sts, sl 1, K1, psso, K3 sts.
Next row P to end.
Rep last 2 rows until 15[17:17:19] sts rem, ending with a P row. Bind off.

Pullover front
Work as given for back until 25[27:27:29] sts rem, ending with a K row.
Shape neck
Next row P9 sts, bind off 7[9:9:11] sts, P to end. Complete this side first. Dec one st at neck edge on next and every other row, *at the same time* cont to dec at raglan edge on every other row as before until 4 sts rem, ending with a P row.
Next row K2 sts, K2 tog.
Next row P3 sts.
Next row K1 st, K2 tog.
Next row P2 tog. Fasten off.
With RS of work facing, attach yarn to rem sts and complete to correspond to first side, reversing all shapings.

Sleeves
Using No.7 needles and A, cast on 27[29:29:31] sts. Work 1¼in rib as given for back, ending with a 2nd row. Change to No.9 needles. Beg with a K row cont in st st, inc one st at each end of 5th and every foll 6th row until there are 39[43:47:51] sts. Cont without shaping until sleeve measures 10 [11½:13:14½]in from beg, ending with a P row.
Shape cap
Bind off 2 sts at beg of next 2 rows. Dec one st at each end of next and every other row as given for back until 5[7:7:9] sts rem ending with a P row. Bind off.
Collar
Join 3 raglan seams, leaving left back seam open. Using No.7 needles, A and with RS of work facing, pick up and K61[61:69:69] sts evenly around neck. Work 4 rows rib as given for back, inc 4[4:5:5] sts evenly across last row. 65[65:74:74] sts. Change to No.9 needles. Work first 13 rows of patt from chart, beg where indicated. Using A, P 1 row.
Next row Using A, P to end to mark fold line. Using A and beg with a P row work 3 rows st st. Bind off.

Finishing
Press each piece under a damp cloth with a warm iron. Join left back raglan and collar seam. Join side and sleeve seams. Sew in sleeves. Turn in hem of collar to WS and sl st down.

Press seams.

Pants right leg
Using No.7 needles and A, cast on 29[33:37:41] sts. Work 1½in rib as given for pullover back, ending with a 2nd row. Change to No.9 needles. Beg with a K row cont in st st for 1½in.

Shape leg
Next row K2 sts, K up 1, K11[13:15:17] sts, K up 1, K3 sts, K up 1, K11[13:15:17] sts, K up 1, K2 sts.
Beg with a P row work 7[7:9:9] rows without shaping.
Next row K2 sts, K up 1, K13[15:17:19] sts, K up 1, K3 sts, K up 1, K13[15:17:19] sts, K up 1, K2 sts.
Beg with a P row work 7[7:9:9] rows without shaping. Cont inc in this way on next and every foll 8th[8th:10th:10th] row until there are 57[61:65:69] sts. Cont without shaping until work measures 12 [14:17:21]in from beg, ending with a P row. Mark each end of last row with colored thread.

Shape gusset
Bind off 2 sts at beg of next 3 rows. P 1 row. Dec one st at each end of next row, then work 7 rows without shaping. Dec one st at end only of next row, then work 7 rows without shaping. Rep last 16 rows once more, then dec one st at each end of next row on 28 and 30in sizes only. 45[49:51:55] sts. Cont without shaping until work measures 7½ [8:8½:9]in from marked point, ending with a K row.

Shape back
Next row P36 sts, turn and K to end.
Next row P24 sts, turn and K to end.
Next row P12 sts, turn and K to end.
Next row P to end.
Change to No.7 needles. Work 1in K1, P1 rib. Bind off in rib.

Pants left leg
Work as given for right leg, reversing all shapings.

Finishing
Press as given for pullover. Join back and front seams. Join leg seams. Sew elastic inside waistband using casing st. Press seams.

Hat
Using No.7 needles and A, cast on 65[73] sts. Work 5 rows rib as given for pullover back. Change to No.9 needles. P 1 row, inc one st at end of row on 2nd size only 65[74] sts. Cont in patt working from chart and beg as indicated, until 14 rows have been completed. Cont in

st st using A only, until work measures 6¼ [7¼]in from beg, ending with a P row.

Shape top
Next row K2 sts, *K2 tog, K1, rep from * to end. 44[50] sts.
Beg with a P row work 5 rows without shaping.
Next row K2 sts, *K2 tog, K1, rep from * to end. 30[34] sts.
Beg with a P row work 3 rows without shaping.
Next row *K2 tog, rep from * to end. 15[17] sts.
P 1 row. Break off yarn, thread through rem sts, draw up and fasten off.

Ear flaps (make 2)
Using No.7 needles and A, cast on 17 sts. Work 2in rib as given for sweater back, ending with a 2nd row.
Next row Rib 6 sts, sl 1, K1, psso, K1, K2 tog, rib to end.
Next row Rib 6 sts, P3 sts, rib to end.
Next row Rib 6 sts, sl 1, K2 tog, psso, rib to end.
Next row Rib to end.
Cont to dec in this way in center of every other row until 3 sts rem. Bind off.

Finishing
Press as given for pullover. Join seam. Sew one ear flap to each side of hat. Make 2 ch cords and sew one to point of each ear flap. Using B and C, make a large pompon and sew to top of hat.

Mittens
Using No.7 needles and A, cast on 25[29] sts. Work 2½[3]in rib as given for pullover back, ending with a 2nd row. Change to No.9 needles. Beg with a K row work 2[4] rows st st.
Next row K12[14] sts, K up 1, K1, K up 1, K to end.
Next row P to end.
Next row K12[14] sts, K up 1, K3, K up 1, K to end.
Next row P to end.
Cont to inc in this way on next and every other row until there are 31[37] sts. Work 3[5] rows without shaping.

Shape thumb
Next row K19[23] sts, cast on one st, turn.
Next row P8[10] sts, cast on one st, turn.
Beg with a K row work 6[8] rows on these 9[11] sts.
Next row K1, *K2 tog, rep from * to end.
Break off yarn, thread through rem sts, draw up and fasten off.
With RS of work facing, attach yarn to rem sts pick up and K 2 sts from cast-on sts at base of

thumb, K to end. 26[30] sts. Cont without shaping until work measures 6½ [8]in from beg, ending with a P row.

Shape top
Next row K1[2] sts, *K2 tog, K1, rep from * to last st, K1. 18[21] sts.
Next row P to end.
Next row *K2 tog, K1, rep from * to end. 12[14] sts.
Next row P to end.
Next row *K2 tog, rep from * to end.
Break off yarn, thread through rem sts, draw up and fasten off.

Finishing
Press as given for pullover. Join seams. Press seams.

22 Pullover with 'Policeman' motif

Sizes
To fit 26 [28:30:32:34]in chest
The figures in brackets [] refer to the 28, 30, 32 and 34in sizes respectively
Length to shoulder, 17 [18½:19½:20¾:22]in
Long sleeve seam, 14½ [14½:15:16:16½]in
Short sleeve seam, 4 [4:4½:5:5]in

Gauge
7½ sts and 9½ rows to 1in over st st worked on No.3 needles

Materials
Bear Brand or Fleisher Winsport
Long sleeved version 4 [4:4:5:5] skeins main color, A
1 skein each contrast colors B, C, D, E and F
Short sleeved version 3 [4:4:4:4] skeins main color, A
1 skein each contrast colors B, C, D, E and F
No.2 knitting needles
No.3 knitting needles
Oddments of yarn and 2 small white beads for features

Note
Wind contrast colors into several small balls and use separate balls of yarn for each color. Always twist yarns at back of work when changing colors to prevent holes.

Back
Using No.2 needles and A, cast on 102 [110:118:124:132] sts. Work 2in K1, P1 rib. Change to No.3 needles. ** Beg with a K row cont in st st until work measures 11 [12:13:14:15]in from beg, ending with a P row.

Shape armholes
Bind off 5[6:7:7:8] sts at beg of next 2 rows. Dec one st at each end every other row 7[8:9:10:11] times. 78[82:86:90:94] sts. Cont without shaping until armholes measure 6 [6¼:6½:6¾:7]in from beg, ending with a P row.

Shape shoulders
Bind off 7[8:8:9:9] sts at beg of next 4 rows; and 8[7:8:7:8] sts at beg of next 2 rows. Slip rem 34[36:38:40:42] sts on holder for back neck.

Front
Work as given for back to **. Beg with a K row work 1 [1½:2:3:4]in st st, ending with a P row. Commence patt.

1st row Using first ball of A, K28[32:36:39:43] sts, using first ball of B, K14 sts, using 2nd ball

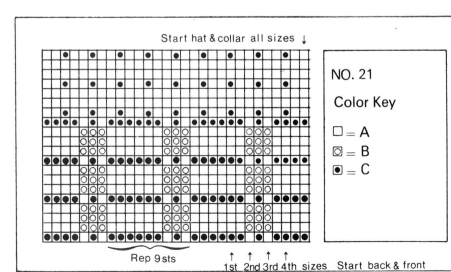

Start hat & collar all sizes ↓

NO. 21
Color Key

□ = A
◎ = B
⊡ = C

Rep 9 sts

↑ 1st ↑ 2nd ↑ 3rd ↑ 4th sizes   Start back & front

of A, K4 sts, using first ball of B, K7 sts, using
2nd ball of A, K to end.
2nd row Using 2nd ball of A, P49[53:57:60:64]
sts, using B, P24 sts, using first ball of A, P
to end.
Cont working from chart on next page in this
way until work measures same as back to
underarm, ending with a P row.

Shape armholes
Keeping patt correct, bind off 5[6:7:7:8] sts at
beg of next 2 rows. Dec one st each end every
other row 7[8:9:10:11] times. 78[82:86:90:94]
sts. Cont without shaping until armholes
measure 4 [4¼:4½:4¾:5]in from beg, using A
only when motif is completed and ending with
a P row.

Shape neck
Next row K29[30:31:32:33] sts, turn and slip
rem sts on holder.
Dec one st at neck edge every other row 7 times.
22[23:24:25:26] sts. Cont without shaping until
armhole measures same as back to shoulder,
ending at armhole edge.

Shape shoulder
At arm edge bind off 7[8:8:9:9] sts twice and
8[7:8:7:8] sts once every other row.
With RS of work facing, sl first 20[22:24:26:28]
sts on holder and leave for center neck, attach
yarn to rem sts and K to end. Complete to
correspond to first side, reversing all shapings.

Long sleeves
Using No.2 needles and A, cast on 50[52:56:
58:60] sts. Work 2in K1, P1 rib. Change to
No.3 needles. Beg with a K row cont in st st,
inc one st at each end of 5th and every foll 8th
row until there are 74[78:82:86:90] sts. Cont
without shaping until sleeve measures 14½ [14½:
15:16:16½]in from beg, ending with a P row.

Shape cap
Bind off 5[6:7:7:8] sts at beg of next 2 rows.
Dec one st at each end of next 2[2:4:4:6] rows,
then each end every other row until 32 sts rem,
ending with a P row. Bind off 2 sts at beg of
next 6 rows; then 3 sts at beg of next 4 rows.
Bind off rem 8 sts.

Short sleeves
Using No.2 needles and A, cast on 66[70:74:
78:82] sts. Work 1in K1, P1, rib. Change to
No.3 needles. Beg with a K row cont in st st,
inc one st at each end of 5th and every foll 6th
row until there are 74[78:82:86:90] sts. Cont
without shaping until sleeve measures 4 [4:4½:
5:5]in from beg, ending with a P row.

Shape cap
Work as given for cap of long sleeves.

Neckband
Join left shoulder seam. Using No.2 needles,
A and with RS of work facing, K across sts of
back neck holder, pick up and K 24 sts down
left side of neck, K across 20[22:24:26:28] sts
of center front holder and pick up and K 24 sts
up right side of neck. 102[106:110:114:118] sts.
Work 2in K1, P1 rib. Bind off loosely in rib.

Finishing
Press each piece on WS under a damp cloth
with a warm iron. Using black yarn, outline
glove and fingers with ch st. Using black, work
eyes in satin st and highlight each eye with
small white bead. Using black, outline nose and
chin strap with stem st. Using pink, fill in
cheeks with satin st. Using brown, work
moustache by cutting lengths of yarn about 1½in
long and with 3 strands tog, knot fringing under
outline of nose. Trim ends of fringe. Join right
shoulder and neckband seam. Join side and
sleeve seams. Sew in sleeves. Turn neckband in
half to WS and sl st down. Press seams.

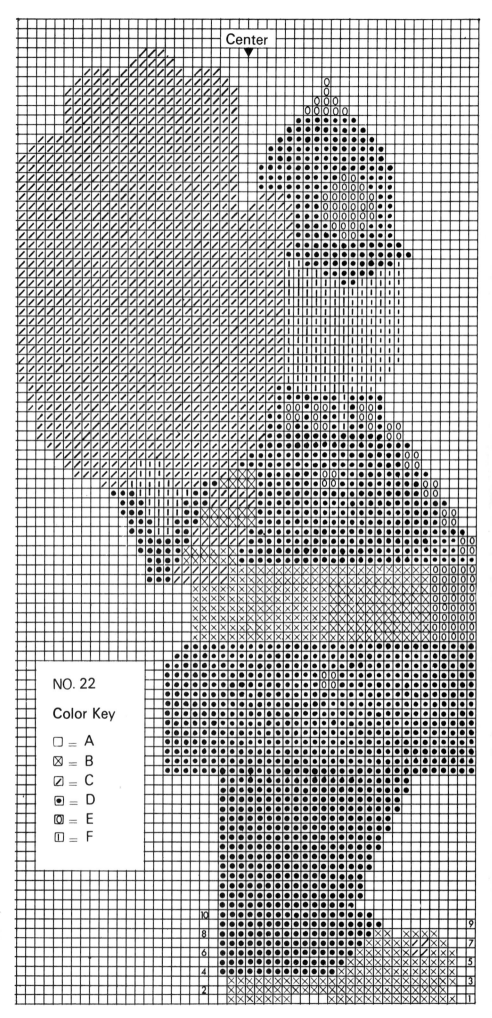

NO. 22

Color Key

☐ = A
☒ = B
◪ = C
◉ = D
◧ = E
⊡ = F

Pullover, trousers, cap and mittens in double seed stitch

Sizes
To fit 24 [26:28:30]in chest
The figures in brackets [] refer to the 26, 28 and 30in sizes respectively
Pullover length to shoulder, 15½ [17:18½:20]in
Sleeve seam, 10 [11½:13:15]in
Trousers inside leg, 12½ [15:17½:20]in

Gauge
5 sts and 6 rows to 1in over double seed st worked on No.8 needles

Materials
9[10:11:12] balls Bernat Berella Germantown in main color, A
1 ball of contrast color, B
No.8 knitting needles; No.6 knitting needles
Set of 4 No.6 double-pointed needles
Waist length of elastic

Pullover back
Using No.6 needles and A, cast on 63[69:75:81] sts.
1st row K1, *P1, K1, rep from * to end.
2nd row P1, *K1, P1, rep from * to end.
Rep these 2 rows 3[4:4:5] times more. Change to No.8 needles. Commence patt.
1st row (P1,K1) 5[6:7:8] times, *(P2, K3) twice, P2, *, K1, (P1, K1) 9[10:11:12] times, rep from * to * once more, (K1, P1) to end.
2nd row (K1 P1) 5[6:7:8] times *(K2, P3) twice, K2, *, P1, (K1, P1) 9[10:11:12] times, rep from * to * once more, (P1, K1) to end.
3rd row (K1, P1) 5[6:7:8] times, rep from * to * as given for 1st row, P1, (K1, P1) 9[10:11:12] times, rep from * to * as given for 1st row, (P1, K1), to end.
4th row (P1, K1) 5[6:7:8] times, rep from * to * as given for 2nd row, K1, (P1, K1) 9[10:11:12] times, rep from * to * as given for 2nd row, (K1, P1) to end.
5th and 6th rows As 1st and 2nd rows.
7th row (K1, P1) 5[6:7:8] times, *P2, K3, P2, K2, P3, *, P1, (K1, P1) 9[10:11:12] times, rep from * to * once more, (P1, K1) to end.
8th row (P1, K1) 5[6:7:8] times, *K3, P2, K2, P3, K2, *, K1, (P1, K1) 9[10:11:12] times, rep from * to * once more, (K1, P1) to end.
9th row (K1, P1) 5[6:7:8] times, *P3, K3, P1, K1, P4, *, K1, (P1, K1) 9[10:11:12] times, rep from * to * once more, (P1, K1) to end.
10th row (K1, P1) 5[6:7:8] times, *K4, P1, K1, P3, K3, *, P1, (K1, P1) 9[10:11:12] times, rep from * to * once more, (P1, K1) to end.
11th row (K1, P1) 5[6:7:8] times, *P4, K3, P5, *, P1, (K1, P1) 9[10:11:12] times rep from * to * once more, (P1, K1) to end.
12th row (P1, K1) 5[6:7:8] times, *K5, P3, K4, *, K1, (P1, K1) 9[10:11:12] times, rep from * to * once more, (K1, P1) to end.
13th row (K1, P1) 5[6:7:8] times, *P5, K3, P4, *, P1, (K1, P1) 9[10:11:12] times, rep from * to * once more, (P1, K1) to end.
14th row (K1, P1) 5[6:7:8] times, *K4, P3, K5, *, P1, (K1, P1) 9[10:11:12] times, rep from * to * once more, (P1, K1) to end.
15th row (K1, P1) 5[6:7:8] times, *P4, K1, P1, K3, P3, *, P1, (K1, P1) 9[10:11:12] times, rep from * to * once more, (P1, K1) to end.
16th row (P1, K1) 5[6:7:8] times, *K3, P3, K1, P1, K4, *, K1, (P1, K1) 9[10:11:12] times, rep from * to * once more, (K1, P1) to end.
17th row (P1, K1) 5[6:7:8] times, *P3, K2, P2, K3, P2, *, K1, (P1, K1) 9[10:11:12] times, rep from * to * once more, (K1, P1) to end.
18th row (K1, P1) 5[6:7:8] times, *K2, P3, K2, P2, K3, *, P1, (K1, P1) 9[10:11:12] times, rep from * to * once more, (P1, K1) to end.

19th and 20th rows As 3rd and 4th rows. These 20 rows form patt. Cont in patt until work measures 10½ [11½:12½:13½]in from beg, or desired length to underarm, ending with a WS row.

Shape armholes
Keeping patt correct, bind off 4 sts at beg of next 2 rows. Work 2 rows. Dec one st at each end of next and every foll 4th row until 45[49:53:57] sts rem. ** Work 1 row after last dec.

Shape shoulders
Bind off 4[5:5:5] sts at beg of next 4 rows and 5[4:5:6] sts at beg of next 2 rows. Slip rem 19[21:23:25] sts on holder.

Pullover front
Work as given for back to **, ending with a RS row.
Shape neck and shoulders
Next row Patt 16[17:18:19] sts, turn and slip rem sts on holder.
Next row K2 tog, patt to end.
Next row Bind off 4[5:5:5] sts, patt to end.
Rep last 2 rows once more, then first of them again. Bind off rem 5[4:5:6] sts.
With WS of work facing, sl first 13[15:17:19] sts on holder and leave for center neck, attach yarn to rem sts, P2 tog, patt to end.
Next row Bind off 4[5:5:5] sts, patt to end.
Complete to correspond to first side.

Sleeves
Using No.6 needles and A, cast on 39[39:43:43] sts. Work 6[6:8:8] rows rib as given for back. Attach B. K 1 row, then rib 3 rows. Break off B. Cont with A only. K 1 row, then rib 1 row, inc one st at end of last row. 40[40:44:44] sts. Change to No.8 needles. Commence patt.
1st row (P1, K1) 7[7:8:8] times, rep from * to * as given for 1st row of back, (K1, P1) to end.
2nd row (K1, P1) 7[7:8:8] times, rep from * to * as given for 2nd row of back, (P1, K1) to end.
3rd row (K1, P1) 7[7:8:8] times, rep from * to * as given for 3rd row of back, (P1, K1) to end.
Cont in patt as given for back as established, inc one st at each end of 5th and every foll 6th row until there are 50[54:58:62] sts and working increased sts into double seed st. Cont without shaping until sleeve measures 10 [11½:13:15]in from beg, or desired length to underarm, ending with a WS row.

Shape cap
Bind off 4 sts at beg of next 2 rows. Dec one st at each end every other row until 28[28:26:26] sts rem, then at each end of every row until 16[16:18:18] sts rem. Cont without shaping on these 16[16:18:18] sts for length of shoulder to neck edge, ending with a WS row. Slip sts on holder.

Neckband
Sew saddle caps of shoulders to front and back shoulders. Using set of 4 No.6 needles, A, and with RS of work facing, K across sts of right sleeve, back neck and left sleeve, K2 tog at each seam, pick up and K4 sts down side of neck, K across center front neck sts, then pick up and K4 sts up other side of neck. 70[74:82:86] sts. Work 1 round K1, P1 rib. Attach B, K 1 round then rib 3 rounds. Break off B, Using A, K 1 round, then cont in rib until work measures 3[3:3:4]in from beg. Bind off loosely in rib.

Finishing
Press each piece under a damp cloth with a warm iron. Sew in sleeves. Join side and sleeve seams. Press seams. Fold neckband in half to WS and sl st down.

Trousers right leg
Using No.6 needles and A, cast on 35[39:43:47] sts. Work 1½in rib as given for pullover back,
ending with a 2nd row. Change to No.8 needles. Cont in double seed st for 4 rows.

Shape leg
Next row Inc in first st, patt 15[17:19:21] sts, K twice into each of next 2 sts, patt 16[18:20:22] sts, inc in last st.
Work 7[7:9:9] rows double seed st.
Next row Inc in first st, patt 17[19:21:23] sts, K twice into each of next 2 sts, patt 18[20:22:24] sts, inc in last st.
Cont to inc in this way on every foll 8th[8th:10th:10th] row until there are 63[67:71:75] sts. Cont without shaping until work measures 12½ [15:17½:20]in from beg, or required leg length, ending with a WS row. Mark each end of last row with colored thread.

Shape crotch
Bind off 4 sts at beg of next 2 rows, and 2 sts once. Work 1 row. Dec one st at each end of next and every foll 4th row until 47[51:55:59] sts rem. Cont without shaping until work measures 7½ [8:8½:9]in from marked point, ending with a RS row.

Shape back
Next row Patt to last 7[11:10:14] sts, turn and patt to end.
Next row Patt to last 15[19:19:23] sts, turn and patt to end.
Cont to work 8[8:9:9] sts less every other row 3 times more. Work 1 row across all sts. Change to No.6 needles. Work 1in rib as given at beg. Bind off in rib.

Trousers left leg
Work as given for right leg, reversing all shapings.

Finishing
Press as given for pullover. Join back and front seams. Join leg seams. Sew elastic inside waistband, using casing st. Press seams.

Cap
Using No.6 needles and A, cast on 79[89] sts. Work 1 row rib as given for pullover back. Attach B, K 1 row, then rib 3 rows. Break off B. Using A only, K 1 row, then cont in rib until work measures 2¾ [3½]in from beg, ending with a 1st row. Change to No.8 needles. Beg with a 1st patt row, cont in double seed st until work measures 8[9]in from beg, ending with a WS row.

Shape top
Next row K2[1] sts, (sl 1, K2 tog, psso, K1) 19[22] times, K1[0]. 41[45] sts.
Beg with a P row work 3 rows st st.
Next row K1, *sl 1, K2 tog, psso, K1, rep from * to end. 21[23] sts.
Beg with a P row work 3 rows st st.
Next row K1, *K2 tog, rep from * to end.
Break off yarn, thread through rem sts, draw up and fasten off.

Finishing
Press as given for pullover. Join seam. Make a pompon and sew to top.

Mittens
Using No.6 needles and A, cast on 29[33] sts. Work 2 [2½]in rib as given for pullover back, ending with a 2nd row. Change to No.8 needles. Work 4 rows double seed st.
Next row Patt 13[15] sts, K up 1, K3 sts, K up 1, patt to end.
Next row Patt 13[15] sts, P5 sts, patt to end.
Next row Patt 13[15] sts, K up 1, K 5 sts, K up 1, patt to end.
Cont to inc in this way twice more, then work 1[3] rows after last inc. 37[41] sts.
Next row Patt 14[16] sts, sl next 9 sts onto holder and leave for thumb, cast on 3 sts, patt to end. 31[35] sts.
Cont in patt for 2½ [3]in, ending with a WS row.

Shape top

Next row K1[2] sts, *K2 tog, K1, rep from * to end. 21[24] sts.

Next row P to end.

Next row *K2 tog, K1, rep from * to end. 14[16] sts.

Next row P to end.

Next row *K2 tog, rep from * to end. Break off yarn, thread through rem sts, draw up and fasten off.

Thumb

Sl 9 sts on holder onto No.8 needle, K up 3 sts from cast-on sts at base of thumb. 12 sts. Cont in st st for 1¼ [1¾]in, ending with a P row.

Shape top

Next row *K2 tog, rep from * to end.

Next row P to end.

Break off yarn, thread through rem sts, draw up and fasten off.

Finishing

Press as given for pullover. Join side and thumb seams. Press seams.

24 *Bulky pullover in broken basket stitch*

Sizes

To fit 24 [26:28:30:32]in chest

The figures in brackets [] refer to the 26, 28, 30 and 32in sizes respectively

Length to shoulder, 14½ [16½:18½:20½:22½]in

Sleeve seam, 10 [11:12:13½:15]in

Gauge

3½ sts and 5 rows to 1in over st st worked on No.10½ needles

Materials

7[8:8:9:10] skeins Bear Brand or Fleisher Four Seasons

No.9 knitting needles; No. 10½ knitting needles

8 buttons

Back

Using No.9 needles cast on 42[50:50:54:54] sts.

1st row K2, *P2, K2, rep from * to end.

2nd row P2, *K2, P2, rep from * to end.

Rep these 2 rows for 2in, ending with a 2nd row and inc one st at each end of last row on 24, 30 and 32in sizes only. 44[50:50:56:56] sts. Change to No.10½ needles. Commence patt.

1st row K1[4:4:1:1] sts, P6, *K6, P6, rep from * to last 1[4:4:1:1] sts, K to end.

2nd row P1[4:4:1:1] sts, K6, *P6, K6, rep from * to last 1[4:4:1:1] sts, P to end.

3rd row K1[4:4:1:1] sts, P1, K4, P1, *K1, P4, K1, P1, K4, P1, rep from * to last 1[4:4:1:1] sts, K to end.

4th row P1[4:4:1:1] sts, K1, P4, K1, *P1, K4, P1, K1, P4, K1, rep from * to last 1 [4:4:1:1] sts, P to end.

5th, 6th, 7th and 8th rows. Rep 3rd and 4th rows twice more.

9th row As 1st.

10th row As 2nd

11th row K7[10:10:7:7] sts, *P6, K6, rep from * to last 1[4:4:1:1] sts, K to end.

12th row P7[10:10:7:7] sts, *K6, P6, rep from * to last 1[4:4:1:1] sts, P to end.

13th row K2[5:5:2:2] sts, P4, K1, *P1, K4, P1, K1, P4, K1, rep from * to last 1[4:4:1:1] sts, K to end.

14th row P2[5:5:2:2] sts, K4, P1, *K1, P4, K1, P1, K4, P1, rep from * to last 1[4:4:1:1] sts, P to end.

15th, 16th, 17th and 18th rows Rep 13th and 14th rows twice more.

19th row As 11th.

20th row As 12th.

These 20 rows form patt. Cont in patt until work measures 8½ [9½:10½:11½:12½]in from beg, ending with a WS row.

Shape armholes

Keeping patt correct, bind off 1[3:1:3:1] sts at beg of next 2 rows. 42[44:48:50:54] sts.

**Next row K2 sts, P2 tog, patt to last 4 sts, P2 tog, K2.

Next row P2 sts, K1, patt to last 3 sts, K1, P2. **

Rep last 2 rows until 12[12:14:14:16] sts rem, ending with a WS row. Slip sts on holder.

Front

Using No.9 needles cast on 50[50:54:54:62] sts.

Work 2in rib as given for back, ending with a 2nd row and inc one st at each end of last row on 28 and 30in sizes only 50[50:56:56:62] sts. Change to No.10½ needles. Commence patt.

1st row K4[4:1:1:4] sts, P6, *K6, P6, rep from * to last 4[4:1:1:4] sts, K to end.

2nd row P4[4:1:1:4] sts, K6, *P6, K6, rep from * to last 4[4:1:1:4] sts, P to end.

3rd row K4[4:1:1:4] sts, P1, K4, P1, *K1, P4, K1, P1, K4, P1, rep from * to last 4[4:1:1:4] sts, K to end.

Cont in patt as given for back keeping 4[4:1:1:4] sts in st st at each end instead of 1[4:4:1:1] sts as on back, until work measures same as back to underarm ending with a WS row.

Shape armholes

Bind off 4[3:4:3:4] sts at beg of next 2 rows. 42[44:48:50:54] sts. Rep from ** to ** as given for back until 24[24:26:26:28] sts rem, ending with a WS row.

Shape neck

Next row K2 sts, P2 tog, patt 6 sts, turn and leave rem sts on holder.

Next row Patt to last 3 sts, K1, P2.

Next row K2 sts, P2 tog, patt to last 2 sts, K2 tog.

Rep last 2 rows once more, then first of them again. 5 sts.

Next row K2 sts, P2 tog, K1.

Next row P1, K1, P2.

Next row K2 sts, P2 tog.

Next row K1, P2.

Next row K1, sl 1, K1, psso.

Next row P2 tog. Fasten off.

With RS of work facing, sl first 4[4:6:6:8] sts on holder and leave for center neck, attach yarn to rem sts and patt to last 4 sts, P2 tog, K2.

Next row P2 sts, K1, patt to end.

Next row Sl 1, K1, psso, patt to last 4 sts, P2 tog, K2.

Complete to correspond to first side, reversing shaping as shown.

Sleeves

Using No.9 needles cast on 22[26:26:30:30] sts. Work 2in rib as given for back, ending with a 2nd row and inc one st at each end of last row on 24, 28 and 32in sizes only. 24[26:28:30:32] sts. Change to No.10½ needles. Commence patt.

1st row K3[4:5:6:1] sts, P6, *K6, P6, rep from * to last 3[4:5:6:1] sts, K to end.

2nd row P3[4:5:6:1] sts, K6, *P6, K6, rep from * to last 3[4:5:6:1] sys, P to end.

3rd row P0[0:0:0:1] st, K0[0:0:1:1] st, P2[3:4:4:4] sts, K1, P1, K4, P1, K1, P4, K1, P1, K4, P1, K1, P2[3:4:4:4] sts, K0[0:0:1:1] st, P0[0:0:0:1] st.

Cont in patt as established, inc one st at each end of every 6th[8th:8th:10th:10th] row until there are 32[34:36:38:40] sts and working increased sts into patt when possible. Cont without shaping until sleeve measures 10 [11:12:13½:15]in from beg, ending with a WS row.

Shape cap

Bind off 3 sts at beg of next 2 rows. 26[28:30:32:34] sts. Work 2 rows without shaping, then work from ** to ** as given for back. Rep last 4 rows 5 times more, then rep from ** to ** as given for back until 8 sts rem, ending with a WS row. Slip.

Front neckband

Using No.9 needles and with RS of work facing, pick up and K 10[10:11:11:12] sts down side of front neck, K across front neck sts, and pick up and K 10[10:11:11:12] sts up other side of front neck.

Next row K3 sts, P2, *K2, P2, rep from * to last 3 sts, K3.

Next row K1, P2, *K2, P2, rep from * to last st, K1.

Rep last 2 rows from 2¾ [2¾:2¾:3¼:3¼]in, ending with a 2nd row.

Next row K1, K2 tog, yrn, *P2, K2, rep from * to last 5 sts, P2, yon, sl 1, K1, psso, K1.

Cont in rib as before until neckband measures 4½ [4½:4½:5¼:5¼]in from beg, ending with a 2nd row. Rep buttonhole row as before, then work 2 more rows rib. Bind off in rib.

Back neckband

Using No.9 needles cast on 3 sts, with RS of work facing K across sts of right sleeve, back neck and left sleeve, K2 tog on each seam on all sizes and inc 2 sts evenly across back neck on 24, 28 and 32in sizes only, then cast on 3 sts. 32[32:36:36:36] sts.

Next row K3 sts, *P2, K2, rep from * to last 5 sts, P2, K3.

Next row K5 sts, *P2, K2, rep from * to last 3 sts, K3.

Rep these 2 rows until back neckband measures same as front. Bind off in rib.

Finishing

Press each piece under a damp cloth with a warm iron. Join raglan seams, leaving front neckband seams open. Sew in sleeves. Sew the 3 cast-on sts at each side of back neckband in front of first sts of front neckband so that when collar turns over to the front, these 3 sts for underflap will be under the sts of front. Join side and sleeve seams. Press seams. Sew on 2 buttons to each side of neckband to correspond with buttonholes, then sew 2 more buttons to each front raglan seam.

25 *Pants suit with double-breasted jacket*

Sizes
To fit 28 [30:32:34]in chest/bust
The figures in brackets [] refer to the 30, 32 and 34in sizes respectively
Sleeve seam, 12 [13½:15:16½]in
Trousers inside leg, 19 [21:23½:26½]in
Gauge
6 sts and 8 rows to 1in over st st worked on No.4 needles
Materials
24[27:30:34] balls Reynolds Cascatelle.
No.4 knitting needles; No.3 knitting needles
8 buttons
Waist length of elastic

Jacket back
Using No.3 needles cast on 89[95:101:107] sts.
1st row K1, *P1, K1, rep from * to end.
2nd row P1, *K1, P1, rep from * to end.
Rep these 2 rows for 1½ [2:2:2½]in, ending with a 2nd row. Change to No.4 needles. Commence patt.
1st row K31[33:35:37] sts, rib 27[29:31:33] sts, K to end.
2nd row P31[33:35:37] sts, rib 27[29:31:33] sts, P to end.
Rep these 2 rows until work measures 14 [15:16:17]in from beg, ending with a WS row.
Shape armholes
Keeping center sts in rib throughout, bind off 5 sts at beg of next 2 rows; then 2 sts at beg of next 2 rows. Dec one st at each end every other row 4[5:6:7] times. 67[71:75:79] sts. Cont without shaping until armholes measure 6[6½:7:7½]in from beg, ending with a WS row.
Shape shoulders
Bind off 4[4:5:5] sts at beg of next 6 rows; then 4[5:3:4] sts at beg of next 2 rows. Bind off rem 35[37:39:41] sts.

Jacket left front
Using No.3 needles cast on 59[63:67:71] sts. Work in rib as given for back for 1½ [2:2:2½]in, ending with a 2nd row. Change to No.4 needles. Commence patt.
1st row K31[33:35:37] sts, rib to end.
2nd row Rib 28[30:32:34] sts, P to end.
Rep these 2 rows until work measures same as back to underarm, ending with a WS row.
Shape armhole
At arm edge, bind off 5 sts; then 2 sts. Dec 1 st at arm edge every other row 4[5:6:7] times. 48[51:54:57] sts. Cont without shaping until armhole measures 3½ [4:4½:5]in from beg, ending with a RS row.
Shape neck
Next row Bind off 26[28:30:32] sts in rib, P to end.
Dec one st at neck edge every other row until 16[17:18:19] sts tem. Cont without shaping until armhole measures same as back to shoulder, ending at armhole edge.
Shape shoulder
At arm edge, bind off 4[4:5:5] sts every other row 3 times and 4[5:3:4] sts once.

Right front
Using No.3 needles cast on 59[63:67:71] sts. Work 1½ [2:2:2½]in rib as given for back, ending with a 2nd row. Change to No.4 needles.
Next row Rib 28[30:32:34] sts, K to end.
Next row P31[33:35:37] sts, rib to end.
Rep these 2 rows until work measures 2½ [3:3½:4]in from beg, ending with a WS row.
Next row (buttonhole row) Rib 3 sts, bind off 3 sts rib 15[17:19:21] sts. bind off 3 sts patt to end.
Next row Patt to end, casting on 3 sts above those bound-off on previous row.
Complete to correspond to left front, reversing all shapings and making 3 more pairs of buttonholes at intervals of 3½in.

Sleeves
Using No.3 needles cast on 41[45:45:49] sts. Work 1½ [2:2:2½]in rib as given for back, ending with a 2nd row. Change to No.4 needles.
Next row K11[13:13:15] sts, rib 19 sts, K to end.
Next row P11[13:13:15] sts, rib 19 sts, P to end.
Keeping center sts in rib throughout, cont in patt inc one st at each end of every 6th[7th:7th:8th] row until there are 63[67:71:75] sts. Cont without shaping until sleeve measures 12 [13½:15:16½]in from beg, ending with a WS row.

Shape cap
Bind off 5 sts at beg of next 2 rows. Dec one st at each end every other row 7[8:9:10] times. Bind off 2 sts at beg of next 10 rows; and 3 sts at beg of next 4 rows; Bind off rem 7[9:7:9] sts,

Collar
Using No.3 needles cast on 89[93:97:101] sts. Work 3½ [4:4½:5]in rib as given for back. Bind off in rib.

Finishing
Press under a dry cloth with a cool iron. Join shoulder seams. Sew in sleeves. Join side and sleeve seams. Sew on collar, beg and ending just inside cast-off sts at neck edge of fronts. Press seams. Sew on buttons.

Pants right half
Using No.3 needles cast on 81[87:93:99] sts. Beg with a K row work 1½in st st, ending with a K row.
Next row K all sts tbl to form hemline.
Change to No.4 needles. Beg with a K row cont in st st until work measures 1½ [2:2½:3] in from hemline, ending with a P row.
Shape leg
Dec one st at each end of next and every foll 10th[12th:14th:16th] row until 71[77:83:89] sts rem. Cont without shaping until work measures 14 [16:18:20]in from hemline, ending with a P row. Inc one st at each end of next and every foll 8th[8th:10th:10th] row until there are 79[85:91:97] sts. Cont without shaping until work measures 19 [21:23½:26½]in from hemline, or desired leg length, ending with a P row.
Shape crotch
Bind off 3 sts at beg of next 2 rows; then 2 sts at beg of next 2 rows. Work 2 rows without shaping. Dec one st at each end of next and every foll 4th row 4 times in all. Cont without shaping until work measures 7½ [8:8½:9]in from beg of crotch, ending with a K row.
Shape back
Next row P32[36:40:44] sts, turn and K to end.
Next row P24[27:30:33] sts, turn and K to end.
Cont to work 8[9:10:11] sts less every other row twice more, then P across all sts. Change to No.3 needles. Work 1¼in rib as given for pullover back. Bind off in rib.

Pants left half
Work as given for right half, reversing shaping at top.

Finishing
Press as given for jacket. Join back and front seams. Join leg seams. Turn hems to WS and sl st down. Press seams. Sew elastic inside waist band using casing- st.

26 *Girl's pants suit, with cable-stitch pullover*

Sizes
To fit 24 [26:28:30:32:34]in chest/bust
26 [28:30:32:34:36]in hips
The figures in brackets [] refer to the 26, 28, 30, 32, 34 and 36in sizes respectively.
Pullover length to shoulder, 16 [17½:19:20½:22:23½]in
Sleeve seam, 10 [11:12:13½:15:16½]in
Pants inside leg, 15 [17½:20:22:24:26]in
Gauge
7 sts and 9 rows to 1in over st st worked on No.4 needles
Materials
18[21:24:27:30:33] balls Unger's English Crepe
No.2 knitting needles
No.4 knitting needles
Set of 4 No.2 double-pointed needles
Waist length of elastic

Pullover back
Using No.2 needles cast on 89[95:103:109:117:123] sts.
1st row K1, *P1, K1, rep from * to end.
2nd row P1, *K1, P1 rep from * to end.
Rep these 2 rows for 1 [1:1¼:1½:1½:1½]in, ending with a 2nd row and inc one st at end of last row. 90[96:104:110:118:124] sts. Change to No.4 needles. Commence patt.
1st row P5[5:3:3:4:4] sts, K2, *P4, K2, rep

from * to last 5[5:3:3:4:4] sts, P to end.
2nd row K5[5:3:3:4:4] sts, P2, *K4, P2, rep from * to last 5[5:3:3:4:4] sts, K to end.
3rd row P5[5:3:3:4:4] sts, put needle behind first st and K 2nd st tbl then K into front of first st and sl both sts off needle tog – called Tw2 –, *P4, Tw2, rep from * to last 5[5:3:3: 4:4] sts, P to end.
4th row As 2nd.
These 4 rows form patt. Cont in patt until work measures 10½ [11½:12½:13½:14½:15½]in from beg, ending with a WS row.
Shape armholes
Bind off 6 sts at beg of next 2 rows.
**Next row P1, P2 tog, patt to last 3 sts, P2 tog, P1.
Next row K2 sts, patt to last 2 sts, K2. ******
Rep last 2 rows until 28[30:32:34:36:38] sts rem, ending with a WS row. Slip sts on holder.

Pullover front
Work as given for back until 42[44:48:50:54: 56] sts rem, ending with a WS row.
Shape neck
Next row P1, P2 tog, patt 11[11:13:13:15:15] sts, turn and slip rem sts on holder.
Next row Patt to last 2 sts, K2.
Next row P1, P2 tog, patt to last 2 sts, P2 tog. Rep last 2 rows 4[4:5:5:6:6] times more, then first of them again. 3 sts.
Next row P1, P2 tog.
Next row K2 tog and fasten off. With RS of work facing, sl first 14[16:16:18:18:20] sts on holder and leave for center neck, attach yarn to rem sts, patt to last 3 sts, P2 tog, P1.
Next row K2 sts, patt to end.
Next row P2 tog, patt to last 3 sts, P2 tog, P1. Complete to correspond to first side, reversing shaping.

Sleeves
Using No.2 needles cast on 51[53:57:59:63:65] sts. Work 1½ [1½:2:2:2½:2½]in rib as given for back, ending with a 2nd row and inc one st at end of last row. 52[54:58:60:64:66] sts. Change to No.4 needles. Commence patt.
1st row P1[2:1:2:1:2] sts, K2, *P4, K2, rep from * to last 1[2:1:2:1:2] sts, P to end.
2nd row K1[2:1:2:1:2] sts, P2, *K4, P2, rep from * to last 1[2:1:2:1:2] sts, K to end.
3rd row P1[2:1:2:1:2] sts, Tw2, *P4, Tw2, rep from * to last 1[2:1:2:1:2] sts, P to end.
4th row As 2nd.
Cont in patt as now set, inc one st at each end of next and every foll 8th row until there are 70[74:80:84:90:94] sts, working extra sts into patt when possible. Cont without shaping until sleeve measures 10 [11:12:13½:15:16½]in from beg, ending with a WS row.
Shape cap
Bind off 6 sts at beg of next 2 rows. Rep from ** to ** as given for back until 8 sts rem, ending with a WS row. Slip sts on holder.

Neckband
Join raglan seams. Using set of No.2 double-pointed needles and with RS of work facing, K across sts of back neck and left sleeve K2 tog at seam, pick up and K 10[10:12:12:14:14] sts down side of front neck, K across sts of center neck, pick up and K 10[10:12:12:14:14] sts up other side of neck, K across sts of right sleeve K2 tog last and first st of back neck. 76[80:86:90:96:100] sts. Join. Cont in rounds of K1, P1 rib for ½ [½:¾:¾:1:1]in. Bind off in rib.

Finishing
Press lightly. Join side and sleeve seams. Sew in sleeves.

Pants right leg
Using No.2 needles cast on 116[124:134:142: 152:160] sts. Beg with a K row work 1 [1:1¼: 1¼:1½:1½]in st st, ending with a K row.
Next row K all sts tbl to mark hemline.
Change to No.4 needles. Beg with a K row cont in st st until work measures 1½ [1½:2:2:2½: 2½]in from hemline, ending with a P row.
Shape leg
Next row K2 sts, K2 tog, K51[55:60:64:69: 73] sts, sl 1, K1, psso, K2 sts, K2 tog, K to last 4 sts, sl 1, K1, psso, K2.
Beg with a P row work 9[9:11:11:13:13] rows without shaping.
Next row K2 sts, K2 tog, K49[53:58:62:67: 71] sts, sl 1, K1, psso, K2 sts, K2 tog, K to last 4 sts, sl 1, K1, psso, K2.
Beg with a P row work 9[9:11:11:13:13] rows without shaping. Cont dec in this way on next and every foll 10th[10th:12th:12th:14th:14th] row until 96[104:110:118:124:132] sts rem. Cont without shaping until work measures 15 [17½:20:22:24:26]in from hemline, ending with a P row.
Shape gusset
Next row Bind off 4 sts, K to end.
Next row Bind off 2 sts, P to end.
Next row Bind off 2 sts, K to end.
Next row P to end.
Next row K1, sl 1, K1, psso, K to last 3 sts, K2 tog, K1.
Rep last 2 rows 4[5:5:6:6:7] times more. Cont to dec in same way on every foll 8th[8th:8th: 6th:6th:6th] row until 70[74:78:82:86:90] sts rem. Cont without shaping until work measures 6½ [7:7½:8:8½:9]in from beg of gusset shaping, ending with a K row.
Shape back
Next row P30[30:36:36:42:42] sts, turn and K to end.
Next row P24[24:30:30:36:36] sts, turn and K to end.
Cont to work 6 sts less every other row in this way 3[3:4:4:5:5] times more. P 1 row across all sts, dec one st at end of row. Change to No.2 needles. Work 1in rib as given for pullover back. Bind off in rib.

Pants left leg
Work as given for right leg, reversing all shapings.

Finishing
Press lightly. Join back and front seams. Join leg seams. Turn hems at lower edge to WS and sl st down. Sew elastic inside waistband using casing st.

27 *Girl's dress with two-color bodice motif*

Sizes
To fit 32 [34:36]in bust
34 [36:38]in hips
The figures in brackets [] refer to the 34in and 36in bust and 36, 38in hip sizes
Length to shoulders, 33[34:35]in.
Sleeve seam, 16½ [17:17½]in
Gauge
6 sts and 8 rows to 1in over st st worked on No.5 needles

Materials
6[6:7] skeins Columbia-Minerva Featherweight Knitting Worsted in main color, A
1 ball each of contrast colors, B and C
No.3 knitting needles
No.5 knitting needles
Note
When working front fair isle patt, use separate balls of A. Always twist yarns at back of work when changing colors to prevent holes.

Back
Using No.3 needles and A, cast on 146[154: 162] sts. Beg with a K row work 1in st st, ending with a K row.
Next row K all sts tbl to form hemline.
Change to No.5 needles. Commence rib patt.
1st row K to end.
2nd row K2 sts, *P16[17:18] sts, K2 rep from * to end.
Rep these 2 rows for 3in, ending with a 2nd row.
Shape skirt
Next row K9[10:10] sts, *K2 tog, K16[17:18] sts, rep from * 6 times more, K2 tog, K9[10:10] sts, Keeping rib patt correct as established, work 23 rows without shaping.
Next row K8[9:9] sts, *K2 tog, K15[16:17] sts, rep from * 6 times more, K2 tog, K8[9:9] sts. Keeping rib patt correct as established, work 23 rows without shaping. Cont to dec in this way on next and every foll 24th row 3 times more. Cont without shaping until work measures 16 [16½:17]in from hemline, ending with a WS row. 106[114:122] sts.
Cont in st st until work measures 26½ [27:27½]in from hemline, ending with a P row.
Shape armholes
Bind off 5 sts at beg of next 2 rows, 4 sts at beg of next 2 rows and 2 sts at beg of next 2 rows. Dec one st at each end every other row 0[1:2] times. 82[88:94] sts. Work even until armholes measure 6½ [7:7½]in from beg, ending with a P row.
Shape shoulders
Bind off 12[13:13] sts at beg of next 2 rows and 13[13:14] sts at beg of next 2 rows. Slip rem 32[36:40] sts on holder.

Front
Work as given for back until work measures 16 rows less than back to underarm, ending with a P row. Commence patt.
Next row Using 1st ball of A, K52[56:60] sts using B, K2, using 2nd ball of A K52[56:60] sts.
Next row Using 2nd ball of A, P51[55:59] sts, P4 B, using 1st ball of A, P51[55:59] sts. Cont to work in patt from chart until 16 rows have been completed.
Shape armholes
Still working in patt from chart, shape armholes as given for back. Cont without shaping until armholes measure 4½ [5:5½]in from beg, ending with a P row.
Shape neck
Next row K34[35:36] sts, turn and slip rem sts on holder.
Bind off 2 sts at neck edge every other row 3 times, then dec one st at neck edge every other row 3 times. Cont without shaping on rem 25[26:27] sts until armhole measures same as back to shoulder, ending with a P row.
Shape shoulder
At arm edge, bind off 12[13:13] sts once and 13[13:14] sts once.
With RS of work facing, sl first 14[18:22] sts on holder and leave for center neck, attach yarn to rem sts and K to end. Complete to correspond to first side, reversing all shapings.

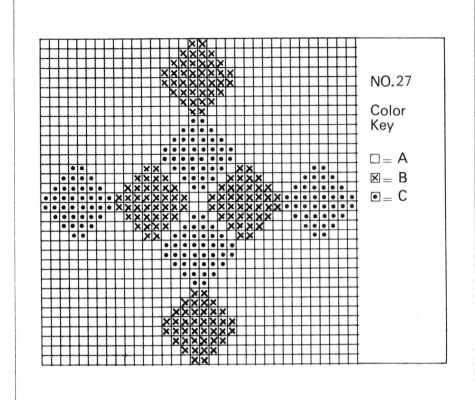

Gauge
6 sts and 8 rows to 1in over st st worked on No.5 needles

Materials
9[9:10] packs of Bear Brand or Fleisher or Botany Twin-Pak Knitting Worsted in main color, A
1 ball each of contrast colors, B and C
No.3 knitting needles; No.5 knitting needles
8 buttons

Cardigan back
Using No.3 needles and A, cast on 106[112:118] sts. Beg with a K row work 1in st st, ending with a K row.
Next row K all sts tbl to form hemline. **
Change to No.5 needles. Beg with a K row cont in st st for 32 rows. Dec one st at each end of next and every foll 20th row until 96[102:108] sts rem. Cont without shaping until work measures 21in from hemline, ending with a P row.
Shape armholes
Bind off 4 sts at beg of next 2 rows, 3 sts at beg of next 2 rows and 2 sts at beg of next 2 rows. Dec one st at each end every other row 2[3:4] times. 74[78:82] sts. Cont without shaping until armholes measure 6 [6½:7]in from beg, ending with a P row.
Shape shoulders
Bind off 10[11:12] sts at beg of next 4 rows. 34 sts. Change to No.3 needles. Beg first row with K2, work 9 rows K2, P2 rib. Bind off in rib.

Cardigan left front
Pocket lining
Using No.5 needles and A, cast on 26 sts. Beg with a K row work 46 rows st st. Slip sts on holder.
Using No.3 needles and A, cast on 54[57:60] sts.
Work as given for back to **. Change to No 5 needles. Beg with a K row work 12 rows st st. Commence patt.
Next row K26 [28:29]A, K1B, K27 [28:30]A.
Next row P25 [27:28]A, P3 B, P26 [27:29]A.
Cont to work in patt from chart 1 until 29 rows have been completed, *at the same time* dec one st at beg of 33rd row from hemline. When 29 rows of patt are completed, work 5 more rows with A, ending with a P row.

Sleeves
Using No.3 needles and A, cast on 54[58:62] sts.
1st row K2, *P2, K2, rep from * to end.
2nd row P2, *K2, P2, rep from * to end.
Rep these 2 rows for 2½in, ending with a 2nd row. Change to No.5 needles. Beg with a K row cont in st st, inc one st at each end of 9th and every foll 12th row until there are 72[76:80] sts. Cont without shaping until sleeve measures 16½ [17:17½]in from beg, ending with a P row.
Shape cap
Bind off 5 sts every other row twice, 4 sts every other row twice and 2 sts every other row twice. Dec one st at each end every other row 12[14:16] times. Bind off 2 sts at beg of next 4 rows. Bind off rem 18 sts.
Neckband
Join right shoulder seam. Using No.3 needles, A and with RS of work facing, pick up and K 20 sts down side of neck, K across sts on front neck holder, pick up and K 20 sts up other side of neck, then K across back neck sts. 86[94:102] sts.
1st row P1, *K2, P2, rep from * to last 3 sts, K2, P1.
2nd row K1, *P2, K2, rep from * to last 3 sts, P2, K1.
Rep these 2 rows for 1½in. Bind off loosely in rib.

Finishing
Press each piece under a damp cloth with a warm iron. Join left shoulder and neckband seam. Sew in sleeves. Join side and sleeve seams. Turn hem at lower edge to WS and sl st down. Fold neckband in half to WS and sl st down. Press seams.

See chart above

28 *Cardigan with diamond motif, and matching hat*

Sizes
To fit 30 [32:34]in bust
The figures in brackets [] refer to the 32 and 34in sizes respectively
Length to shoulder, 27 [27½:28]in
Sleeve seam, 16½ [17:17½]in

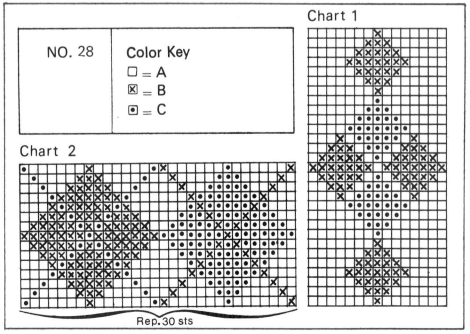

Place pocket
Next row K13[14:16] sts, sl next 26 sts onto holder, K across pocket lining sts, K to end. Cont in st st, dec one st at side edge on every foll 20th row from last dec until 49[52:55] sts rem. Cont without shaping until work measures 6 rows less than back to underarm, ending with a P row.
Shape front edge
Dec one st at end of next row; and on next 3rd row. Work 2 rows without shaping.
Shape armhole
Cont dec at front edge on every 3rd row, bind off every other row 4 sts once, 3 sts once and 2 sts once. Dec one st at armhole edge every other row 2 [3:4] times. Cont dec at front edge only until 20[22:24] sts rem. Cont without shaping until armhole measures same as back to shoulder, ending at armhole edge.
Shape shoulder
At arm edge, bind off 10[11:12] sts every other row twice.

Right front
Work as given for left front, reversing all shapings.

Sleeves
Using No.3 needles and A, cast on 46[50:54] sts. Beg first row with K2, work 2½in K2, P2 rib, ending with a 2nd row. Change to No.5 needles. Beg with a K row cont in st st, inc one st at each end of 9th and every foll 10th row until there are 68[70:74] sts. Cont without shaping until sleeve measures 16½ [17:17½]in from beg, ending with a P row.
Shape cap
Bind off 4 sts at beg of next 2 rows, 3 sts at beg of next 2 rows; then 2 sts at beg of next 2 rows. Dec one st each end every other row 11[12:13] times. Bind off 2 sts at beg of next 4 rows. Bind off rem 20 sts.

Left front edge
. Turn hem to WS and tack in place. Using No.3 needles, A, and with RS of work facing, pick up and K 214[218:222] sts down front edge. Beg first row with P2, work 8 rows K2, P2 rib. Bind off in rib. Mark positions for 8 buttons on left front, first to come on 5th and 6th sts from lower edge and last to come ½in below beg of front shaping, with 6 more evenly spaced between.

Right front edge
Work to correspond to left front edge, working buttonholes on 4th row by binding off 2 sts as each marker is reached, and casting on 2 sts above those bound-off on 5th row.

Pocket tops
Sl 26 pocket top sts on to No.3 needles, using A and with RS of work facing, beg first row with P2 and work 8 rows K2, P2 rib. Bind off in rib.
Finishing
Press each piece under a damp cloth with a warm iron. Join shoulder seams. Sew in sleeves. Join side and sleeve seams. Sew down pocket linings. Sl st hem to WS. Fold pocket tops in half to outside and sew down sides. Press seams. Sew on buttons.

Hat
Using No.3 needles and A, cast on 122 sts. Work as given for cardigan back to **. Change to No.5 needles. Cont in st st, working from chart 2 until 15 rows have been completed, keeping one st at each end in A throughout for seam. Cont with A only until work measures 6in from hemline, ending with a P row.
Shape top

Next row K2 sts, *K2 tog, K1, rep from * to end. 82 sts.
Beg with a P row work 5 rows st st.
Next row *K2 tog, rep from * to end. 41 sts.
Beg with a P row work 5 rows st st.
Next row K1, *K2 tog, rep from * to end. 21 sts. Break off yarn, thread through rem sts, draw up and fasten off.

Finishing
Press as given for cardigan. Join seam. Turn hem to WS and sl st down. Press seam. Make a pompon using A and sew to top of hat.

29 *Lace overblouse and shaped skirt*

Sizes
To fit 34[36:38:40:42]in bust
36[38:40:42:44]in hips
The figures in brackets [] refer to the 36, 38, 40 and 42 and 44in sizes respectively
Overblouse length to shoulder, 22½[23:23½:24:24½] in adjustable
Skirt length, 20[20½:21:21½:22]in adjustable
Gauge
5 sts and 7 rows to 1in over st st worked on No.5 needles
Materials
9[10:11:12:13] balls Bernat Sesame
No.4 knitting needles
No.5 knitting needles
Set of 4 No.4 double-pointed needles
Waist length of elastic
One 7in zipper

Overblouse back
Using No.4 needles cast on 90[94:98:102: 110] sts.
1st row K2, *P2, K2, rep from * to end.
2nd row P2, *K2, P2, rep from * to end.
Rep these 2 rows until work measures 2in from beg, ending with a 2nd row and dec one st at end of last row on 34, 36 and 42in sizes, and inc one st at end of last row on 38 and 40in sizes. 89[93:99:103:109] sts.
Change to No.5 needles. Commence patt.
1st row K11[12:14:15:17] sts, *ytf, K6, sl 1, K2 tog, psso, K6, ytf, K11[12:13:14:15] sts, rep from * once more, ytf, K6, sl 1, K2 tog, psso, K6, ytf, K11[12:14:15:17] sts.
2nd and every other row P to end.
3rd row K12[13:15:16:18] sts, *ytf, K5, sl 1, K2 tog, psso, K5, ytf, K13[14:15:16:17] sts, rep from * once more, ytf, K5, sl 1, K2 tog, psso, K5, ytf, K to end.
5th row K13[14:16:17:19] sts, *ytf, K4, sl 1, K2 tog, psso, K4, ytf, K15[16:17:18:19] sts, rep from * once more, ytf, K4, sl 1, K2 tog, psso, K4, ytf, K to end.
7th row K14[15:17:18:20] sts, *ytf, K3, sl 1, K2 tog, psso, K3, ytf, K17[18:19:20:21] sts, rep from * once more, ytf, K3, sl 1, K2 tog, psso, K3, ytf, K to end.
9th row K15[16:18:19:21] sts, *ytf, K2, sl 1, K2 tog, psso, K2, ytf, K19[20:21:22:23] sts, rep from * once more, ytf, K2, sl 1, K2 tog, psso, K2, ytf, K to end.
11th row K16[17:19:20:22] sts, *ytf, K1, sl 1, K2 tog, psso, K1, ytf, K21[22:23:24:25] sts, rep from * once more, ytf, K1, sl 1, K2 tog, psso, K1, ytf, K to end.
13th row K17[18:20:21:23] sts, * ytf, sl 1, K2 tog, psso, ytf, K23[24:25:26:27] sts, rep from

* once more, ytf, sl 1, K2 tog, psso, ytf
K to end.
14th row P to end.
These 14 rows form patt. Cont in patt until work measures 14½in from beg, or desired length to underarm ending with a P row.
Shape armholes
Bind off 3[3:4:4:4] sts at beg of next 2 rows; 3[3:3:3:4] sts at beg of next 2 rows; then 3 sts at beg of next 2 rows. 71[75:79:83:87] sts. Cont without shaping until armholes measure 8[8½:9:9½: 10]in from beg, ending with a P row.
Shape shoulders
Bind off at beg of next 6 rows 5[5:6:6:6] sts and 6[7:5:6:7] sts at beg of next 2 rows. Slip rem 29[31:33:35:37] sts on holder.

Overblouse front
Work as given for back until work measures 1½in less than back to underarm, ending with a P row.
Divide for neck
Next row Patt 44[46:49:51:54] sts, turn and slip rem sts on holder.
Next row P to end.
Next row Patt to last 3 sts, K2 tog, K1.
Cont to dec at neck edge in this way on every foll 4th row until work measures same as back to underarm, ending at armhole edge.
Shape armhole
Cont dec at neck edge as before, binding off at arm edge 3[3:4:4:4] sts once, then 3[3:3:3:4] sts once and 3 sts once. Cont to dec at neck edge on every 4th row until 21[22:23:24:25] sts rem. Cont without shaping until armhole measures same as back to shoulder, ending at armhole edge.
Shape shoulder
Bind off 5[5:6:6:6] sts at arm edge every other row 3 times. Work 1 row. Bind off rem 6[7:5:6:7] sts. With RS of work facing, leave first st on holder, attach yarn to rem sts and patt to end.
Next row P to end.
Next row K1, sl 1, K1, psso, patt to end.
Complete to correspond to first side, reversing shaping.

Neckband
Join shoulder seams. Using No.4 double-pointed needles and with RS of work facing, K across sts of back neck holder, pick up and K 70[73:76:79:82] sts down front neck, K center front neck st and pick up and K 71[74:77:80:83] sts up other side of front neck. 171[179:187:195:203] sts.
Next round P0[0:1:0:0], K1[2:2:0:1], (P2,K2) 24[25:26:28:29] times, P2 tog, K1, P2 tog, (K2, P2) 17[18:18:19:20] times, K1[0:2:2:1], P0[0:1:0:0].
Work 4 more rounds in rib as set, P2 sts tog at each side of center st on every round. Bind off in rib still dec at center front.

Armbands
Using No.4 needles and with RS of work facing, pick up and K 122[126:130:134:138] sts around armhole. Beg with a 2nd row, work 5 rows rib as given for back. Bind off in rib.

Finishing
Press each piece under a damp cloth with a warm iron. Join side seams. Press seams.

Skirt back
Using No.4 needles cast on 64[68:74:78:84] sts and beg at waist. Beg with a K row work 1½in st st, ending with a K row.
Next row K all sts tbl to mark foldline.
Change to No.5 needles. Beg with a K row cont in st st until work measures 2in from foldline, ending with a P row.
Shape darts
Next row K21[22:24:26:28] sts, pick up loop lying between sts and K tbl – called inc 1 –, K1, inc 1, K20[22:24:24:26] sts, inc 1, K1, inc 1,

64

K21[22:24:26:28] sts.
Beg with a P row work 7 rows st st.
Next row K22[23:25:27:29] sts, inc 1, K1, inc 1, K22[24:26:26:28] sts, inc 1, K1, inc 1, K22[23:25:27:29] sts.
Beg with a P row work 7 rows st st.
Cont inc in this way on next and every foll 8th row until there are 96[100:106:110:116] sts. Cont without shaping until work measures 20[20½:21:21½:22]in from foldline, or desired length from beg, ending with a K row.
Next row K all sts tbl to mark hemline.
Change to No.4 needles. Beg with a K row work 1½in st st. Bind off loosely.

Skirt front
Work as given for back.

Finishing
Press as given for overblouse. Join side seams, leaving 7in from foldline open on left seam for zipper. Turn waistband and hem to WS and sl st down. Press seams. Thread elastic through waistband and secure. Sew in zipper.

Beret and scarf

Sizes
Beret to fit an average head
Scarf 8in wide by 68in long
Gauge
6 sts and 12 rows to 1in over g st worked on No.4 needles
Materials
Bernat Nylo Sports
Beret 1 ball each of 4 colors, A, B, C and D
Scarf 1 ball each of 4 colors, A, B, C and D
No.4 knitting needles

Beret
Using No.4 needles and A, cast on 44 sts.
1st row (RS) K to end.
2nd row K40 sts, turn.
3rd row K32, sts, turn.
4th row K28 sts, turn.
5th row K24 sts, turn.
6th row K20 sts, turn.
7th row As 5th.
8th row As 4th.
9th row K36 sts to end.
10th row As 2nd.
11th row K40 sts to end.
12th row K44 sts to end. Do not break yarn.
Rep these 12 rows using B, C and D. These 48 rows form patt and are rep throughout. Work pattern 6 times more. Bind off.

Finishing
Run in all ends. With WS of work facing, join back seam and using running sts, draw up center crown. Press seam lightly. Using A, B, C and D make a pompon and sew to top.

Scarf
Using No.4 needles and A, cast on 360 sts. Work in garter st working 12 rows each of A, B, C and D. Rep these 48 rows once more.
Bind off loosely.

Finishing
Run in all ends. With WS of work facing and using running sts, draw up each short end of scarf and fasten off. Make 2 pompoms as given for beret and sew one to each short end.

Sleeveless or puff sleeved weskit and hat

Sizes
To fit a 32[34:36:38:40]in bust
The figures in brackets [] refer to the 34, 36, 38 and 40in sizes respectively
Length at center back, 19½[19¾:20:20¼:20½]in adjustable
Sleeve seam, 5in adjustable

Gauge
7½ sts and 8 rows to 1in over patt when blocked worked on No.4 needles
Materials
Bernat Mohairlaine
Sleeveless version 13[14:14:16:16]
Puff sleeved version 19[20:20:22:22] balls
Hat 2 balls
No.2 knitting needles
No.4 knitting needles
Six buttons

Back
Using No.2 needles, cast on 117[125:133:141: 149] sts.
1st row Sl 1, *P1, K1, rep from * to end.
2nd row Sl 1, *K1, P1, rep from * to last 2 sts, K2.
Rep these 2 rows until work measures 4in from beg, ending with a 2nd row.
Next row Inc in first st, rib to last 2 sts, inc in next st, K1. 119[127:135:143:151] sts.
Change to No.4 needles. Commence patt. **.
1st row (WS) Sl 1, K1 tbl, *insert needle p-wise into next 3 sts as if to P3 tog but P1, K1 tbl, P1 all into these 3 sts and sl them off left hand needle – called M3 –, K1 tbl, rep from * to last st, K1.
2nd row Sl 1, P to last st, K1.
These 2 rows form patt. Cont in patt until work measures 11in from beg for sleeveless version, or 12in for puff sleeved version, or desired length to underarm ending with a WS row.

Shape armholes
Keeping patt correct bind off 7[7:8:8:9] sts loosely at beg of next 2 rows. Dec one st at each end of next 6 rows, then each end every other row until 83[87:91:95:99] sts rem for sleeveless version, or 91[95:99:103:107] sts for puff sleeved version. Cont without shaping until armholes measure 7¾[8:8¼:8½:8¾]in from beg for sleeveless version, or 6¾[7:7¼:7½:7¾]in for puff sleeved version, . ending with a WS row.

Shape shoulders
Bind off 6 sts at beg of next 4 rows for sleeveless version, or 8 sts at beg of next 4 rows for puff sleeved version, and 7[8:9:10:11] sts at beg of next 2 rows for both versions.
Slip rem sts on holder.

Front
Work as given for back to **.
Divide for front
1st row (WS) Sl 1, K1 tbl, *M3, K1 tbl, rep from * 12[13:14:15:16] times more, K1, turn.
Complete right front on these 55[59:63:67:71] sts.
2nd row Sl 1, P to last st, K1.
Cont in patt until work measures same as back to underarm, ending at armhole edge.

Shape armhole
Keeping patt correct bind off 7[7:8:8:9] sts loosely at beg of next row. Work 1 row. Dec one st at armhole edge on next 6 rows, then every other row until 37[39:41:43:45] sts rem for

sleeveless version, or 41[43:45:47:49] sts remain for puff sleeved version. Cont without shaping until armhole measures 3[3¼:3½:3¾:4]in from beg for sleeveless version, or 2[2¼:2½:2¾:3]in for puff sleeved version, ending at front edge.

Shape neck
Next row Sl 1, patt 7[8:9:10:11] sts and sl these 8[9:10:11:12] sts onto holder and leave for center neck, patt to last st, K1.
Cont in patt, dec one st at neck edge on every row 10 times in all. 19[20:21:22:23] sts for sleeveless version, or 23[24:25:26:27] sts for puff sleeved version. Cont without shaping until armhole measures same as back to shoulder, ending at armhole edge.

Shape shoulder
Bind off 6 sts every other row twice for sleeveless version, or 8 sts every other row twice for puff sleeved version. Work 1 row. Bind off rem 7[8:9:10:11] sts.
With WS of work facing, sl next 9 sts onto holder and leave for front band. Attach yarn to rem sts and complete to correspond to right front, reversing all shapings.

Puff sleeves
Using No.2 needles cast on 75[79:83:87:91] sts. Work 1in rib as given for back, ending with a 2nd row.
Next row Rib 2[4:6:8:10] sts, *inc in next st, rib 1, rep from * to last 3[5:7:9:11] sts, inc in next st, rib to end. 111[115:119:123:127] sts. Change to No.4 needles. Work in patt as given for back until sleeve measures 5in from beg, or desired length to underarm ending with a WS row.
Shape cap
Keeping patt correct bind off 7[7:8:8:9] sts loosely at beg of next 2 rows. Dec one st at each end of next 6 rows, then each end every other row until 61 sts rem, then each end of every row until 45 sts rem, ending with a RS row.
32, 36 and 40in sizes only
Next row Sl 1, *K3 tog, K1 tbl, rep from * to end. 23 sts.
34 and 38in sizes only
Next row Sl 1, P1, *K1 tbl, K3 tog, rep from * to last 3 sts, K1 tbl, P1, K1. 25 sts.
All sizes
Next row Sl 1, *P2 tog, rep from * to end.
Bind off loosely.

Buttonhole band
Mark positions for 6 buttons on left front, first to come 1in above waist ribbing and 6th to come in neckband. Using No.2 needles and with WS of work facing, attach yarn to sts on holder and work in rib as given for back, making buttonholes as markers are reached as foll:
Next row (RS row) Rib 3, bind off 2 sts, rib 4.
Next row Rib to end, casting on 2 sts above those bound off on previous row.
Work in rib until band measures same as right front opening to neck shaping, when very slightly stretched. Slip sts on holder.

Button band
Using No.2 needles cast on 9 sts. Work as given for buttonhole band, omitting buttonholes.

Neckband
Join shoulder seams. Using No.2 needles and with RS of work facing, rib across sts of buttonhole band and center neck holders, pick up and K 38[40:42: 44:46] sts, rib across sts of back neck holder, pick up and K 38[40:42:44:46] sts, rib across sts of center neck holder and button band holder. 155 [163:171:179:187] sts.
Work 1in rib as given for back, working buttonhole as before on 4th and 5th rows.
Bind off in rib.

Armbands for sleeveless version
Using No.2 needles and with RS of work facing, pick up and K 139[143:147:151:155] sts around armhole. Work 1in rib as given for back, dec one st at each end of every other row.
Bind off in rib.

Finishing
Press each piece lightly on WS under a damp cloth with a warm iron, omitting ribbing. Join side seams. Join sleeve seams for puff sleeved version and sew in sleeves. Oversew front bands to fronts, catching down button band at bottom of button. hole band.
Press seams.
Sew on buttons.

Hat
Using No.3 needles, cast on 135 sts. Work 1in rib as given for back, ending with a 2nd row.
Next row Rib 1, *rib 10, inc in next st, rep from * to last 2 sts, rib 2. 147 sts.
Change to No.5 needles. Cont in patt as given for back until work measures 5½in from beg, ending with a RS row.
Shape top
Next row Sl 1, K1 tbl, *insert needle p-wise into next 3 sts as if to P3 tog but P1, K1 tbl into them and sl off left-hand needle, K1 tbl, rep from * to last st, K1. 111 sts.
Next row Sl 1, P to last st, K1.
Next row Sl 1, K1 tbl, *insert needle p-wise into next 2 sts as if to P2 tog but P1, K1 tbl into them and sl off left-hand needle, K1 tbl, rep from * to last st, K1.
Rep last 2 rows twice more, then first of these rows once more.
Next row Sl 1, K1 tbl, *P2 tog, K1 tbl, rep from * to last st, K1. 75 sts.
Next row Sl 1, *P2 tog, rep from * to end. 38 sts.
Next row Sl 1, *P2 tog, rep from * to last st, K1. 20 sts.
Next row *P2 tog, rep from * to end. 10 sts.
Break yarn and thread through rem sts, draw up and fasten off.

Finishing
Press as for weskit. Join back seam. Press seam.

32 *Two-piece dress with striped yoke*

Sizes
To fit 34[36:38]in bust
36[38:40] hips
The figures in brackets [] refer to the 36 and 38in sizes respectively
Jumper length to shoulder, 25[25½:26]in
Sleeve seam, 8in
Skirt length, 23in adjustable
Gauge
4½ sts and 5½ rows to 1in over st st worked on No.9 needles
Materials
12[13:14] skeins Botany Jiffy
in main color, A
2[2-3] skeins in contrast color, B
No.7 knitting needles
No.9 knitting needles
Set of 4 No.7 double-pointed needles
Waist length of elastic
One 8in zipper

Overblouse back
Using No.7 needles and A, cast on 88[92:96] sts.

Beg with a K row work 1½in st st, ending with a K row.
Next row K all sts tbl to form hemline.
Change to No.9 needles. Beg with a K row cont in st st until work measures 14in from hemline.
Dec one st at each end of next and every foll 6th row until 80[84:88] sts rem. Cont without shaping until work measures 18in from hemline, ending with a P row.
Shape armholes
Bind off 5 sts at beg of next 2 rows. Dec one st at each end every other row 3[4:5] times. 64[66:68] sts. Cont without shaping until armholes measure 7[7½:8]in from beg, ending with a P row.
Shape shoulders
Bind off 5 sts at beg of next 4 rows; then 4[5:6] sts at beg of next 2 rows.
Slip rem 36 sts on holder.

Front
Work as given for back until front measures 7in from hemline, ending with a P row.
Divide for front opening
Next row K44[46:48] sts, turn and slip rem sts on holder.
Complete this side first, shaping side edge to match back and dec one st at center front edge on every foll 5th row until work measures same as back to underarm, ending at armhole edge.
Shape armhole
Bind off 5 sts at beg of next row. Work 1 row. Dec one st at arm edge every other row 3[4:5] times. Keeping armhole edge straight, cont to dec at front edge as before until 14[15:16] sts rem. Cont without shaping until armhole measures same as back to shoulder, ending at armhole edge
Shape shoulder
At arm edge bind off 5 sts every other row twice and 4[5:6] sts once. With RS of work facing, attach yarn to rem sts and work to correspond to first side, reversing shaping.

Sleeves
Using No.7 needles and A, cast on 46[48:50] sts. Beg with a K row 1in st st, ending with a K row.
Next row K all sts tbl to form hemline.
Change to No.9 needles. Beg with a K row cont in st st, inc one st at each end of 3rd and every foll 4th row until there are 62[64:66] sts. Cont without shaping until sleeve measures 8in from hemline, ending with a P row.
Shape cap
Bind off 5 sts at beg of next 2 rows. Dec one st at each end every other row until 30 sts rem.
Bind off 2 sts at beg of next 8 rows; then 3 sts at beg of next 2 rows. Bind off rem 8 sts.

Neckband
Join shoulder seams. Using set of No.7 double-pointed needles, B and with RS of work facing, K across sts on back neck holder, pick up and K 72[74:76] sts down side of front neck and 72[74:76] sts up other side of front neck. 180[184:188] sts.
Next round K to 2 sts before center front, sl 1, K1, psso, K2 tog, K to end.
Rep this round 5 times more, then P1 around still dec at center front.
Next round K to 2 sts before center front, K twice into next st, K2, K twice into next st, K to end.
Rep this round 4 times more. Bind off loosely, still inc at center front.

Striped yoke
Using No.9 needles and A, cast on 4 sts. Beg with a K row work 8 rows st st, inc one st at each end of 3rd and foll 4th row. Cont in st st, working 6 rows B, 6 rows A, and inc at each end of every foll 4th row until there are 50 sts. Cont without shaping until 5th row of 8th stripe in B has been worked. 97 rows in all. Change to No.7 needles. K 1 row.
Beg with a K row, cont with B and work 5 more rows. Bind off loosely.

Finishing
Press each piece under a damp cloth with a warm iron. Sew in sleeves. Join side and sleeve seams. Turn all hems to WS and sl-st down. Sew in striped yoke to front opening. Press seams.

Skirt back
Using No.7 needles and A, cast on 90[94:98] sts and beg at hem. Beg with a K row work 1½in st st, ending with a K row.
Next row K all sts tbl to form hemline.
Change to No.9 needles. Beg with a K row cont in st st, working (6 rows A, 6 rows B) twice. Cont in st st using A only until work measures 14in from hemline, or desired length to waist less 9in, ending with a P row.
Next row K22[23:24] sts, K2 tog, K42[44:46] sts, sl 1, K1, psso, K22[23:24] sts.
Beg with a P row work 3 rows st st.
Next row K22[23:24] sts, K2 tog, K40[42:44] sts, sl 1, K1, psso, K22[23:24] sts.
Beg with a P row work 3 rows st st.
Cont dec in this way on next and every foll 4th row until 66[70:74] sts rem. Cont without shaping for further 1in, ending with a K row. Change to No.7 needles.
Next row K all sts tbl to mark fold line.
Beg with a K row cont in st st for 1in. Bind off loosely.

Skirt front
Work as given for back.

Finishing
Press as given for overblouse. Join side seams leaving 8in open from fold line on left side for zipper. Sew in zipper. Fold hem and waistband to WS and sl-st down. Press seams. Thread elastic through waistband and fasten at each end.

33 *Striped maxi dress*

Sizes
To fit 32[34:36:38:40]in bust
34[36:38:40:42]in hips
Length to shoulder, 46[47:48:49:50]in
The figures in brackets [] refer to the 34, 36, 38 and 40in sizes respectively
Length to shoulder, 46[47:48:49:50]in
Gauge
6 sts and 8 rows to 1in over st st worked on No.4 needles
Materials
11[12:13:15:16] balls. Reynolds Kermesse in main color, A
2[2:2:2:3] balls of contrast color, B
No.4 knitting needles
No. D crochet hook
20 buttons
Back
Using No.4 needles and A, cast on 158[164:170:176:182] sts. Beg with a K row work 4in st st, ending with a P row.
Shape skirt
Next row K19 sts, sl 1, K1, psso, K40[42:44:46: 48] sts, sl 1, K1, psso, K32[34:36:38:40] sts, K2 tog, K40[42:44:46:48] sts, K2 tog, K19 sts.
Beg with a P row cont in st st until work measures

5in from beg, then work 2 rows with B. Cont with A until 17 rows in all have been worked from last dec row.

Next row K19 sts, sl 1, K1, psso, K38[40:42:44:46] sts, sl 1, K1, psso, K32[34:36:38:40] sts, K2 tog, K38[40:42:44:46] sts, K2 tog, K19 sts.

Cont to dec in this way on every foll 18th row until 98[104:110:116:122] sts rem, *at the same time* work in stripes as foll: 4½in A, 2 rows B, 4in A, 2 rows B, 3½in A, 2 rows B, 3in A, 2 rows B, 2½in A, 2 rows B, 2in A, 2 rows B, 1½in A, 2 rows B. Complete back working in 8 rows A and 2 rows B throughout. Cont without shaping until work measures 38[38½:39:39½:40]in from beg.

End with a P row.

Shape armholes

Bind off 8 sts at beg of next 2 rows; then 2[2:3:3:4] sts at beg of next 2 rows. Dec one st at each end every other row 4[5:5:6:6] times. 70[74:78:82:86] sts. Cont without shaping until armholes measure 7[7½:8:8½:9]in from beg, ending with a P row.

Shape neck and shoulders

Next row K19[20:21:22:23] sts, turn and slip rem sts on holder.

Next row Bind off 4 sts, P to end.

Next row Bind off 6[6:7:7:8] sts, K to end.

Next row Bind off 4 sts, P to end.

Bind off rem 5[6:6:7:7] sts. With RS of work facing, attach yarn to rem sts and bind off 32[34:36:38:40] sts, K to end. P 1 row. Work to correspond to first side reversing shaping.

Left front

Using No.4 needles and A, cast on 79[82:85:88:91] sts. Beg with a K row work 4in st st, ending with a P row.

Shape skirt

Next row K19 sts, sl 1, K1, psso, K40[42:44:46:48] sts, sl 1, K1, psso, K to end.

Cont working in striped sequence as given for back, dec in this way on every foll 18th row until 49[52:55:58:61] sts rem. Cont without shaping until work measures same as back to underarm, ending at armhole edge.

Shape armhole

At arm edge; bind off 8 sts, then 2[2:3:3:4] sts. Dec one st at armhole edge every other row 4[5:5:6:6] times. 35[37:39:41:43] sts. Cont without shaping until armhole measures 3[3½:4:4½:5]in from beg, ending at front edge.

Shape neck

Bind off 9[9:10:10:11] sts once, 5[6:6:7:7] sts once, 4 sts once and 2 sts every other row twice. Dec one st at neck edge every other row twice. Cont without shaping until armhole measures same as back to shoulder.

End at armhole edge.

Shape shoulder

Bind off at neck edge; 6[6:7:7:8] sts; then 5[6:6:7:7] sts once.

Right front

Work as given for left front, reversing shaping.

Finishing

Press each piece under a damp cloth with a warm iron. Join shoulder and side seams.

Armbands Using No.D crochet hook, A and with RS of work facing, work 1 round sc around armhole. Join with a ss.

Next round Ch2, *ch1, skip 1sc, 1sc into next sc, rep from * to end. Join with ss to 2nd of first ch2.

Rep last round 4 times more. Fasten off.

Borders Mark positions for 20 buttons on left front, first to come 1½in from lower edge and last level with neck shaping with 18 spaced at equal intervals. Work around all edges as given for armbands, working 1sc, ch1, 1sc into each corner on every row and making buttonholes on 4th row as markers are reached by working ch3 and skipping 3 sts, and working 3 sts in to each ch3 sp on 5th row.

Press all seams. Sew on buttons.

34 *Candy-striped shirt*

Sizes

To fit 34[36:38:40:42]in bust

The figures in brackets [] refer to the 36, 38, 40 and 42in sizes respectively

Length to shoulder, 26½[27:27½:28:28½]in

Sleeve seam, 14[14½:15:15½:16]in

Gauge

5½ sts and 7 rows to 1in over st st worked on No.5 needles

Materials

6[7:8:8:9] balls Reynolds Danksyarn in main color, A

2 balls each in contrast colors B and D

4 balls in contrast color, C

No.3 knitting needles

No.5 knitting needles

Four buttons

Back

Using No.3 needles and A, cast on 97[103:109:115:121] sts. Beg with a K row work 1½in st st, ending with a K row.

Next row K all sts tbl to form hemline.

Change to No.5 needles. Beg with a K row, cont in st st working 2 rows B, 2 rows C, 2 rows A, 2 rows D, then cont in A only until work measures 2in from hemline, ending with a P row.

Shape sides

Dec one st at each end of next and every foll 12th row until 85[91:97:103:109] sts rem, *at the same time* work striped patt, as foll: Cont in A until work measures 7¼in from hemline, **2 rows D, 2 A, 2 D, 2 A, 2 C, 2 A, 4 B, 2 A, 2 B, 2 D, 2 A, 8 C, 2 A, 4 D, **, then cont in A only until work measures 17in from hemline, ending with a P row. Work 4 rows B, 6 A.

Shape armholes

Using C, bind off 3 sts at beg of next 2 rows. 79[85:91:97:103] sts.

3rd row Using A, K1, K2 tog, K to last 3 sts, K2 tog tbl, K1.

4th row Using A, P to end.

5th and 6th rows Using B, work 2 rows without shaping.

7th and 8th rows Using A, as 3rd and 4th rows.

9th and 10th rows Using A, as 5th and 6th rows.

11th and 12th rows Using A, as 3rd and 4th rows.

13th and 14th rows Using D, as 5th and 6th rows.

15th and 16th rows Using D, as 3rd and 4th rows.

Rep 3rd and 4th rows until 27[29:31:33:35] sts rem, working 2 rows B, 2 A, 16 C, 2 D, then cont in A only, ending with a P row.

Bind off.

Front

Work as given for back until work measures 17in from beg, ending with a K row and 1 row less of stripe in A.

Divide for front opening

Next row Using A, P40[43:46:49:52] sts, bind off 5 sts, P to end. Complete this side first. Cont in striped patt until work measures same as back to underarm, ending at armhole edge.

Shape armhole

Keeping striped patt correct, bind off 3 sts at beg of next row. Work 1 row.

Next row K1, K2 tog, K to end.

Beg with a P row work 3 rows st st.

Rep last 4 rows twice more, then cont to dec at beg of every other row until 18[19:20:21:22] sts rem, ending at front edge.

Shape neck

Next row Bind off 4(5:6:7:8] sts, P to end.

Next row K1, K2 tog, K to last 2 sts, K2 tog.

Next row P to end.

Rep last 2 rows 4 times more. Cont to dec at armhole edge only every other row until 2 sts rem, ending with a K row.

Next row P2 tog. Fasten off.

With RS of work facing, attach yarn to rem sts and complete to correspond to first side, reversing shaping.

Sleeves

Using No.3 needles and A, cast on 45[45:47:47:49] sts.

1st row K1, *P1, K1, rep from * to end.

2nd row P1, *K1, P1, rep from * to end.

Rep these 2 rows for 2in, ending with a 2nd row and inc 4 sts evenly across last row. 49[49:51:51:53] sts. Change to No.5 needles. Beg with a K row, cont in st st inc one st at each end of 7th and every foll 8th row until there are 69[71:73:75:77] sts, *at the same time* working in stripes as foll: Cont in A until work measures 3¼[3½:3¾:4:4¼]in, work as given for back from ** to **, then cont in A until sleeve measures 12½[13:13½:14:14½]in from beg, ending with a P row. Work 4 rows B, 6 A.

Shape cap

Working in stripes to match back, bind off 3 sts at beg of next 2 rows.

Next row K1, K2 tog, K to last 3 sts, K2 tog tbl, K1.

Beg with a P row work 3 rows st st. Cont to dec on every 4th row 1[2:3:4:5] times more. 59 sts. P 1 row. Dec one st at each end of next and every other row until 7 sts rem, ending with a P row. Bind off.

Buttonhole band

Using No.3 needles and A, cast on 55[57:61:63:67] sts. Beg with a 2nd row work 3 rows rib as given for sleeves.

Next row Rib 4[6:7:9:10] sts, *bind off 2 sts, rib 13[13:14:14:15] sts, rep from * twice more, bind off 2 sts, rib to end.

Next row Rib to end, casting on 2 sts above those bound off on previous row.

Work 3 more rows in rib. Bind off in rib.

Button band

Work as given for buttonhole band, omitting buttonholes.

Collar

Using No.3 needles and C, cast on 35[37:39:41:43] sts. Work 1 row K1, P1 rib. Cont in rib, casting on 8 sts at beg of next 6 rows and 10 sts at beg of next 4 rows. 123[125:127:129:131] sts. Cont in rib until work measures 3[3:3¼:3¼:3½]in from beg. Break off C. Attach B and K 1 row, then rib 1 row. Break off B. Attach A and K 1 row, then rib 3 rows. Bind off loosely in rib.

Finishing

Press each piece under a damp cloth with a warm iron. Join raglan seams. Join side and sleeve seams. Sew on front bands. Sew in sleeves. Sew on collar. Turn hem to WS at hemline and sl-st down. Press all seams. Sew on buttons.

35 *Pullover and striped sleeveless jacket*

Sizes

To fit 32[34:36:38:40]in bust

The figures in brackets [] refer to the 34, 36, 38 and 40in sizes respectively

Pullover length to shoulder, 24[24½:25:25½:26]in

Sleeve seam, 17in

Jacket length to shoulder, 29[29½:30:30½:31]in

Gauge

6 sts and 8 rows to 1 in over st st worked on No.4 needles

Materials

Pullover 8[8:9:10:10] skeins Bear Brand or Fleisher or Botany Winsom in main color, A

Jacket 5[6:6:6:7] skeins main color, A
3[3:3:3:3] skeins in contrast color, B
No.4 knitting needles; No.2 knitting needles
Set of 4 No.2 double-pointed needles

Pullover back

Using No.4 needles cast on 98[104:110:116:122] sts.

1st row K14[17:20:23:26] sts, P14, (K14, P14) twice, K14[17:20:23:26] sts.

2nd row P14[17:20:23:26] sts, K14, (P14, K14) twice, P14[17:20:23:26] sts.

These 2 rows form patt. Cont in patt until work measures 4in from beg, ending with a 2nd row. Keeping patt correct, dec one st at each end of next and every foll 12th row until 88[94:100:106:112] sts rem. Cont without shaping until work measures 17½in from beg, ending with a WS row.

Shape armholes

Bind off 4 sts at beg of next 2 rows. Dec one st at each end of every other row 6[7:8:9:10] times. 68[72:76:80:84] sts. Cont without shaping until armholes measure 6½[7:7½:8:8½]in from beg, ending with a WS row.

Shape shoulders

Bind off 6[6:7:7:7] sts at beg of next 4 rows; then 6[7:6:7:8] sts at beg of next 2 rows. Slip rem sts on holder.

Front

Work as given for back until armhole shaping is completed. Cont without shaping until armholes measure 4½[5:5½:6:6½]in from beg, ending with a WS row.

Shape neck

Next row Patt 26[27:28:29:30] sts, turn and slip rem sts on holder.

Complete this side first. At neck edge, bind off 2 sts every other row twice, then dec one st at neck edge on every other row until 18[19:20:21:22] sts rem. Cont without shaping until armhole measures same as back to shoulder, ending at armhole edge.

Shape shoulder

Bind off 6[6:7:7:7] sts every other row twice and 6[7:6:7:8] sts once.

With RS of work facing, sl first 16[18:20:22:24] sts on holder and leave for center neck, attach yarn to rem sts and patt to end. Complete to correspond to first side, reversing shaping.

Sleeves

Using No.2 needles cast on 42[44:46:48:50] sts.

1st row K0[1:2:3:4] sts, P14, K14, P14, K0[1:2:3:4] sts.

2nd row P0[1:2:3:4] sts, K14, P14, K14, P0[1:2:3:4] sts.

Cont in patt as established until sleeve measures 1½in from beg. Change to No.4 needles. Cont in patt, inc one st at each end of next and every foll 8th row until there are 70[72:74:76:78] sts. Cont without shaping until sleeve measures 17in from beg, or desired length to underarm; end with a WS row.

Shape cap

Bind off 4 sts at beg of next 2 rows. Dec one st at each end of next and every other row until 48 sts rem. Bind off 2 sts at beg of next 10 rows; 3 sts at beg of next 4 rows and 4 sts at beg of next 2 rows. Bind off rem 8 sts.

Neckband

Join shoulder seams. Using No.2 double-pointed needles, K across sts on back neck holder pick up and K 20 sts down side of front neck, K across sts on center front neck holder and pick up and K 20 sts up other side of neck. 88[92:96:100:104] sts. Join 1½in in rounds of K1, P1 rib. Bind off in rib.

Finishing

Press each piece under a damp cloth with a warm iron. Sew in sleeves. Join side and sleeve seams. Press seams.

Jacket back

Using No.2 needles and A, cast on 106[112:118:124:130] sts. Beg with a K row work 1½in st st, ending with a K row.

Next row K all sts tbl for hemline.

Change to No.4 needles. Beg with a K row cont in st st working throughout in stripes of 20 rows A and 4 rows B. Cont in patt until work measures 4in from hemline, ending with a P row. Dec one st at each end of next and every foll 10th row until 90[96:102:108:114] sts rem. Cont without shaping until work measures 22in from hemline, ending with a P row.

Shape armholes

Bind off 5 sts at beg of next 2 rows. Dec one st each end every other row 6[7:8:9:10] times. 68[72:76:80:84] sts. Cont without shaping until armholes measure 7[7½:8:8½:9]in from beg, ending with a P row.

Shape shoulders

Work as given for pullover back. Bind off rem 32[34:36:38:40] sts.

Jacket left front

Using No.2 needles and A, cast on 57[60:63:66:69] sts. Work as given for back until work measures 4in from hemline, ending with a P row. Dec one st at beg of next and every foll 10th row until 49[52:55:58:61] sts rem. Cont without shaping until work measures same as back to underarm, less 3in, ending with a P row.

Shape front edge

Dec one st at end of next and every foll 4th row until work measures same as back to underarm, ending at armhole edge.

Shape armhole

Cont to dec at front edge as before, binding off 5 sts at beg of next row. Work 1 row. Dec one st at armhole edge every other row 6[7:8:9:10] times. Cont dec at front edge only as before until 18[19:20:21:22] sts rem. Cont without shaping until armhole measures same as back to shoulder, ending at armhole edge.

Shape shoulder

Bind off at arm edge; 6[6:7:7:7] sts every other row; then 6[7:6:7:8] sts once.

Jacket right front

Work as given for left front, reversing shaping.

Armbands

Join shoulder seams. Using No.2 needles, A and with RS of work facing, pick up and K85[91:97:103:109] sts around armhole. Beg 1st row with P1, work in K1, P1 rib for ¾in. Bind off in rib.

Front band

Using No.2 needles and B, cast on 11 sts. Work in K1, P1 rib until band is long enough to fit up right front, around back neck and down left front. Bind off in rib.

Finishing

Press as given for pullover. Join side seams. Turn hem to WS and sl st down. Sew on front band. Press seams.

36 *Tunic with front lacing*

Sizes

To fit 32[34:36:38:40]in bust
The figures in brackets [] refer to the 34, 36, 38 and 40in sizes respectively
Length to shoulder, 25½[26:26½:27:27½]in
Sleeve seam, 17[17:17½:17½:18]in

Gauge

6 sts and 8 rows to 1 in over st st worked on No.4 needles

Materials

6[7:7:8:8] balls Bernat Nylo Sports
No.2 knitting needles
No.4 knitting needles

Back

Using No.2 needles cast on 114 [120:126:132:138] sts. Beg with a K row work 1½in st st, ending with a K row.

Next row K all sts tbl to mark hemline.

Change to No.4 needles. Beg with a K row cont in st st until work measures 4in from hemline, ending with a P row.

Shape darts

Next row K1, K2 tog, K36[38:40:42:44] sts, K2 tog, K32[34:36:38:40] sts, sl 1, K1, psso, K36[38:40:42:44] sts, sl 1, K1, psso, K1. Beg with a P row work 9 rows st st.

Next row K1, K2 tog, K35[37:39:41:43] sts, K2 tog, K30[32:34:36:38] sts, sl 1, K1, psso, K35[37:39:41:43] sts, sl 1, K1, psso, K1. Dec in same way on foll 10th row. 102[108:114:120:126] sts. Cont without shaping until work measures 18½in from hemline, ending with a P row.

Shape armholes

Bind off 6 sts at beg of next 2 rows.

Next row K1, K2 tog, K to last 3 sts, sl 1, K1, psso, K1.

Next row P to end.

Rep last 2 rows 3[4:5:6:7] times more. 82[86:90:94:98] sts. Cont without shaping until armholes measure 7[7½:8:8½:9]in from beg, ending with a P row.

Shape neck and shoulders

Next row Bind off 4[5:5:5:6] sts, K17[17:18:19:19] sts, turn and slip rem sts on holder.

Next row Bind off 2 sts, P to end.

Next row Bind off 4 sts, K to end.

Rep last 2 rows once more, then first of these 2 rows once. Bind off rem 3[3:4:5:5] sts. With RS of work facing, sl first 40[42:44:46:48] sts on holder and leave for back neck, attach yarn to rem sts and K to end. Complete to correspond to first side, reversing shaping.

Front
Work as given for back until front measures 7[7:6½:6½:6]in less than back to underarm, ending with a K row.
Divide for front opening
Next row P50[53:56:59:62] sts, bind off 2 sts, P to end.
Next row K to end, turn and cast on 4 sts. 54[57:60:63:66] sts.
Next row P to end.
Next row K to last 4 sts, sl 1, K3.
Rep last 2 rows for 1½in, ending with a P row.
Next row (eyelet hole) K to last 8 sts, ytf, K2 tog, K2, sl 1, K3.
Keeping sl st correct on every K row, cont to make eyelet holes in this way at intervals of 1½in from the previous eyehole, until work measures same as back to underarm ending at armhole edge.
Shape armhole
Bind off 6 sts at beg of next row. Work 1 row.
Next row K1, K2 tog, patt to end.
Next row Patt to end.
Rep last 2 rows 3[4:5:6:7] times more. Cont without shaping, working eyelet holes as before until 7 in all have been made, then cont for a further 1½in, ending at neck edge. 44[46:48:50:52] sts.
Shape neck
Bind off 3 sts, P to end.
Next row K21[22:23:24:25] sts, turn and slip rem 20[21:22:23:24] sts on holder.
Bind off 2 sts at neck edge every other row 3 times; then cont without shaping until armhole measures same as back to shoulder, ending at armhole edge.
Shape shoulder
At arm edge bind off 4[5:5:5:6] sts once, 4 sts every other row twice; then 3[3:4:5:5] sts once.
With RS of work facing attach yarn to rem sts, cast on 4 sts, K3, sl 1, K to end. Complete to correspond to first side, reversing shaping and noting that eyelet hole row will be worked as foll: K3, sl 1, K2, sl 1, K1, psso, ytf, K to end.

Sleeves
Using No.2 needles cast on 49[51:53:55:57] sts.
1st row K1, *P1, K1, rep from * to end.
2nd row P1, *K1, P1, rep from * to end.
Rep these 2 rows for 1¼in, ending with a 2nd row.
Change to No.4 needles and work in st st.
1st row K1[2:3:4:5] sts, (K twice into next st, K4) 9 times, K twice into next st, K2[3:4:5:6] sts. 59[61:63:65:67] sts.
Beg with a P row work 3 rows st st.
5th row K2[3:4:5:6] sts, (K twice into next st, K5) 9 times, K twice into next st, K2[3:4:5:6] sts. 69[71:73:75:77] sts.
Beg with a P row work 3 rows st st.
9th row K2[3:4:5:6] sts, (K twice into next st, K6) 9 times, K twice into next st, K3[4:5:6:7] sts. 79[81:83:85:87] sts.
Beg with a P row work 3 rows st st.
13th row K0[1:2:3:4] sts, (K twice into next st, K6) 11 times, K twice into next st, K1[2:3:4:5] sts. 91[93:95:97:99] sts.
Beg with a P row cont without shaping until sleeve measures 7in from beg, ending with a P row.
Next row K12[13:14:15:16] sts, (K2 tog, K14) 4 times, K2 tog, K to end.
Beg with a P row work 11 rows st st. Cont to dec 5 sts evenly in this way on next and every foll 12th row until 71[73:75:77:79] sts rem. Cont without shaping until sleeve measures 17[17:17½:17½:18]in from beg, ending with a P row.
Shape cap
Bind off 6 sts at beg of next 2 rows. Dec at each end of next and every other row as for back until 31[33:35:37:39] sts rem. Bind off 2 sts at beg of next 4[4:6:6:6] rows; then 3 sts at beg of next 4 rows. Bind off rem 11[13:11:13:15] sts.

Neckband
Join shoulder seams. Using No.2 needles and with RS of work facing K across sts of right front neck, pick up and K 18[20:20:22:22] sts up side of front neck, K up 9 sts down back neck, K across sts of back neck, dec one st in center, pick up and K 9 sts up back neck, pick up and K18[20:20:22:22] sts down side of front neck and K across sts of left front neck. 133[141:145:153:157] sts. Beg with a 2nd row work 1in in rib as given for sleeves.
Bind off in rib.

Finishing
Press each piece under a damp cloth with a warm iron. Sew in sleeves. Join side and sleeve seams. Turn hem to WS and sl st down. Fold front facings to WS at sl st line and sl st down. Press seams. Make a twisted cord 60in long and thread through eyelet holes to tie at neck edge.

37 *Pullover with cable panels and saddle-top sleeves*

Sizes
To fit 32[34:36:38:40]in bust
The figures in brackets [] refer to the 34, 36, 38 and 40in sizes respectively
Length to shoulder, 22[22½:23:23½:24]in
Sleeve seam, 16½[17:17:17½:18]in
Gauge
5¾ sts and 7½ rows to 1in over st st worked on No.5 needles
Materials
7[7:8:8:9] balls Unger's Les Coraux in main color, A
1 ball each in contrast colors, B and C
No.3 knitting needles
No.5 knitting needles
Set of 4 No.3 double-pointed needles
Cable needle

Back
Using No.3 needles and A, cast on 102[106:114:118:126] sts.
1st row K2, *P2, K2, rep from * to end.
2nd row P2, *K2, P2, rep from * to end.
Rep these 2 rows 5 times more, inc one st at each end of last row on 34 and 38in sizes only. 102[108:114:120:126] sts. Change to No.5 needles.
Commence patt.
1st row P4[5:6:7:8] sts, *K6, P6, K4[5:6:7:8] sts, P6, rep from * 3 times more, K6, P4[5:6:7:8] sts.
2nd row K4[5:6:7:8] sts, *P6, K6, P4[5:6:7:8] sts, K6, rep from *3 times more, P6, K4[5:6:7:8] sts.
3rd row As 1st.
4th row As 2nd.
5th row P4[5:6:7:8] sts, *sl next 3 sts onto cable needle and hold at front of work, K3 sts, then K3 sts from cable needle – called C6F –, P6, K4[5:6:7:8] sts, P6, rep from * 3 times more, C6F, P4[5:6:7:8] sts.
6th row As 2nd.
7th row As 1st.
8th row As 2nd
These 8 rows form patt. Cont in patt until work measures 14½in from beg, ending with a WS row.
Shape armholes
Bind off 2 sts at beg of next 2 rows. Dec one st at each end of next and every foll 4th row until 76[80:84:88:92] sts rem, then work even for 2 rows after last dec ending with a WS row.
Shape shoulders
Bind off 25[25:27:27:29] sts, patt 26[30:30:34:34] sts, bind off rem 25[25:27:27:29] sts. Slip sts on holder for center neck.

Front
Work as given for back.

Sleeves
Using No.3 needles and B, cast on 50[54:54:58:58] sts. Work 2 rows rib as given for back. Break off B. Attach A, K 1 row, then rib 2 rows. Break off A. Attach C, P 1 row, then rib 1 row. Break off C. Using A only, P 1 row, then cont in rib until sleeve measures 3½in from beg, ending with a 2nd row and inc one st at each end of last row on 32, 36 and 40in sizes only. 52[54:56:58:60] sts. Change to No.5 needles. Beg with a K row cont in st st, inc one st at each end of 5th and every foll 8th row until there are 72[74:78:80:84] sts. Cont without shaping until sleeve measures 16½[17:17:17½:18]in from beg, ending with a P row.
Shape cap
Bind off 2 sts at beg of next 2 rows. 68[70:74:76:80] sts.
Next row K3 sts, K2 tog, K to last 5 sts, sl 1, K1, psso, K3 sts.
Beg with a P row work 3 rows st st.
Cont to dec in this way on next and every foll 4th row 0[1:1:2:2] times more, then on every other row until 24 sts rem.
Saddle top
Cont in st st without shaping until saddle top measures same as top of shoulder on back and front, ending with a P row. Slip sts on holder.

Neckband
Sew saddle top of sleeves to shoulders of back and front. Using No.3 double-pointed needles, A and with RS of work facing, K across all sts on holders, K2 tog at each seam. Cont in rounds of K2, P2 rib, as foll: Work 2 rounds A. With C, K 1 round, then rib 1 round. With A, K 1 round, then rib 2 rounds. With B, K 1 round, then rib 1 round. Bind off in rib with B.

Finishing
Press each piece lightly on WS under a damp cloth with a cool iron. Sew in sleeves. Join side and sleeve seams. Press seams.

38 *Boat-neck pullover*

Sizes
To fit 32[34:36:38:40:42]in bust
The figures in brackets [] refer to the 34, 36, 38, 40 and 42in sizes respectively
Length to shoulder, 20½[21:21½:22:22½:23]in
Sleeve seam, 12in
Gauge
9 sts and 14 rows to 2in over st st worked on No.6 needles
Materials
10[10:10:11:11:12] skeins Bernat Venetian Boucle
No.4 knitting needles; No.6 knitting needles

Back
Using No.4 needles cast on 76[80:86:90:96:100] sts. Beg with a K row work 9 rows st st.
Next row K all sts tbl to mark hemline.
Change to No.6 needles. Beg with a K row cont in st st until work measures 14in from hemline, ending with a P row.
Shape armholes
Bind off 4 sts at beg of next 2 rows; then 2 sts at beg of next 2 rows. Dec 1 st each end every other

row 2[2:3:3:4:4] times. 60[64:68:72:76:80] sts.
Cont without shaping until armholes measure
6½[7:7½:8:8½:9]in from beg, ending with a P row.
Shape shoulders
Bind off 4 sts at beg of next 3 rows.
Next row (neckline) Bind off 4 sts, work to end.
Change to No.3 needles. Beg with a K row work
5 rows st st, inc one st at each end of every row.
Bind off.

Front
Work as given for back.

Sleeves
Using No.4 needles cast on 44[46:48:50:52:54]
sts. Work hem as given for back. Change to No.6
needles. Beg with a K row cont in st st, inc one st at
each end of 5th and every foll 8th row until there
are 58[60:62:64:66:68] sts. Cont without shaping
until sleeve measures 12in from hemline, ending
with a P row.
Shape cap
Bind off 4 sts at beg of next 2 rows. K2 tog at each
end of next and every other row until 28 sts rem.
Bind off 2 sts at beg of next 6 rows; then 3 sts at
beg of next 2 rows.
Bind off rem 10 sts.

Finishing
Press each piece under a damp cloth with a warm
iron. Join shoulder, side and sleeve seams. Sew in
sleeves. Fold hems at lower and neck edges to
WS and sl-st down. Press seams.

Dress with smocked sleeves and sleeveless jacket

Sizes
To fit 32 [34:36:38]in bust
34[36:38:40]in hips
The figures in brackets [] refer to the 34, 36 and
38in sizes respectively
Dress length to shoulder, 40[40½:41:41½]in
Sleeve seam, 17[17:17½:17½]in
Jacket length to shoulder, 20[20½:21:21½]in
Gauge
7 sts and 9 rows to 1in over st st worked on No.3
needles
Materials
Dress 14[15:16:18] skeins Brunswick Fairhaven
Fingering
Jacket 4[5:6:6] skeins
No.2 knitting needles
No.3 knitting needles
Set of 4 No.2 double-pointed needles
No.B crochet hook. Six buttons

Dress back
Using No.2 needles cast on 158[164:172:178] sts.
Beg with a K row work 1½in st st, ending with a K
row.
Next row K all sts tbl to mark hemline.
Change to No.3 needles. Beg with a K row cont in
st st until work measures 5in from hemline, ending
with a P row.
Shape darts
Next row K38[40:42:44] sts, sl 1, K1, psso, K to
last 40[42:44:46] sts, K2 tog, K to end.
Beg with a P row work 7 rows st st.
Cont to dec in this way on next and every foll 8th
row until 110[116:124:130] sts rem. Cont without
shaping until work measures 33in from hemline,
ending with a P row.
Shape armholes

Bind off 5 sts at beg of next 2 rows; then 3[3:4:4]
sts at beg of next 2 rows. Dec 1 st each end every
other row 3[4:5:6] times. 88[92:96:100] sts. Cont
without shaping until armholes measure 7[7½:8:
8½]in from beg.
End with a P row.
Shape shoulders
Bind off 8 sts at beg of next 4 rows; then
6[7:8:9] sts at beg of next 2 rows. Slip rem
44[46:48:50] sts on holder

Dress front
Work as given for back until armhole shaping is
completed. Cont without shaping until armholes
measure 5[5½:6:6½]in from beg, ending with a P
row.
Shape neck
Next row K30[31:32:33] sts, turn and slip rem
sts on holder.
At neck edge; bind off 3 sts; then 2 sts.
Dec one st at neck edge every other row until
22[23:24:25] sts rem. Cont without
shaping until armhole measures same as back to
shoulder.
End at armhole edge.
Shape shoulder
At arm edge; bind off 8 sts every other row twice
then 6[7:8:9] sts once.
With RS of work facing, sl first 28[30:32:34] sts on
holder and leave for center neck, attach yarn to
rem sts and K to end. Complete to correspond to
first side, reversing shaping.

Sleeves
Using No.3 needles cast on 94[96:98:100] sts.
1st row P1[2:3:4] sts, (K1, P6) 13 times, K1,
P1[2:3:4] sts.
2nd row K1[2:3:4] sts, (P1, K6) 13 times, P1,
K1[2:3:4] sts.
Rep these 2 rows until sleeve measures 2in from beg
ending with a 2nd row. Cont in patt, inc one st at
each end of next and every foll 10th row until there
are 104[106:108:110] sts. Cont without shaping
until work measures 11in from beg, ending with a
WS row. Dec one st at each end of next and every
other row until 84[86:88:90] sts rem. Cont without
shaping until sleeve measures 17[17:17½:17½]in
from beg, ending with a WS row.
Shape cap
Bind off 2 sts at beg of every row until 8 sts rem.
Bind off.

Neckband
Join shoulder seams. Using No.2 double-pointed
needles and with RS of work facing, K across back
neck sts, pick up and K 20 sts down side of neck, K
across front neck sts and pick up and K 20 sts up
other side of neck. Join. Work in rounds of K1, P1
rib for 8in. Bind off loosely in rib.

Finishing
Press each piece under a damp cloth with a warm
iron.
Sleeve smocking Beg above cast-on edge
using darning needle and one strand of yarn,
join 1st and 2nd K sts tog, take yarn behind work
and join 2nd and 3rd K sts tog approx 1in above
2 sts already joined, take yarn behind work again
and join 3rd and 4th K sts tog at cast-on edge, cont
in this way across sleeve. Fasten off. Beg again
with 1st and 2nd K ridges 2in from beg and 2nd
and 3rd K ridges 3in from beg. Cont in this way
until 8 lines of smocking have been worked.
Join side and sleeve seams. Sew in sleeves. Turn
hem to WS and sl-st down. Press seams.

Jacket back
Using No.2 needles cast on 120[126:134:140] sts.
Work hem as given for dress back. Change to No.3
needles. Beg with a K row cont in st st until work
measures 12in from hemline, ending with a P row.
Shape armholes

Bind off 5 sts at beg of next 2 rows; 4 sts at beg of
next 2 rows; then 2[2:3:3] sts at beg of next 2 rows.
Dec one st at each end of every other row 5[6:7:8]
times. 88[92:96:100] sts. Cont without shaping
until armholes measure 8[8½:9:9½]in from beg,
ending with a P row.
Shape shoulders
Bind off 7 sts at beg of next 4 rows; then 6[7:8:9]
sts at beg of next 2 rows. Bind off rem 48[50:52:54]
sts.

Jacket left front
Using No.2 needles cast on 62[65:69:72] sts.
Work as given for back until front measures same
as back to underarm, ending at armhole edge.
Shape armhole and front edge
Next row Bind off 5 sts, K to last 3 sts, K2 tog, K1.
Next row P to end.
Next row Bind off 4 sts, K to end.
Next row P1, P2 tog, P to end.
Next row Bind off 2[2:3:3] sts, K to end.
Next row P to end.
Dec one st at armhole edge on next and foll 4[5:6:
7] alt rows, *at the same time* cont to dec at front edge
on every 3rd row until 20[21:22:23] sts rem. Cont
without shaping until armhole measures same as
back to shoulder, ending at armhole edge.
Shape shoulder
Bind off 7 sts every other row twice; then 6[7:8:9]
sts once.

Jacket right front
Work as given for left front, reversing all shaping.

Finishing
Press as given for dress. Join shoulder and side
seams. Turn hem to WS and sl-st down. Using
No.B crochet hook and with RS of work facing,
work 2 rounds sc around armholes. Work 2 rows
sc up right front edge, around neck and down left
front edge, making 6 button loops on right front on
2nd row by working ch4 and skipping 4 sts, the
first to come 5in above lower edge and the last just
below beg of neck shaping, with 4 more evenly
spaced between. Press seams. Sew on buttons.

Two-piece suit with midi-skirt

Sizes
To fit 34[36:38:40]in bust
36[38:40:42]in hips
The figures in brackets [] refer to the 36, 38 and
40in sizes respectively
Pullover length to shoulder, 23[23½:24:24½]in
Sleeve seam, 16½[17:17½:18]in
Skirt length, 27½[28:28½:29]in, adjustable
Gauge
6 sts and 7½ rows to 1in over st st worked on No.4
needles
Materials
21[23:24:25] balls Spinnerin Wintuk Fingering
No.2 knitting needles
No.4 knitting needles
Set of 4 No.2 double-pointed needles
Waist length of elastic
One 7in zipper

Skirt back
Using No.2 needles cast on 77[83:89:95] sts and
beg at waist.
1st row K1, *P1, K1, rep from * to end.
2nd row P1, *K1, P1, rep from * to end.

Rep these 2 rows for 1½in, ending with a 2nd row and inc one st at end of last row. 78[84:90:96] sts. Change to No.4 needles. Beg with a K row work 4 rows st st.

Shape darts
Next row K3 sts, K up 1, K20[22:24:26] sts, K up 1, K32[34:36:38] sts, K up 1, K20[22:24:26] sts, K up 1, K3 sts.
Beg with a P row work 7 rows st st.
Next row K3 sts, K up 1, K21[23:25:27] sts, K up 1, K34[36:38:40] sts, K up 1, K21[23:25:27] sts, K up 1, K3 sts.
Beg with a P row work 7 rows st st.
Cont inc in this way on next and every foll 8th row until there are 110[116:122:128] sts, then on every foll 20th row until work measures 27½[28:28½:29]in from beg, or required length to hem, ending with a K row. Change to No.3 needles.
Next row K all sts tbl to form hemline.
Beg with a K row work 1in st st. Bind off loosely.

Skirt front
Work as given for back.

Finishing
Press each piece under a damp cloth with a warm iron. Join side seams leaving 7in open at top of left seam for zipper. Sew in zipper. Sew elastic inside waist edge with casing st. Turn hem to WS at hemline and sl-st down. Press seams.

Pullover back
Using No.2 needles cast on 106[110:118:122] sts.
1st row K2, *P2, K2, rep from * to end.
2nd row P2, *K2, P2, rep from * to end.
Rep these 2 rows for 1½in, ending with a 2nd row and inc one st at each end of last row on 36 and 40in sizes only. 106[112:118:124] sts. Change to No.4 needles. Commence patt.
1st row K13[16:19:22] sts, P2, K4, P2, (K10, P2, K4, P2) 4 times, K13[16:19:22] sts.
2nd row P13[16:19:22] sts, K2, P4, K2, (P10, K2, P4, K2) 4 times, P13[16:19:22] sts.
These 2 rows form patt. Cont in patt until work measures 16in from beg, ending with a WS row.
Shape armholes
Keeping patt correct, at arm edges, bind off 6 sts every other row twice; then 2 sts every other row twice. Dec one st at each end every other row 6[7:8:9] times. 78[82:86:90] sts. Cont without shaping until armholes measure 7[7½:8:8½]in from beg, ending with a WS row.
Shape neck and shoulders
Next row Patt 25[26:27:28] sts, turn and slip rem sts on holder.
Next row Bind off 2 sts, patt to end.
Next row Bind off 5 sts, patt to end.
Rep last 2 rows twice more. Work 1 row. Bind off rem 4[5:6:7] sts.
With RS of work facing, sl first 28[30:32:34] sts on holder, attach yarn to rem sts and patt to end. Complete to correspond to first side, reversing shaping.

Pullover front
Work as given for back until armhole shaping is completed. Cont without shaping until armholes measure 4½[5:5½:6]in from beg. End with a WS row.
Shape neck
Next row Patt 31[32:33:34] sts, turn and slip rem sts on holder.
At neck edge, bind off 2 sts every other row 3 times. Dec one st at neck edge every other row until 19[20:21:22] sts rem. Cont without shaping until armhole measures same as back to shoulder, ending at armhole edge.
Shape shoulder
At arm edge, bind off 5 sts every other row 3 times and 4[5:6:7] sts once.
With RS of work facing, sl first 16[18:20:22] sts on holder and leave for center neck, attach yarn to rem sts, patt to end. Complete to correspond to first side, reversing shaping.

Sleeves
Using No.2 needles cast on 50[50:54:54] sts. Work 3in K2, P2 rib as given for back. Change to No.4 needles. Cont in K2, P2 rib, inc one st at each end of next and every foll 8th row until there are 74[76:78:80] sts. Cont without shaping until sleeve measures 16½[17:17½:18]in from beg, ending with a WS row.
Shape cap
Bind off 6 sts at beg of next 2 rows. Dec one st each end every other row 12[13:14:15] times. 38 sts. Bind off 2 sts at beg of next 8 rows; then 3 sts at beg of next 4 rows. Bind off rem 10 sts.

Collar
Join shoulder seams. Using No.2 double-pointed needles and with RS of work facing, K across back neck sts on holder, pick up and K 10 sts up side of back neck and 30 sts down side of front neck, K across front neck sts on holder, pick up and K 30 sts up front of neck and 10 sts down back neck. 124[128:132:136] sts. Join. Work in rounds of K2, P2 rib for 8in. Bind off loosely in rib.

Finishing
Press as given for skirt. Sew in sleeves. Join sides and sleeve seams. Press seams.

41 *Aran tunic with slit sides*

Sizes
To fit 34[36:38:40:42]in bust
The figures in brackets [] refer to the 36, 38, 40 and 42in sizes respectively
Length to shoulder, 27[27¼:27½:27¾:28]in

Gauge
4 sts and 6 rows to 1in over st st worked on No.7 needles
Materials
11[12:13:13:14] balls Reynolds Irish Fisherman Yarn
No.5 knitting needles
No.7 knitting needles
Cable needle
12 small wooden beads for belt

Front panel
Using No.7 needles cast on 55[57:59:61:63] sts. Work 4 rows K1, P1 rib. Commence patt.
1st row (RS) (K1, P1) twice, P2[3:4:5:6] sts, sl next 2 sts onto cable needle and hold at back of work, K2 sts from left hand needle then K 2 from cable needle – called C4B –, P1, K into front then into back of next st – called M2 –, P1, M2, (P1, K1, P1, K1) all into next st, turn and K4, turn and P4, lift 2nd, 3rd and 4th sts over 1st st and off needle – called B1 –, P1, M2, P1, M2, P6, sl next 3 sts onto cable needle and hold at front of work, K2 sts from left hand needle, sl 1st st on cable needle onto left hand needle and P it, then K2 sts from cable needle – called Cr5 –, P6, M2, P1, M2, P1, B1, M2, P1, M2, P1, sl next 2 sts onto cable needle and hold at front of work, K2 sts from left hand needle then K2 sts from cable needle – called C4F –, P2[3:4:5:6] sts, (P1, K1) twice.
2nd row (P1, K1) twice, K2[3:4:5:6] sts, P4, K1, P2 tog, K1, P2 tog, K2, P2 tog, K1, P2 tog, K6, P2, K1, P2, K6, P2 tog, K1, P2 tog, K2, P2 tog, K1, P2 tog, K1, P4, K2[3:4:5:6] sts, (K1, P1) twice.
3rd row (K1, P1) twice, P2[3:4:5:6] sts, K4, P1, M2, P1, M2, P2, M2, P1, M2, P5, sl next st onto cable needle and hold at back of work, K2 sts from left hand needle then P1 from cable needle – called C3B –, P1, sl next 2 sts onto cable needle and hold at front of work, P1 from left hand needle then K2 sts from cable needle – called C3F –, P5, M2, P1, M2, P2, M2, P1, M2, P1, K4, P2[3:4:5:6] sts, (P1, K1) twice.
4th row (P1, K1) twice, K2[3:4:5:6] sts, P4, K1, P2 tog, K1, P2 tog, K2, P2 tog, K1, P2 tog, K5, P2, K3, P2, K5, P2 tog, K1, P2 tog, K2, P2 tog, K1, P2 tog, K1, P4, K2[3:4:5:6] sts, (K1, P1) twice.
5th row (K1, P1) twice, P2[3:4:5:6] sts, K4, P1, M2, P1, M2, P2, M2, P1, M2, P4, C3B, P3, C3F, P4, M2, P1, M2, P2, M2, P1, M2, P1, K4. P2[3:4:5:6] sts, (P1, K1) twice.
6th row (P1, K1) twice, K2[3:4:5:6] sts, P4, K1, P2 tog, K1, P2 tog, K2, P2 tog, K1, P2 tog, K4, P2, K5, P2, K4, P2 tog, K1, P2 tog, K2, P2 tog, K1, P2 tog, K1, P4, K2[3:4:5:6] sts, (K1, P1) twice.
7th row (K1, P1) twice, P2[3:4:5:6] sts, C4B, P1, M2, P1, M2, P1, B1, M2, P1, M2, P3, C3B, P2, K into front, then into back, then into front, then into back of next st – called M4 –, P2, C3F, P3, M2, P1, M2, B1, P1, M2, P1, M2, P1, C4F, P2[3:4:5:6] sts, (P1, K1) twice.
8th row (P1, K1) twice, K2[3:4:5:6] sts, P4, K1, P2 tog, K1, P2 tog, K2, P2 tog, K1, P2 tog, K3, P2, K3, P4, K3, P2, K3, P2 tog, K1, P2 tog, K2, P2 tog, K1, P2 tog, K1, P4, K2[3:4:5:6] sts, (K1, P1) twice.
9th row (K1, P1) twice, P2[3:4:5:6] sts, K4, P1, M2, P1, M2, P2, M2, P1, M2, P2, C3B, P3, K4, P3, C3F, P2, M2, P1, M2, P2, M2, P1, M2, P1, K4, P2[3:4:5:6] sts, P(1, K1) twice.
10th row (P1, K1) twice, K2[3:4:5:6] sts, P4, K1, P2 tog, K1, P2 tog, K2, P2 tog, K1, P2 tog, K2, P2, K4, P4 tog, K4, P2, K2, P2 tog, K1, P2 tog, K2, P2 tog, K1, P2 tog, K1, P4, K2[3:4:5:6] sts, (K1, P1) twice.
11th row (K1, P1) twice, P2[3:4:5:6] sts, K4, P1, M2, P1, M2, P2, M2, P1, M2, P1, C3B, P1, M4, P5, M4, P1, C3F, P1, M2, P1, M2, P2, M2, P1, M2, P1, K4, P2[3:4:5:6] sts, (P1, K1) twice.
12th row (P1, K1) twice, K2[3:4:5:6] sts, P4, K1, P2 tog, K1, P2 tog, K2, P2 tog, K1, P2 tog, K1, P2, K2, P4, K5, P4, K2, P2, K1, P2 tog, K1, P2

71

tog, K2, P2 tog, K1, P2 tog, K1, P4, K2[3:4:5:6] sts, (K1, P1) twice.

13th row (K1, P1) twice, P2[3:4:5:6] sts, C4B, P1, M2, P1, M2, B1, P1, M2, P1, M2, P1, C3F, P1, K4, P5, K4, P1, C3B, P1, M2, P1, M2, P1, B1, M2, P1, M2, P1, C4F, P2[3:4:5:6] sts, (P1, K1) twice.

14th row (P1, K1) twice, K2[3:4:5:6] sts, P4, K1, P2 tog, K1, P2 tog, K2, P2 tog, K1, P2 tog, K2, P2, K1, P4 tog, K5, P4 tog, K1, P2, K2, P2 tog, K1, P2 tog, K2, P2 tog, K1, P2 tog, K1, P4, K2[3: 4:5:6] sts, (K1, P1) twice.

15th row (K1, P1) twice, P2[3:4:5:6] sts, K4, P1, M2, P1, M2, P2, M2, P1, M2, P2, C3F, P3, M4, P3, C3B, P2, M2, P1, M2, P2, M2, P1, M2, P1, K4, P2[3:4:5:6] sts, (P1, K1) twice.

16th row As 8th.

17th row (K1, P1) twice, P2[3:4:5:6] sts, K4, P1, M2, P1, M2, P2, M2, P1, M2, P3, C3F, P2, K4, P2, C3B, P3, M2, P1, M2, P2, M2, P1, M2, P1, K4, P2[3:4:5:6] sts, (P1, K1) twice.

18th row (P1, K1) twice, K2[3:4:5:6] sts, P4, K1, P2 tog, K1, P2 tog, K2, P2 tog, K1, P2 tog, K4, P2, K2, P4 tog, K2, P2, K4, P2 tog, K1, P2 tog, K2, P2 tog, K1, P2 tog, K1, P4, K2[3:4:5:6] sts, (K1, P1) twice.

19th row (K1, P1) twice, P2[3:4:5:6] sts, C4B, P1, M2, P1, M2, P1, B1, M2, P1, M2, P4, C3F, P3, C3B, P4, M2, P1, M2, B1, P1, M2, P1, M2, P1, C4F, P2[3:4:5:6] sts, (P1, K1) twice.

20th row As 4th.

21st row (K1, P1) twice, P2[3:4:5:6] sts, K4, P1, M2, P1, M2, P2, M2, P1, M2, P5, C3F, P1, C3B, P5, M2, P1, M2, P2, M2, P1, M2, P1, K4, P2[3:4: 5:6] sts, (P1, K1) twice.

22nd row As 2nd.

23rd row (K1, P1) twice, P2[3:4:5:6] sts, K4, P1, M2, P1, M2, P2, M2, P1, M2, P6, K2, P1, K2, P6, M2, P1, M2, P2, M2, P1, M2, P1, K4, P2[3:4: 5:6] sts, (P1, K1) twice.

24th row (P1, K1) twice K2 [3:4:5:6] sts, P4, K1, P2 tog, K1, P2 tog, K2, P2 tog, K1, P2 tog, K6, P5, K6, P2 tog, K1, P2 tog, K2, P2 tog, K1, P2 tog, K1, P4, K2[3:4:5:6] sts, (K1, P1) twice.

These 24 rows form patt. Cont in patt until work measures 6in from beg, ending with a WS row.

Next row Inc in first st, P5[6:7:8:9] sts, patt to last 6[7:8:9:10] sts, P5[6:7:8:9] sts, inc in last st. 57[59:61:63:65] sts.

Keeping 7[8:9:10:11] sts at each end in reversed st st, cont in patt until work measures 24¾[25:25¼: 25½:25¾]in from beg, ending with a WS row.**

Shape neck

Next row Patt 20[21:22:23:24] sts, turn and slip rem sts on holder.

Dec one st at neck edge on next 3 rows, then dec one st at same edge every other row until 14[15:16: 17:18] sts rem. Cont without shaping until work measures 27[27¼:27½:27¾:28]in from beg, ending at armhole edge.

Shape shoulder

Bind off 7 sts at beg of next row. Work 1 row. Bind off rem 7[8:9:10:11] sts.

With RS of work facing, sl next 17 sts onto holder, attach yarn to rem sts and patt to end. Complete to correspond to first side, reversing shaping.

Back panel

Work as given for front panel to **. Cont in patt until work measures same as front to shoulder, ending with a WS row.

Shape shoulders

Bind off 7 sts at beg of next 2 rows; then 7[8:9:10:11] sts at beg of next 2 rows. Slip rem 29 sts on holder.

Side panel (make 2)

Using No.7 needles cast on 29[31:33:35:37] sts. Work 4 rows K1, P1 rib, dec one st in center of last row. 28[30:32:34:36] sts. Commence patt.

1st row (RS) (K1, P1) twice, P6[7:8:9:10] sts, M2, P1, M2, B1, P1, M2, P1, M2, P6[7:8:9:10] sts,

(P1, K1) twice.

2nd row (P1, K1) twice, K6[7:8:9:10] sts, P2 tog, K1, P2 tog, K2, P2 tog, K1, P2 tog, K6[7:8:9:10] sts, (K1, P1) twice.

3rd row (K1, P1) twice, P6[7:8:9:10] sts, M2, P1, M2, P2, M2, P1, M2, P6[7:8:9:10] sts, (P1, K1) twice. Rep 2nd and 3rd rows once more, then 2nd row once.

7th row (K1, P1) twice, P6[7:8:9:10] sts, M2, P1, M2, P1, B1, M2, P1, M2, P6[7:8:9:10] sts, (P1, K1) twice. Rep 2nd and 3rd rows twice more, then 2nd row once.

These 12 rows form patt. Cont in patt until work measures 6in from beg, ending with a WS row.

Next row Inc in first st, P9[10:11:12:13] sts, patt 8, P9[10:11:12:13] sts, inc in last st. 30[32:34:36: 38] sts. Keeping 11[12:13:14:15] sts in reversed st st at each end, cont in patt until work measures 8in from beg, ending with a RS row.

Shape sides

Next row K9[10:11:12:13] sts, sl 1, K1, psso, patt 8, K2 tog, K to end.

Work 1 row.

Next row K8[9:10:11:12] sts, sl 1, K1, psso, patt 8, K2 tog, K to end.

Work 1 row.

Cont dec in this way on next and every other row until 12[14:16:18:20] sts rem. Cont without shaping until work measures 12½in from beg, ending with a RS row.

Next row K2[3:4:5:6] sts, pick up loop lying between sts and K tbl – called inc 1 –, patt 8, inc 1, K to end.

Work 3 rows.

Next row K3[4:5:6:7] sts, inc 1, patt 8, inc 1, K to end.

Work 3 rows.

Cont inc in this way on next and every 4th row until there are 26[28:30:32:34] sts. Cont without shaping until work measures 19in from beg, ending with a WS row.

Shape underarm

Next row Patt 9[10:10:11:11] sts, turn and slip rem sts on holder.

Dec one st at beg of next and at same edge on every row until all sts are worked off.

With RS of work facing, sl first 8[8:10:10:12] sts on holder, attach yarn to rem sts and patt to end. Dec one st at end of next and at same edge on every row until all sts are worked off.

Armbands

Press pieces under a damp cloth with a warm iron. Join side panels to back and front panels from top of ribbing of slits. Using No.5 needles and with RS of work facing, beg at shoulder and pick up and K 43[45:47:49:51] sts down armhole, K across sts on holder, dec one st in center, and pick up and K 43[45:47:49:51] sts to shoulder. 93[97:103:107: 113] sts. Work 4 rows K1, P1 rib, working 3 sts tog in center of every other row. Bind off in rib, still dec at center.

Neckband

Join right shoulder and armband seam. Using No.5 needles and with RS of work facing K across 29 sts at center back neck inc in first st, pick up and K 18[20:22:24:26] sts down front neck, K17 sts on holder and pick up and K 19[21:23:25:27] sts up front neck. 84[88:92:96:100] sts. Work 4 rows K1, P1 rib. Bind off in rib.

Finishing

Join left shoulder and armband seam. Press seams.

Make belt

Cut 12 lengths of yarn 90in long. (Take 2 ends tog and knot at one end, thread on bead) 6 times. Tie tog 10in from beaded end. Form into 3 strands and plait to within 16in of other end. Knot tog at end of plait, (take 2 ends tog, thread on bead and knot at end) 6 times. Trim ends.

42,43

A button-to-the-neck
cardigan and pullover,
both featuring the
traditional Fair Isle yoke.
Both are long and ribbed
on all edges. Knit them in
Shetland yarn, in
contrasting colors.

Knit
Sizes 34-40 inch bust.

44

Right A casual
car coat, with
comfortable raglan
sleeves and roomy
pockets. Contrasting
bands of color on all
edgings make it
come alive!

Knit
Sizes 34-42 inch bust.

45

A casual classic that's
easy to wear.
This charming cardigan
suit has a wide-ribbed
classic jacket
and plain stockinette
stitch skirt.

Knit
Sizes 34-40 inch bust.

46

Right Soft and
feminine—that's how
you'll feel in this mohair
sleeveless top with
cowl neck. Shown here
in both vivid and
pastel colors.

Knit
Sizes 32-40 inch bust.

47

Center A delightful
diagonal-patterned
classic with short sleeves.
Wear it under a suit, or
as a top over a skirt
or slacks.

Knit
Sizes 32-40 inch bust.

48

Far right A neatly fitting
pullover worked in double
ribbing. The v-neck insert
and high turtleneck
are worked separately
and then assembled.

Knit
Sizes 32-38 inch bust.

49

*Elegant
evenings in this delicate
lacy cardigan with high
polo collar. Wear it to
button either at the
front or back.*

*Knit
Sizes 34-38 inch bust.*

50

*Sparkle all
through the evening in
this glamorous two-piece
cocktail suit, worked
in glitter yarn in
simple stockinette stitch.*

*Knit
Sizes 34-42 inch bust.*

51

Two versions of an Aran cardigan for father and son. The boy's version has saddle cap sleeves and the man's has raglan sleeves.

Knit
Boy's to fit 26 [28:30] inch chest
Man's to fit 38 [40:42] inch chest.

52

Cardigan worked in an
unusual arrowhead
pattern with a
zipper and bands of
two contrasting colors on
the lower edge, cuffs and
collar

Knit
Sizes to fit 36(38:40:
42) inch chest

53

Pullovers for the family using
variations of cables and
seed stitches.
Pullover A is shown on
the smaller child, pullover
B on the woman and
pullover C on the man and
the older child

Knit
Sizes to fit 24(26:28:
30:32:34:36:38:40:
42:44) inch chest

54

Bulky Aran cardigan
with deep pockets
and raglan
sleeves

Knit
Sizes to fit 34(36:38:
40:42) inch chest

55

Cardigan with smoothly
fitted shawl collar,
worked in an unusual
check pattern in two
colors. The collar and
all edges are worked in
single ribbing

Knit
Sizes to fit 38(40:42:
44:46) inch chest

56

*Textured patterned
sleeveless vests
for either a man
or woman*

*Knit
Sizes to fit 32(34:36:
38:40:42:44) inch
chest*

57

*Cardigans, buttoned to
the neck with picot-
trimmed mandarin collar,
for mother and daughter.
Simple crossed basket
weave stitch gives an
interesting texture.*

*Knit
Sizes: to fit 24 [27:30:
33:36] inch chest.*

58

Warm ribbed winter
playsuit and matching hat.
It has saddle shoulders
and zippered front.

Knit
Sizes: to fit 22 [24]
inch chest.

59

Warm and pretty suit
teamed with matching
beret and socks worked
in distinctive lobster
claw stitch.
Knit
Sizes: to fit 28 [31:34]
inch chest.

60

Crisp, short sleeved summer dress. The skirt is in stockinette stitch and the bodice is worked in cable panels.

Knit
Sizes: to fit 22 [24:26 :28] inch chest.

61

Casual wrapover judo dressing gown, suitable for a boy or girl. This is worked in a simple broken rib stitch and edges are in a contrasting color.

Knit
Sizes: to fit 24 [26:28] inch chest.

Ideas for the home

62

For knitters in a hurry—
a plaid blanket to make
in record time with jumbo
knitting pins and a
jumbo crochet hook.

Knit and crochet
Size: 72 × 71 inches.

63

Spherical lampshade
shows off the decorative
quality of an intricate
stitch. You may prefer
to cover the frame with
cotton to diffuse the
light before putting on
the knitted cover.

Knit
Shade diameter: 24
inches.

64

Big bold bunny makes a jolly pajama case or soft washable toy— (remember to unstitch the felt trimmings before washing).

Knit
Length : 15 inches.

65

Choose chevron stripes to give a hot water bottle cover a bright, fashionable look.

Knit and crochet
Size : $11\frac{1}{2} \times 10\frac{1}{2}$ inches.

66

This dog's sweater is definitely not designed for Great Danes, so check his chest measurement before you start knitting!

Knit
Chest : $13\frac{1}{2}$ ($17\frac{3}{4}$: $21\frac{1}{4}$) inches.

67

Brighten up the bathroom with a facecloth, embroidered with the owner's initial.

Knit
Size : 12 inches square.

68

Left: bright, Mexican pinks and alternating rib direction give this blanket made in easy ribbed squares a glamorous look. Try it in a mixture of brown, camel and beige for a cooler effect.

Knit
Size: 30 × 40 inches, or as required.

69

This time, a blanket in boldly contrasting patches, trimmed with pompons.

Knit
Size: 50 × 80 inches.

70, 71

A 'Fair Isle' toaster cover (to keep the dust out) and matching oven mitt in washable, cotton yarn.

Knit
Toaster cover :
9 × 7 × 5 inches.
Pot holder : 30 inches long.

72, 73

Patchwork cozies for coffee pots (left) and the traditional tea pot (right). The joining trim on both is crocheted.

Knit and crochet
Coffee cozy : 8 inches high.
Tea cozy : 6½ inches high.

74, 75

Two covers, designed to fit over square foam rubber pillows and forms to be used as floor pillows.

Knit
Size: 18 inches square, 3½ inches deep.

Instructions for designs 42-75

42 Cardigan with Fair Isle yoke

Sizes
To fit 34[36:38:40]in bust
The figures in brackets [] refer to the 36, 38 and 40in sizes respectively
Length to shoulder, 21½[22:22½:23]in
Sleeve seam, 16½[17½:18½:19½]in

Gauge
6½ sts and 8½ rows to 1in over st st worked on No.4 needles

Materials
Reynolds Cashmere Lamb 8[8:9:10] balls main color, A
1 ball each contrast colors B, C, D, E and F
1 ball of additional contrast color, if desired, instead of A as background color of yoke
No.2 and No.4 knitting needles
Five stitch holders
Ten buttons.

Back
Using No.2 needles and A, cast on 109[113:117:121] sts. Work in K1, P1 rib for 4in. Change to No.4 needles. Beg with a K row cont in st st, inc one st at each end of 7th and every foll 8th row until there are 115[121:127:133] sts. Cont without shaping until work measures 15in from beg, ending with a P row.

Shape armholes
Bind off 6 sts at beg of next 2 rows. 103[109:115:121] sts.

36, 38 and 40in sizes only
Dec one st at each end of every other row until 103 sts rem, ending with a P row.

All sizes
Next row K2 tog, K33 sts, K2 tog, turn and slip rem 66 sts on holder.
Complete this side first. Dec one st at each end of every K row until 3 sts rem, ending with a P row.
Next row K2 tog, K1.
Next row P2 sts.
Next row K2 tog and fasten off.
With RS facing, sl first 29 sts onto holder and leave for yoke, attach yarn to rem 37 sts, K2 tog, K33 sts, K2 tog. Complete to correspond to first side.

Left front
Using No.2 needles and A, cast on 50[52:54:56] sts. Work 4in K1, P1 rib. Change to No.4 needles. Beg with a K row cont in st st, inc one st at beg of 7th and every foll 8th row until there are 57[60:63:66] sts. Cont without shaping until work measures same as back to underarm, ending at armhole edge.

Shape armhole
Bind off 6 sts at beg of next row. 51[54:57:60] sts
36, 38 and 40in sizes only
Next row P to end.
Next row K2 tog, K to end.
Rep last 2 rows until 51 sts rem for front yoke.
All sizes
Next row P14 sts and slip on holder, P37 sts.
Next row K2 tog, K to last 2 sts, K2 tog.
Next row P to end.
Rep last 2 rows until 3 sts rem. Complete as given for back.

Right front
Work as given for left front, reversing all shaping.

Sleeves
Using No.2 needles and A, cast on 58[60:62:64] sts. Work 4½in K1, P1 rib. Change to No.4 needles. Beg with a K row cont in st st, inc one st at

each end of 5th and every foll 6th row until there are 84[90:96:102] sts. Cont in st st without shaping until sleeve measures 18½[19½:20½:21½]in from beg, or desired length to underarm allowing 2in for turn back cuff, ending with a P row.

Shape cap
Bind off 6 sts at beg of next 2 rows. 72[78:84:90] sts.
Next row K2 tog, K to last 2 sts, K2 tog.
Next row P to end.
Rep last 2 rows until 36 sts rem. Slip sts on holder for yoke.

Yoke
Join raglan seams. Using No.4 needles, A and with RS of work facing, K14 sts from right front holder, pick up and K 28[31:34:37] sts up right neck edge, K36 sts from sleeve holder, pick up and K 28[31:34:37] sts down right back neck, K29 sts from center back holder, pick up and K 28[31:34:37] sts up left back neck, K36 sts from sleeve holder, pick up and K 28[31:34:37] sts down left front neck and K14 sts from left front holder. 241[253:265:277] sts.
Next row P to end, inc one st at center back. 242[254:266:278] sts.
Next row Work from Chart 1 as foll : *K2 B, K2 A, rep from * to last 2 sts, K2 B.
Next row *P2A, P2B, rep from * to last 2sts, P2A.
Using A and beg with a K row work 2 rows st st, dec one st at center back. 241[253:265:277] sts.
Cont in Fair Isle patt, working from charts as foll :
34, 36 and 38in sizes only
Skip first 18[12:6] sts of Chart 2 and beg on 19th [13th:7th] st of Chart 2, K rem 7[13:19] sts of Chart 2, K full patt of 42 sts of Charts 3 and 2 five times, then K17 sts of Chart 3 once, then K first 7[13:19] sts of Chart 2.
Cont working rem 24 rows of Charts, taking care to beg K rows on the 19th[13th:7th] sts and all P rows on the 7th[13th:19th] sts at front edge.
40in size only
Working from Charts, K 1st row of Chart 2, foll by 1st row of Chart 3 right across work, ending with 25 sts of Chart 2.
All sizes
Note that the dec on Chart 3 on 9th and foll alt rows are made by K first 2 sts tbl.
When 25 rows of Charts have been worked, break off all colors except A and the color used for Chart 1.
Next row Using A, P to end.
Next row Using A, K10[7:4:1] sts, *K2 tog, K1, rep from * to last 9[6:3:0] sts, K2 tog, K7[K2 tog, K4: K2 tog, K1:K0]. 102[108:114:120] sts.
Beg with a P row work 2 rows of Chart 1. Cont using A only.
Next row P to end.
Next row K1[2:2:2] sts, *K2 tog, K3, rep from * to last 1[1:2:3] sts, K1[1:2:3]. 82[87:92:97] sts.
Change to No.2 needles. Work 2in K1, P1 rib.
Bind off loosely in rib. Fold ribbing in half to WS and sl st bound-off edge to 1st row of ribbing.

Button band
Using No.2 needles and A, cast on 11 sts.
1st row *K1, P1, rep from * to last st, K1.
Rep this row until band is same length as front edge when slightly stretched. Bind off. Sew on button band and mark positions for 10 buttons, first to come ½in above cast-on edge and last to come ½in below bound-off edge.

Buttonhole band
Work as given for button band, making buttonholes as markers are reached, as foll :
Next row Seed st 4, bind off 3 sts, seed st 4.
Next row Work in seed st to end, casting on 3 sts above those bound-off on previous row.

Finishing
Press each piece under a damp cloth with a warm iron. Join side and sleeve seams. Sew in sleeves. Press seams.
Sew on buttons.

43 Pullover with Fair Isle yoke

Sizes
To fit 34[36:38:40]in bust
The figures in brackets [] refer to the 36, 38 and 40in sizes respectively
Length to shoulder, 21½[22:22½:23]in
Long sleeve seam, 16½[17½:18½:19½]in
Short sleeve seam, 4½[5:5½:6]in

Gauge
As given for cardigan (design 42)

Materials
Reynolds Cashmere Lamb
Long sleeved version 8[8:8:9] balls main color, A
Short sleeved version 5[5:6:7] balls main color, A
See materials for cardigan for contrast colors
No.2 knitting needles
No.3 knitting needles
One set of 4 No.3 double-pointed needles
One 4½in zipper

Front
Work as given for back of cardigan. (No. 42.)

Back
Using No.2 needles and A, cast on 108[112:116:120] sts and work as given for cardigan back (No. 42) until there are 114[120:126:132] sts. Cont without shaping until work measures 15in from beg, ending with a P row.

Shape armholes
Work as given for cardigan back until 102 sts rem. Work shaping as given for cardigan back, leaving 28 sts for yoke.

Short sleeves
Using No.2 needles and A, cast on 78[80:82:84] sts. Work 1in K1, P1 rib. Change to No.3 needles. Beg with a K row cont in st st, inc one st at each end of 3rd and every foll 4th row until there are 84[90:96:102] sts. Cont without shaping until sleeve measures 4½[5:5½:6]in from beg, ending with a P row.

Shape cap
Work as given for cap of cardigan sleeve.

Long sleeves
Work as given for sleeves of cardigan (No. 42).

Yoke
Join raglan seams. With RS of work facing leave first 14 sts of back on holder. Using first needle of No.3 needles and A, beg at center back and K rem 14 sts of back, pick up and K 28[31:34:37] sts up left back neck, K36 sts from sleeve, using 2nd needle pick up and K 28[31:34:37] sts down left front neck, K29 sts from center front holder, pick up and K 28[31:34:37] sts up right neck, using 3rd needle K36 sts from other sleeve, pick up and K 28[31:34:37] sts down right back neck, then K rem 14 sts from center back neck. 241[253:265:277] sts.
Work as given for cardigan yoke until neckband is reached. Change to No.2 needles. Work 8 rows K1, P1 rib.
Bind off loosely in rib.

Finishing
Press as for cardigan. Join side and sleeve seams. Sew in sleeves. Press seams. Sew back opening leaving 4½in open for zipper. Sew in zipper.

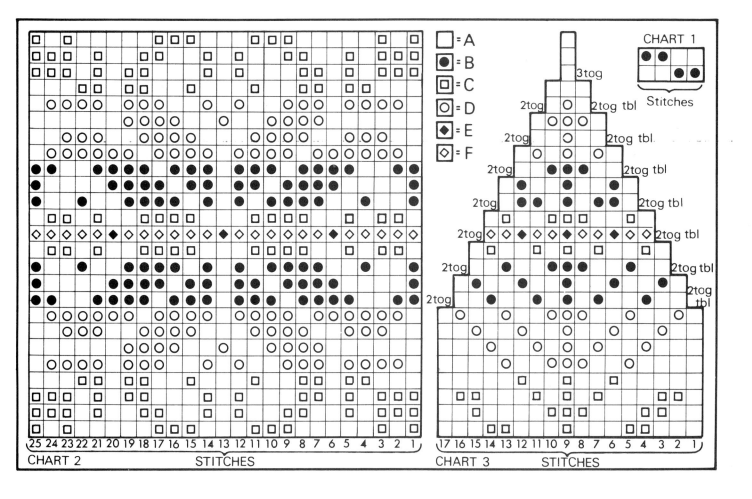

	= A
●	= B
⊡	= C
⊙	= D
◈	= E
◇	= F

CHART 1

Stitches

3tog

2tog 2tog tbl

2tog 2tog tbl

2tog 2tog tbl

2tog 2tog tbl

2tog 2tog tbl

2tog 2tog tbl

2tog 2tog tbl

2tog 2tog tbl

|25|24|23|22|21|20|19|18|17|16|15|14|13|12|11|10|9|8|7|6|5|4|3|2|1|

CHART 2   STITCHES

|17|16|15|14|13|12|11|10|9|8|7|6|5|4|3|2|1|

CHART 3   STITCHES

Length to shoulder, 33[33½:34:34½:35]in, adjustable.

Sleeve seam, 16½[17:17:17½:18]in, adjustable

Gauge

4 sts and 5 rows to 1in over st st worked on No.10 needles

Materials

11[12:13:13:14] balls Unger Regatta in main color, A

1 ball of contrast color, B

No.10 knitting needles

No.8 knitting needles

7 buttons

Back

Using No.8 needles and A, cast on 107[111:115:119:123] sts.

1st row K1, *P1, K1, rep from * to end.

2nd row P1, *K1, P1, rep from * to end.

Rep these 2 rows twice more. Change to No.10 needles. Beg with a K row cont in st st for 2½in, ending with a P row.

Shape darts

Next row K1, K2 tog, K19[20:21:22:23] sts, sl 1, K1, psso, K59[61:63:65:67] sts, K2 tog, K19[20:21:22:23] sts, sl 1, K1, psso, K1.

Beg with a P row work 11 rows st st.

Next row K1, K2 tog, K18[19:20:21:22] sts, sl 1, K1, psso, K57[59:61:63:65] sts, K2 tog, K18[19:20:21:22] sts, sl 1, K1, psso, K1.

Beg with a P row work 11 rows st st.

Cont dec in this way on next and every foll 12th row until 75[79:83:87:91] sts rem. Cont without shaping until work measures 25in from beg, or desired length to underarm.

End with a P row.

Shape armholes

Bind off 3 sts at beg of next 2 rows.

Next row K3 sts, K2 tog, K to last 5 sts, sl 1, K1, psso, K3 sts.

Next row P to end.

Rep last 2 rows until 29[29:31:31:33] sts rem, ending with a K row. **Attach B and change to No.8 needles. P 1 row, then work 1st row of rib. Attach A. P 1 row, then rib 6 rows. Attach B. K 1 row.

Bind off loosely in rib. **

Left front

Using No.10 needles and A, cast on 23 sts for pocket lining. Beg with a K row work 4in st st, ending with a P row. Slip sts on holder. Using No.8 needles and A, cast on 53[55:57:59:61] sts. Work 6 rows rib as given for back. Change to No.10 needles. Beg with a K row cont in st st for 2½in.

End with a P row.

Shape darts

Next row K1, K2 tog, K19[20:21:22:23] sts, sl 1, K1, psso, K to end.

Beg with a P row work 11 rows st st.

Next row K1, K2 tog, K18[19:20:21:22] sts, sl 1, K1, psso, K to end.

Beg with a P row work 11 rows st st.

Cont dec in this way on next and every foll 12th row until work measures 8in from beg, ending with a P row.

Insert pocket

Next row K to last 33[33:34:34:35] sts, sl next 23 sts onto holder, K across pocket lining sts, K to end.

Cont to dec on every foll 12th row as before until 37[39:41:43:45] sts rem. Cont without shaping until work measures 10 rows less than back to underarm. End with a P row.

Shape front edge

Next row K to last 3 sts, K2 tog, K1.

Beg with a P row work 5 rows st st.

Next row K to last 3 sts, K2 tog, K1.

Beg with a P row work 3 rows st st.

44 *Casual car coat*

Sizes

To fit 34[36:38:40:42]in bust

36[38:40:42:44]in hips

The figures in brackets [] refer to the 36, 38, 40 and 42 and 44in sizes respectively

Shape armhole
Next row Bind off 3 sts, K to end.
Next row P to end.
Next row K3 sts, K2 tog, K to last 3 sts, K2 tog, K1. Cont to dec at front edge on every foll 6th row 7[7:8:8:9] times more, *at the same time* dec at raglan edge on every other row until 4 sts rem, ending with a P row.
Next row K2 sts, K2 tog.
Next row P3 sts.
Next row K1 st, K2 tog.
Next row P2 tog. Fasten off.

Right front
Work as given for left front, reversing position of pocket and all shaping.

Sleeves
Using No.8 needles and A, cast on 33[35:37:39:41] sts. Work 4in rib as given for back, ending with a 2nd row. Change to No.10 needles. Beg with a K row cont in st st, inc one st at each end of first and every foll 6th row until there are 53[57:59:63:65] sts. Cont without shaping until sleeve measures 16½[17:17:17½:18]in from beg, or desired length to underarm ending with a P row. Mark each end of last row with colored thread. Work 4 more rows.
Shape cap
Next row K3 sts, K2 tog, K to last 5 sts, sl 1, K1, psso, K3 sts.
Next row P to end.
Rep last 2 rows until 7 sts rem, ending with a K row. Work as given for back from ** to **.

Left front band
Using No.8 needles and A, with RS of work facing pick up and K 125[127:129:131:133] sts along front edge.
Work as given for back from ** to **.
Mark positions for 7 buttons, first to come 1½in from lower edge and last to come ½in below beg of front shaping, with 5 more evenly spaced between.

Right front band
Work as given for left front band, making buttonholes on 3rd row of rib in A as foll: Rib to first marker, (bind off 2 sts, rib to next marker) 6 times, bind off 2 sts, rib to end.
Next row Rib to end, casting on 2 sts above those bound off on previous row.

Pocket edging
Using No.8 needles and with WS of work facing, sl 23 sts from holder onto needle and work as given for back from ** to **, inc one st at each end of first row.

Finishing
Press each piece under a damp cloth with a warm iron. Join raglan seams, sewing last 4 rows of sleeves to bound-off sts at underarm. Join side and sleeve seams. Sew down pocket edges and pocket linings. Press all seams. Sew on buttons.

45 *Classic two-piece suit*

Sizes
To fit 34[36:38:40]in bust
36[38:40:42]in hips
The figures in brackets [] refer to the 36, 38 and 40 and 42in sizes respectively
Jacket length to shoulder, 21[21½:22:22½]in
Sleeve seam, 16½[17:17½:18]in
Skirt length, 19½[20:20½:21]in
Gauge
5 sts and 7 rows to 1in over rib worked on No.4 needles

Materials
30[31:34:36] skeins Bernat Venetian Highlights
No.2 knitting needles
No.4 knitting needles
Five buttons
Waist length of elastic
One 7in zipper

Jacket back
Using No.2 needles cast on 87[92:97:102] sts.
1st row P2, *K3, P2, rep from * to end.
2nd row K2, *P3, K2, rep from * to end.
These 2 rows form patt. Cont in patt until work measures 1½in from beg. Change to No.4 needles and cont in patt until work measures 14in from beg, ending with a 2nd row.
Shape armholes
Bind off 5 sts at beg of next 2 rows. Dec one st at each end every other row 5[6:7:8] times. 67[70:73:76] sts. Cont without shaping until armholes measure 7[7½:8:8½]in from beg, ending with a WS row.
Shape shoulders
Bind off 7 sts at beg of next 4 rows; then 5[6:7:8] sts at beg of next 2 rows.
Bind off rem 29[30:31:32] sts.

Jacket left front
Using No.4 needles cast on 21 sts for pocket lining. Beg with a K row work 4in st st, ending with a K row.
Next row P3 sts, *P twice into next st, P2, rep from * to end. 27 sts. Slip sts on holder.
Using No.2 needles cast on 51[54:56:59] sts.
1st row *P2, K3, rep from * to last 11[9:11:9] sts, P2[0:2:0] sts, K4, sl 1, K4.
2nd row P9 sts, K2[0:2:0] sts. *P3, K2, rep from * to end.
Rep these 2 rows for 1½in. Change to No.4 needles and cont in patt until work measures 5in from beg, ending with a WS row.
Insert pocket
Next row Rib 10 sts, sl next 27 sts onto holder for pocket top, rib across sts of pocket lining, rib to end. Cont in patt until work measures same as back to underarm, ending with a WS row.
Shape armhole and front edge
Next row Bind off 5 sts, patt to last 11 sts, K2 tog, K4, sl 1, K4.
Next row Patt to end.
Next row K2 tog, patt to end.
Next row P9 sts, P2 tog, patt to end.
Cont dec at armhole edge every other row 4[5:6:7] times more, *at the same time* cont to dec at front edge on every 3rd row until 28[29:30:31] sts rem. Cont without shaping until armhole measures same as back to shoulder, ending at armhole edge.
Shape shoulder
Bind off 7 sts every other row twice and 5[6:7:8] sts once. Cont on rem 9 sts until strip is long enough to reach center back neck. Bind off.

Right front
Work pocket lining as given for left front.
Using No.2 needles cast on 51[54:56:59] sts.
1st row K4, sl 1, K4, P2[0:2:0] sts, *K3, P2, rep from * to end.
2nd row *K2, P3, rep from * to last 11[9:11:9] sts, K2[0:2:0] sts, P9.
Cont as given for left front until work measures 2½in from beg, ending with a WS row.
Next row (buttonhole) K1, bind off 2 sts, K1, sl 1, K1, bind off 2 sts, patt to end.
Next row Patt to end, casting on 2 sts above those bound off on previous row. Complete to correspond to left front, reversing position of pocket and all shaping and making 4 more buttonholes in same manner at intervals of 2½in from previous one.

Sleeves
Using No.2 needles cast on 32[37:37:42] sts. Work

in rib as given for back for 1½in. Change to No.4 needles and cont in rib, inc one st at each end of next and every foll 6th row until there are 62[67:71:74] sts. Cont without shaping until sleeve measures 16½[17:17½:18]in from beg, ending with a WS row.
Shape cap
Bind off 5 sts at beg of next 2 rows. Dec one st at each end every other row 7[9:11:12] times. Bind off 2 sts at beg of next 8 rows; then 3 sts at beg of next 4 rows. Bind off rem 10[11:11:12] sts.

Pocket tops
Using No.2 needles and with RS of work facing, work across pocket top sts, as foll: K3 sts, *K2 tog, K2, rep from * to end. 21 sts. Beg with a P row work 4 rows st st.
Next row K all sts tbl to mark fold line.
Beg with a K row work 4 rows st st. Bind off.

Finishing
Press lightly. Join shoulder seams. Sew in sleeves. Join side and sleeve seams. Join ends of front band. Fold front bands in half to WS and sl-st down and sew to back neck. Buttonhole-st around buttonholes. Sew pocket tops and linings in place. Sew on buttons.

Skirt back
Using No.2 needles cast on 66[70:74:78] sts and beg at waist.
1st row K2, *P2, K2, rep from * to end.
2nd row P2, *K2, P2, rep from * to end.
Rep these 2 rows for 1½in, ending with a 2nd row. Change to No.4 needles. Beg with a K row cont in st st for 4 rows.
Shape darts
Next row K21[22:23:24] sts, K twice into next st, K24[26:26:28] sts, K twice into next st, K21[22:23:24] sts.
Beg with a P row work 3 rows st st.
Next row K21[22:23:24] sts, K twice into next st, K24[26:28:30] sts, K twice into next st, K21[22:23:24] sts.
Beg with a P row work 3 rows st st.
Cont to inc in this way on next and every foll 4th row until there are 96[100:104:108] sts, then on every foll 8th row until work measures 19½[20:20½:21]in from beg, ending with a K row. Change to No.2 needles.
Next row K all sts tbl to form hemline.
Beg with a K row work 1½in st st. Bind off loosely.
Skirt front
Work as given for back.

Finishing
Press lightly. Join side seams leaving 7in open at top of left seam for zipper. Sew in zipper. Sew elastic inside waist edge with casing st. Turn hem to WS and sl—st down.

46 *Sleeveless mohair top with cowl neck*

Sizes
To fit 32[34:36:38:40]in bust
The figures in brackets [] refer to the 34, 36, 38 and 40in sizes respectively
Length to shoulder, 20½[21:21½:22:22½]in adjustable
Gauge
4 sts and 5 rows to 1in over rib worked on No.11 needles
Materials
7[8:9:9:10] balls Bernat Jaeger Mohair-Spun
No.4 knitting needles
No.11 knitting needles
No.G crochet hook

Back

Using No.4 needles cast on 67[71:75:79:83] sts.
1st row K1, *P1, K1, rep from * to end.
2nd row P1, *K1, P1, rep from * to end.
Rep these 2 rows twice more.
Change to No. 11 needles. Cont in rib until work measures 14in from beg, or desired length to underarm ending with a WS row.
Shape armholes
Bind off 5 sts at beg of next 2 rows. Dec one st at each end every other row 3[3:4:4:5] times. 51[55:57:61:63] sts. Cont without shaping until armholes measure 6[6½:7:7½:8]in from beg, ending with a WS row.
Shape neck
Next row Rib 17[18:19:20:21] sts, bind off 17[19:19:21:21] sts, rib to end.
Complete this side first. Dec one st at neck edge every other row 3 times. Bind off rem sts. With WS of work facing, attach yarn to rem sts and complete to correspond to first side, reversing shaping.

Front
Work as given for back.

Collar
Using No.4 needles cast on 99[101:103:105:107] sts. Work 6 rows rib as given for back. Change to No.11 needles and cont in rib until work measures 6½in from beg. Bind off very loosely in rib.

Finishing
Press lightly. Join shoulder and side seams. Join collar seam, then sew around neck with seam at center back. Using No.G crochet hook work a row of sc around each armhole.

47 Diagonal patterned sweater

Sizes
To fit 32[34:36:38:40]in bust
The figures in brackets[] refer to the 34, 36, 38 and 40in sizes respectively
Length to shoulder, 22[22½:23:23½:24] in
Sleeve seam, 6 in
Gauge
7 sts and 9 rows to 1in over st st worked on No.3 needles
Materials
6[7:8:8:9] balls Spinnerin Mona
No.2 knitting needles; No.3 knitting needles
Set of 4 No.2 double-pointed needles

Back
Using No.2 needles cast on 110[118:126:134:142] sts.
1st row K2, *P2, K2, rep from * to end.
2nd row P2, *K2, P2, rep from * to end.
Rep these 2 rows until work measures 2in from beg, ending with a 1st row. Change to No.3 needles. Beg with a P row cont in st st until work measures 15½in from beg, ending with a P row.
Shape armholes
Bind off 6 sts at beg of next 2 rows; then 2[3:3:4:4] sts at beg of next 2 rows. Dec one st at each end every other row 4[5:6:7:8] times. 86[90:96:100:106] sts. Cont without shaping until armholes measure 6½[7:7½:8:8½]in from beg, ending with a P row.
Shape shoulders
Bind off 6[6:7:8:8] sts at beg of next 6 rows; then 6[8:7:6:8] sts at beg of next 2 rows. Slip rem 38[38:40:40:42] sts on holder.

Front
Using No.2 needles cast on 110[118:126:134:142]

sts. Work in rib as given for back for 2in, ending with a 1st row and inc 10[10:11:11:9] sts evenly across last row. 120[128:137:145:151] sts. Change to No.3 needles. Commence patt.
1st row (WS) P18[22:16:20:23] sts, *(P1, K1) 7 times, P1, K6, rep from * 3[3:4:4:4] times more, P to end.
2nd row K18[22:16:20:23] sts, *P5, yrn, P1, (K1, P1) 6 times, K first and 3rd sts on left hand needle tog and let first st drop off needle, P 2nd st then let 2nd and 3rd sts drop off needle – called Tw3–, rep from * 3[3:4:4:4] times more, K to end.
3rd row P18[22:16:20:23] sts, K1, *rib 15, K6, rep from * 2[2:3:3:3] times more, rib 15, K5, P to end.
4th row K18[22:16:20:23] sts, P4, yrn, P1, *rib 12, Tw3, P5, yrn, P1, rep from * 2[2:3:3:3] times more, rib 12, Tw3, P1, K to end.
5th row P18[22:16:20:23] sts, K2, *rib 15, K6, rep from * 2[2:3:3:3] times more, rib 15, K4, P to end.
6th row K18[22:16:20:23] sts, P3, yrn, P1, *rib 12, Tw3, P5, yrn, P1, rep from * 2[2:3:3:3] times more, rib 12, Tw3, P2, K to end.
7th row P18[22:16:20:23] sts, K3, *rib 15, K6, rep from * 2[2:3:3:3] times more, rib 15, K3, P to end.
8th row K18[22:16:20:23] sts, P2, yrn, P1, *rib 12, Tw3, P5, yrn, P1, rep from * 2[2:3:3:3] times more, rib 12, Tw3, P3, K to end.
9th row P18[22:16:20:23] sts, K4, *rib 15, K6, rep from * 2[2:3:3:3] times more, rib 15, K2, P to end.
10th row K18[22:16:20:23] sts, P1, yrn, P1, *rib 12, Tw3, P5, yrn, P1, rep from * 2[2:3:3:3] times more, rib 12, Tw3, P4, K to end.
11th row P18[22:16:20:23] sts, K5, *rib 15, K6, rep from * 2[2:3:3:3] times more, rib 15, K1, P to end.
12th row K18[22:16:20:23] sts, yrn, P1, *rib 12, Tw3, P5, yrn, P1, rep from * 2[2:3:3:3] times more, rib 12, Tw3, P5, yon, K to end.
13th row P19[23:17:21:24] sts, *K6, rib 15, rep from * 3[3:4:4:4] times more, P to end.
14th row K18[22:16:20:23] sts, *rib 12, Tw3, P5, yrn, P1, rep from * 3[3:4:4:4] times more, K to end.
15th row P19[23:17:21:24] sts, K1, P1, *K6, rib 15, rep from * 2[2:3:3:3] times more, K6, rib 13, P to end.
16th row K18[22:16:20:23] sts, rib 10, Tw3, *P5, yrn, P1, rib 12, Tw3, rep from * 2[2:3:3:3] times more, P5, yrn, P1, K1, P1, K to end.
17th row P19[23:17:21:24]sts, (K1, P1) twice, *K6, rib 15, rep from * 2[2:3:3:3] times more, K6, rib 11, P to end.
18th row K18[22:16:20:23] sts, rib 8, Tw3, *P5, yrn, P1, rib 12, Tw3, rep from * 2[2:3:3:3] times more, P5, yrn, P1, rib 4, K to end.
19th row P19[23:17:21:24] sts, rib 6, *K6, rib 15, rep from * 2[2:3:3:3] times more, K6, rib 9, P to end.
20th row K18[22:16:20:23] sts, rib 6, Tw3, *P5, yrn, P1, rib 12, Tw3, rep from * 2[2:3:3:3] times more, P5, yrn, P1, rib 6, K to end.
21st row P19[23:17:21:24] sts, rib 8, *K6, rib 15, rep from * 2[2:3:3:3] times more, K6, rib 7, P to end.
22nd row K18[22:16:20:23] sts, rib 4, Tw3, *P5, yrn, P1, rib 12, Tw3, rep from * 2[2:3:3:3] times more, P5, yrn, P1, rib 8, K to end.
23rd row P19[23:17:21:24] sts, rib 10, *K6, rib 15, rep from * 2[2:3:3:3] times more, K6, rib 5, P to end.
24th row K18[22:16:20:23] sts, rib 2, Tw3, *P5, yrn, P1, rib 12, Tw3, rep from * 2[2:3:3:3] times more, P5, yrn, P1, rib 10, K to end.
25th row P19[23:17:21:24] sts, rib 12, *K6, rib 15, rep from * 2[2:3:3:3] times more, K6, rib 3, P to end.
26th row K18[22:16:20:23] sts, Tw3, *P5, yrn, P1, rib 12, Tw3, rep from * 2[2:3:3:3] times more, P5, yrn, P1, rib 12, K to end.

27th row P19[23:17:21:24] sts, rib 14, *K6, rib 15, rep from * 2[2:3:3:3] times more, K6, P1, P to end.
28th row K18[22:16:20:23] sts, P2 tog, P4, yrn, P1, *rib 12, Tw3, P5, yrn, P1, rep from * 2[2:3:3:3] times more, rib 12, Tw3, K to end.
Rows 3 to 28 form patt. Cont in patt until work measures same as back to underarm, ending with a WS row.
Shape armholes
Keeping patt correct, bind off 6 sts, at beg of next 2 rows; 2[3:3:4:4] sts at beg of next 2 rows. Dec one st at each end every other row 4[5:6:7:8] times. 96[100:107:111:115] sts. Note that when working patt between 12th and 27th rows there will be one more st. Cont without shaping until armholes measure 4½[5:5½:6:6½]in from beg, ending with a WS row.
Shape neck
Next row Patt 37[39:41:43:45] sts, turn and slip rem sts on holder. At neck edge, bind off 2 sts every other row 3 times, then dec one st at neck edge every other row 4 times. Cont without shaping until armhole measures same as back to shoulder, ending at armhole edge.
Shape shoulder
Bind off 6[7:7:8:9] sts every other row 3 times. Work 1 row. Bind off rem 9[8:10:9:8] sts. With RS of work facing, sl first 22[22:25:25:27] sts on holder, attach yarn to rem sts and patt to end, noting that when working patt between 12th and 27th rows there will be one more st. Complete to correspond to first side, reversing shaping.

Sleeves
Using No.2 needles cast on 66[66:70:70:74] sts. Work 2½in rib as given for back, ending with a 2nd row and inc one st at each end of last row on 34 and 38in sizes only. 66[68:70:72:74] sts. Change to No.3 needles. Beg with a K row cont in st st, inc one st at each end of 5th and every foll 6th row until there are 72[74:76:78:80] sts. Cont without shaping until sleeve measures 6in from beg; end with P row.
Shape cap
Bind off 6 sts at beg of next 2 rows. Dec one st at each end every other row until 34 sts rem. Bind off 2 sts at beg of next 6 rows; 3 sts at beg of next 2 rows; then 4 sts at beg of next 2 rows. Bind off rem 8 sts.

Neckband
Join shoulder seams. Using No. 2 double-pointed needles and with RS of work facing, K across sts on back neck holder, pick up and K 22 sts down side of neck, K across sts on front neck holder dec one st in center on 36, 38 and 40in sizes only, then pick up and K 22 sts up other side of neck. 104[104:108:108:112] sts. Note that if sts were left on holder for front neck between 12th and 27th patt rows, dec one more st. Join. Work 1in in rounds of K2, P2 rib. Bind off in rib.

Finishing
Press each piece under a damp cloth with a warm iron. Join side and sleeve seams. Sew in sleeves. Press seams.

48 Ribbed turtle-neck pullover

Sizes
To fit 32[34:36:38]in bust
The figures in brackets [] refer to the 34, 36 and 38in sizes respectively
Length to shoulder, 24[25:26:27]in
Sleeve seam, 17[17½:18:18½]in
Gauge 6 sts and 7½ rows to 1in over rib patt worked on No.5 needles

Materials

Spinnerin Wintuk Fingering
15[16:16:18] skeins
No.3 knitting needles
No.5 knitting needles

Back

Using No.3 needles cast on 102[106:114:118] sts.
1st row K2, *P2, K2, rep from * to end.
2nd row P2, *K2, P2, rep from * to end.
Rep these 2 rows until work measures 4in from beg, ending with a 2nd row and inc one st in center of last row on 34 and 38in sizes, and dec one st in center of last row on 32 and 36in sizes. 101 [107:113:119] sts. Change to No.5 needles.
Next row K2, *P1, K2, rep from * to end.
Next row P2, *K1, P2, rep from * to end.
Rep last 2 rows until work measures 16½[17:17½:18]in from beg, ending with a WS row.
Shape armholes
Bind off 3 sts at beg of next 8 rows. 77[83:89:95] sts. Cont without shaping until armholes measure 7½[8:8½:9]in from beg, ending with a WS row.
Shape shoulders
Bind off 5[6:6:7] sts at beg of next 6 rows; then 6[5:7:6] sts at beg of next 2 rows. Bind off rem 35[37:39:41] sts.

Front

Work as given for back until 12 rows less than back to armholes, ending with a WS row.
Divide for neck
Next row Patt 50[53:56:59] sts, turn and slip rem sts on holder.
Next row Patt to end.
Next row Patt to last 4 sts, P2 tog, K2.
Next row P2, K1, patt to end.
Next row Patt to last 3 sts, P1, K2.
Next row P2, K1, patt to end.
Rep last 4 rows once more, then first 2 of these last 4 rows once.
Shape armhole
Bind off 3 sts at neck edge every other row 4 times, *at the same time* cont to dec at neck edge on every 4th row until 21[23:25:27] sts rem. Cont without shaping until work measures same as back to shoulder, ending at armhole edge.
Shape shoulder
At arm edge bind off 5[6:6:7] sts every other row 3 times. Work 1 row. Bind off rem 6[5:7:6] sts. With RS of work facing, attach yarn to rem sts, K2 tog, patt to end.
Next row Patt to end.
Next row K2, P2 tog, patt to end.
Next row Patt to last 3 sts, K1, P2.
Complete to correspond to first side, reversing all shaping.

Sleeves

Using No.3 needles cast on 50[54:54:58] sts.
Work first 2 rows rib as given for back until work measures 4in from beg, ending with a 2nd row and dec one st in center of last row on 34in size ,inc one st at each end of last row on 36in size and one st in center of last row on 38in size. 50[53:56:59] sts.
Change to No.5 needles and cont in patt as given for back, inc one st at each end of 7th and every foll 8th row and working extra sts into patt, until there are 74[77:80:83] sts. Cont without shaping until sleeve measures 17[17½:18:18½]in from beg, ending with a WS row.
Shape cap
Bind off 2 sts at beg of every row until 10[9:8:7] sts rem. Bind off.

Front insert and collar

Using No.5 needles cast on 6 sts.
1st row K2, P2, K2.
2nd row P2, K2, P2.
Cont in rib, inc one st at each end of next and every foll 4th row and working the extra sts into rib patt, until there are 38[40:42:44] sts. Cont without shaping until work measures 6½[7:7½:8]in from beg, ending with a WS row. Slip sts on holder to be worked later. Break off yarn.
Using No.3 needles cast on 48[50:52:54] sts. Sl sts on holder to be worked later. Break off yarn. Using No.3 needles cast on 12 sts.
Next row Rib 12 sts, rib across 38[40:42:44] sts on holder, then rib across 48[50:52:54] sts on holder. 98[102:106:110] sts.
Cont in K2, P2 rib until collar measures 4in from cast-on sts. Change to No.5 needles and cont in rib for 8in more.
Bind off loosely in rib.

Finishing

Press each piece lightly under a damp cloth with a warm iron. Join shoulder seams. Sew in sleeves. Join side and sleeve seams. Join seam of collar. Sew insert and collar to neck edge, having collar seam to left shoulder seam and point of insert to center front neck. Press seams.

49 *Back—buttoned evening cardigan*

Sizes

To fit 34[36:38]in bust
The figures in brackets [] refer to the 36 and 38in sizes respectively
Length to shoulder, 20in adjustable
Sleeve seam, 16½in adjustable

Gauge

6 sts and 9 rows to 1in over main patt worked on No.4 needles

Materials

15[16:17] balls of Bucilla Brocade
No.2 knitting needles
No.3 knitting needles
No.4 knitting needles
Circular needles No.2, No.3 and No.4
14 buttons

Front

Using No.2 straight needles cast on 111[119:127] sts. Work 10 rows K1, P1 rib. Change to No.4 needles. Commence main patt.
1st row K2 sts, *ytf, K2 tog, rep from * to last st, K1.
This row forms main patt. Cont in patt until work measures 13in from beg, or desired length to underarm, ending with a WS row.
Shape armholes
Bind off 6[8:8] sts at beg of next 2 rows. Dec one st at each end every other row 6[8:10] times. Work 1 row.
Slip rem 87[87:91] sts on holder.

Left back

Using No.2 needles cast on 60[64:68] sts.
1st row K6 sts, *P1, K1, rep from * to end.
2nd row *P1, K1, rep from * to last 6 sts, P1, K5 sts.
Rep these 2 rows 3 times more, then 1st row once.
Next row Work in rib until 5 sts rem, turn slipping rem 5 sts on holder for front band. 55[59:63] sts.
** Change to No.4 needles. Work in patt as given for back until work measures same as back to underarm, ending at armhole edge.
Shape armhole
Bind off 6[8:8] sts at beg of next row. Dec one st at armhole edge every other row 6[8:10] times. Work 1 row.
Slip rem 43[43:45] sts on holder. **

Right back

Using No.2 needles cast on 60[64:68] sts.
1st row *K1, P1, rep from * to last 6 sts, K6.
2nd row K5 sts, P1, *K1, P1, rep from * to end.
Rep these 2 rows 3 times more, then 1st row once.
Next row K5 sts and slip these sts on holder, rib to end.
Complete as given for left back from ** to **.

Sleeves

Using No.2 needles cast on 57[61:67] sts. Work 2in K1, P1 rib. Work main patt as given for front until work measures 3in from beg. Change to No.3 needles and cont in main patt until work measures 4in from beg. Change to No.4 needles and cont in main patt, inc one st at each end of 9th and every foll 8th row 8[10:10] times in all, then on every foll 12th row 4 times in all. 81[89:95] sts.
Cont in main patt without shaping until sleeve measures 16½in from beg, or desired length to underarm.
End with a WS row.
Shape cap
Bind off 6[8:8] sts at beg of next 2 rows. Dec one st at each end every other row 6[8:10] times. Work 1 row. Slip rem 57[57:59] sts on holder.

Yoke

34 and 36in sizes only

1st row Using No.4 circular needle, across 43 sts of left back K2, (ytf, K2 tog) 20 times then sl rem st onto beg of 57 sts of one sleeve, ytf, K3 tog, (ytf, K2 tog) 27 times, ytf, K1, across 87 sts of front (ytf, K2 tog) 43 times then sl rem st onto beg of 57 sts of 2nd sleeve, ytf, K3 tog, (ytf, K2 tog) 27 times, ytf, K1, across 43 sts of right back (ytf, K2 tog) 21 times, K last st. 287 sts. Do not join.
Work 3 rows main patt.

38in size only

1st row Using No.4 circular needle, across 45 sts of left back K2, (ytf, K2 tog) 21 times, ytf, K1, across the 59 sts of one sleeve (ytf, K2 tog) 29 times, ytf, K1, across 91 sts of front (ytf, K2 tog) 45 times, ytf, K1, across 59 sts of 2nd sleeve, (ytf, K2 tog) 29 times, ytf, K1, across 45 sts of right back (ytf, K2 tog) 22 times, K1. 303 sts.
Work 3 rows main patt, inc one st in 2nd st, one st in center and one st in 2nd st from end of last row. 306 sts.

All sizes

Commence yoke patt.
1st row K1, *sl 1, K1, psso, K3, (ytf, sl 1, K1, psso) twice, ytf, K1, ytf, (K2 tog, ytf) twice, K3, K2 tog, rep from * to last st, K1.
2nd and every other row P to end.
3rd, 5th and 7th rows As 1st row.
9th row K1, *sl 1, K1, psso, K2, (ytf, K2 tog) twice, ytf, K3, ytf, (sl 1, K1, psso, ytf) twice, K2, K2 tog, rep from * to last st, K1.
11th row K1, *sl 1, K1, psso, K1, (ytf, K2 tog) twice, ytf, K5, ytf, (sl 1, K1, psso, ytf) twice, K1, K2 tog, rep from * to last st, K1.
13th row K1, *sl 1, K1, psso, (ytf, K2 tog) twice, ytf, K7, ytf, (sl 1, K1, psso, ytf) twice, K2 tog, rep from * to last st, inc one in last st.
15th row *Sl 1, K1, psso, (ytf, K2 tog) twice, ytf, K3, K2 tog, K4, ytf, (sl 1, K1, psso, ytf) twice, rep from * to last 3 sts, sl 1, K1, psso, K1.
16th row P to end.
Change to No.3 circular needle.
17th row K1, *(ytf, K2 tog) twice, ytf, K3, K2 tog, sl 1, K1, psso, K3, ytf, (sl 1, K1, psso, ytf) twice, K1, rep from * to last st, K1.
19th, 21st and 23rd rows As 17th row.
25th row K1, *K1, (ytf, sl 1, K1, psso) twice, ytf, K2, K2 tog, sl 1, K1, psso, K2, (ytf, K2 tog) twice, ytf, K2, rep from * to last st, K1.
27th row K1, *K2, (ytf, sl 1, K1, psso) twice, ytf, K1, K2 tog, sl 1, K1, psso, K1, ytf, (K2 tog, ytf) twice, K3, rep from * to last st, K1.
29th row K1, *K3, (ytf, sl 1, K1, psso) twice, ytf, K2 tog, sl 1, K1, psso ytf, (K2 tog, ytf) twice, K4, rep from * to last st, K1.

31st row K1, *K4, (ytf, sl 1, K1, psso) 3 times, ytf, (K2 tog, ytf) twice, K3, K2 tog, rep from * to last st, K1.
32nd row P to end.
Change to No.2 circular needle. Rep 1st to 7th patt rows once more.
1st dec row P5, *P2 tog, P2 tog, P3, P2 tog, P2 tog, P8, rep from * ending last rep P5. 227[227: 242] sts.
2nd dec row K1, sl 1, K1, psso, K4, *sl 1, K2 tog, psso, K5, sl 1, K1, psso, K5, rep from * to last 10 sts, sl 1, K2 tog, psso, K4, sl 1, K1, psso, K1. 181[181: 193] sts.
1st rib row K2, *P1, K1, rep from * to last st, K1.
2nd rib row K1, *P1, K1, rep from * to end.
Rep these 2 rows twice more.
3rd dec row K2, *sl 1, P2 tog, psso, rib 5, rep from * to last 3[3:7] sts, P1, K2[P1, K2: rib 5, K2].
Work 7 rows rib.
4th dec row K2, P1, K1, *sl 1, K2 tog, psso, rib 7, rep from * to last 3 sts, P1, K2. 111[111:119] sts.
Work 4 rows rib. Mark each end of last row with colored thread.

Work collar
Cont in rib on these sts for 11in more. Bind off in rib.

Button band
Using No.2 needles and with WS of work facing attach yarn to 5 sts left on holder of left back and cont in garter (g) st until band is long enough, when slightly stretched, to fit up center back edge to colored marker. Do not bind off. Mark positions for 11 buttons, first to come 4 rows below sts on needle and rem 10 at 2in intervals. Cont in g st for a further 11in to match edge of collar.
Bind off.
Sew on band.

Buttonhole band
Using No.2 needles and with RS of work facing attach yarn to 5 sts left on holder of right back and work as given for button band making first 11 buttonholes as markers are reached as foll:
Buttonhole row K1, bind off 2 sts, K2.
Next row K2, cast on 2 sts, K1.
When 11th buttonhole has been worked, K2 rows g st, when band should reach colored marker. Work 1in g st.
** Work 2 buttonhole rows, then work 2in g st.** Rep from ** to ** once more. Work 2 buttonhole rows then work 1in g st. Rep from ** to ** twice more. Work 2 buttonhole rows then work 1in g st. Bind off.
Sew on band.

Finishing
Do not press. Sew in sleeves. Join side and sleeve seams. Fold collar in half to RS so that 3 double-buttonholes match. Buttonhole-st around buttonholes. Sew on buttons.

Two-piece cocktail suit

Sizes
To fit 34[36:38:40:42]in bust
36[38:40:42:44]in hips
The figures in brackets [] refer to the 36, 38, 40, 42 and 44in sizes respectively
Jacket length to shoulder, 23[23½:24:24½:25]in
Sleeve seam, 6in
Skirt length, 20[20½:21:21½:22]in
Gauge
7 sts and 9 rows to 1in over st st worked on No.3 needles

Materials
20[21:22:24:26] balls Reynolds Grand Cotillion
No.2 knitting needles
No.3 knitting needles
Six buttons; Waist length of elastic
One 7in zipper

Jacket back
Using No.2 needles cast on 123[129:137:143:151] sts.
1st row K1, *P1, K1, rep from * to end.
2nd row P1, *K1, P1, rep from * to end.
Rep these 2 rows for 1in, ending with a 2nd row and inc one st at end of last row on 36 and 40in sizes only. 123[130:137:144:151] sts.
Change to No.3 needles. Beg with a K row cont in st st until work measures 16in from beg, ending with P row.
Shape armholes
Bind off 6 sts at beg of next 2 rows; then 2[2:3:3:4] sts at each end for next 4 rows. Dec one st at each end every other row 6[8:8:10:10] times. 91[94: 97:100:103] sts. Cont without shaping until armholes measure 7[7½:8:8½:9]in from beg, ending with a P row.
Shape neck and shoulders
Next row K30[31:32:33:34] sts, turn and slip rem sts on holder.
Next row Bind off 4 sts, P to end.
Next row Bind off 6[6:7:7:7] sts, K to end.
Rep last 2 rows once more, then first of them once more. Bind off rem 6[7:6:7:8] sts. With RS of work facing, sl first 31[32:33:34:35] sts on holder, attach yarn to rem sts and K to end. Work to correspond to first side, reversing shaping.

Jacket left front
Using No.2 needles cast on 75[79:83:87:91] sts.
1st row *K1, P1, rep from * to last 21 sts, K10, sl 1, K10.
2nd row P21 sts, *K1, P1, rep from * to end.
Rep these 2 rows for 1in, ending with a 2nd row. Change to No.3 needles.
Next row K to last 11 sts, sl 1, K10.
Next row P to end.
Rep last 2 rows until work measures same as back to underarm, ending at armhole edge.
Shape armhole
At arm edge, bind off 6 sts once;
then 2[2:3:3:4] sts every other row twice, ending at armhole edge.
Shape neck
Next row K2 tog, K to last 29[30:31:32:33] sts, turn and slip rem sts on holder.
Dec one st at armhole edge every other row 5[7:7:9:9] times, *at the same time* bind off at neck edge every other row 4 sts once, 3 sts once, 2 sts once and one st 3 times. 18[19:20:21:22] sts. Cont without shaping until armhole measures same as back to shoulder, ending at armhole edge.
Shape shoulder
At arm edge, bind off 6[6:7:7:7]sts every other row twice and 6[7:6:7:8] sts once. Mark positions for 6 buttons, the first to come ½in above hem and last to come in neckband ½in above sts on holder, with 4 more evenly spaced between.

Jacket right front
Using No.2 needles cast on 75[79:83:87:91]sts.
1st row K10, sl 1, K10, *P1, K1, rep from * to end.
2nd row *P1, K1, rep from * to last 21 sts, P21.
Rep these 2 rows once more.
Next row (buttonhole row) K3 sts, bind off 4 sts, K2, sl 1, K3, bind off 4 sts, patt to end.
Next row Patt to end, casting on 4 sts above those bound-off on previous row.
Complete to correspond to left front, reversing all shaping and making buttonholes as markers are reached, as before.

Sleeves
Using No.2 needles cast on 69[73:77:81:85] sts. Work 1in rib as given for back, ending with a 2nd row. Change to No.3 needles. Beg with a K row cont in st st, inc one st at each end of 5th and every foll 6th row until there are 83[87:91:95:99] sts. Cont without shaping until sleeve measures 6in from beg, ending with a P row.
Shape cap
Bind off 6 sts at beg of next 2 rows. Dec one st at each end every other row 12[13:14:15:16] times. Bind off at beg of next and every row 2 sts 10[10:12: 12:14] times, 3 sts 4 times and 4 sts twice. Bind off rem 7[9:7:9:7] sts.

Neckband
Join shoulder seams. Using No.2 needles and with RS of work facing, patt across sts of right front neck, pick up and K 45 sts up side of front neck and 20 sts down side of back neck, K across back neck sts inc one st in center on 36 and 40in sizes only, pick up and K 20 sts up side of back neck and 45 sts down side of front neck, patt across sts of left front neck. 219[223:225:229:231] sts.
Next row P21 sts, rib to last 21 sts, P21.
Next row K10, sl 1, K10, rib to last 21 sts, K10, sl 1, K10.
Rep last 2 rows for 1in making buttonholes as before on 5th and 6th rows. Bind off in patt.

Finishing
Press lightly under a dry cloth with a cool iron. Sew in sleeves. Join side and sleeve seams. Fold front bands in half to WS and sl st down. Buttonhole-st around double buttonholes. Press seams. Sew on buttons.

Skirt back
Using No.2 needles cast on 91[97:105:111:119] sts and beg at waist. Work 1in rib as given for jacket back, ending with a 2nd row and inc one st at end of last row on 36 and 40in sizes only. 91[98: 105:112:119] sts. Change to No.3 needles.
Beg with a K row work 4 rows st st.
Shape darts
Next row K14 sts, pick up loop between sts and K tbl – called inc 1 –, K19[21:23:25:27] sts, inc 1, K25[28:31:34:37] sts, inc 1, K19[21:23:25:27] sts, inc 1, K14 sts.
Beg with a P row work 9 rows st st.
Next row K14 sts, inc 1, K20[22:24:26:28] sts, inc 1, K27[30:33:36:39] sts, inc 1, K20[22:24:26:28] sts, inc 1, K14 sts.
Beg with a P row work 9 rows st st.
Cont inc in this way on next and every foll 10th row until there are 143[150:157:164:171] sts. Cont without shaping until work measures 20[20½: 21:21½:22]in from beg, ending with a P row and inc one st at end of last row on 36 and 40in sizes only.
Next row (picot edge) K1, *ytf, K2 tog, rep from * to end.
Change to No.2 needles. Beg with a P row work 1½in st st. Bind off.

Skirt front: Work as given for back.

Finishing
Press as given for jacket. Join side seams leaving 7in open at top of left seam for zipper. Turn hem to WS at picot row and sl st down. Sew in zipper. Sew elastic inside waist ribbing with casing st. Press seams.

51 *Aran cardigans for father and son*

Sizes
Boy's cardigan to fit 26[28:30]in chest
Length to shoulder, 14[15:16]in
Sleeve seam, 9½ [10½:11½]in
Man's cardigan to fit 38 [40:42]in chest
The figures in brackets [] refer to the 28 and 30in boy's sizes and 40 and 42in mens' sizes respectively
Length to shoulder, 25[26:27]in
Sleeve seam, 18 [18½:19]in
Gauge
6 sts and 8 rows to 1in over st st worked on No.4 knitting needles
Materials
Columbia-Minerva Nantuk Sports
Boy's cardigan 5 [5:6] 2oz skeins
Man's cardigan 9 [9:10] 2 oz skeins
No.2 knitting needles
No.4 knitting needles
One cable needle
6 buttons for boy's cardigan
7 buttons for man's cardigan
Note
Abbreviations are given in patt rows of boy's cardigan

Boy's cardigan back
Using No.2 needles cast on 81 [87:93] sts.
1st row K1, *P1, K1, rep from * to end.
2nd row P1, *K1, P1, rep from * to end.
Rep these 2 rows for 1¼in, ending with a 2nd row and inc one st in center of last row. 82[88:94] sts. Change to No.4 needles. Commence patt.
1st row P9 [11:13] sts, (insert needle behind first st and K 2nd st then K first st and sl both sts off tog – called Tw2L –) twice, K1, P7, K3, P1, K1, P11 [12:13], K4, P11 [12:13:], K3, P1, K3, P7, K1, (insert needle in front of first st and K 2nd st then K first st and sl both sts off tog – called Tw2R –) twice, P9 [11:13] sts.
2nd row K9 [11:13] sts, P5, K7, P3, K1, P3, K11 [12:13], sl next 2 sts onto cable needle and hold at front of work to WS, P2 then P2 from cable needle – called C4P –, K11 [12:13], P3, K1, P3, K7, P5, K9 [11:13] sts.
3rd row P9 [11:13] sts, K1, (Tw2L) twice, P7, sl 1, K2, P1, K2, sl 1, P10 [11:12], sl next st onto cable needle and hold at back of work, K2 then P1 from cable needle – called Cr3R –, sl next 2 sts onto cable needle and hold at front of work, P1 then K2 from cable needle – called Cr3L –, P10 [11:12] sts, sl 1, K2, P1, K2, sl 1, P7, (Tw2R) twice, K1, P9 [11:13] sts.
4th row K9 [11:13] sts, P5, K7, sl 1, P2, K1, P2, sl 1, K10 [11:12], P2, K2, P2, K10 [11:12], sl 1, P2, K1, P2, sl 1, K7, P5, K9 [11:13] sts.
5th row P9 [11:13] sts, (Tw2L) twice, K1, P7, sl next st onto cable needle and hold at front of work, K2 then K1 from cable needle – called C3F –, P1, sl next 2 sts onto cable needle and hold at back of work, K1 then K2 sts from cable needle – called C3B –, P9 [10:11], Cr3R, P2, Cr3L, P9 [10:11], C3F, P1, C3B, P7, K1, (Tw2R) twice, P9 [11:13] sts.
6th row K9 [11:13] sts, P5, K7, P3, K1, P3, K9 [10:11] P2, K4, P2, K9 [10:11] P3, K1, P3, K7, P5, K9 [11:13] sts.
7th row P9 [11:13] sts, K1, (Tw2L) twice, P7, sl 1, K2, P1, K2, sl 1, P8[9:10], Cr3R, P4, Cr3L, P8 [9:10], sl 1, K2, P1, K2, sl 1, P7, (Tw2R) twice, K1, P9 [11:13] sts.
8th row K9 [11:13] sts, P5, K7, sl 1, P2, K1, P2, sl 1, K8 [9:10] P2, K6, P2, K8 [9:10], sl 1, P2, K1, P2, sl 1, K7, P5. K9 [11:13] sts.
9th row P9 [11:13] sts, (Tw2L) twice, K1, P7, C3F, P1, C3B, P7 [8:9], Cr3R, P6, Cr3L, P7 [8:9], C3F, P1, C3B, P7, K1, (Tw2R) twice, P9 [11:13] sts.
10th row K9 [11:13] sts, P5, K7, P3, K1, P3, K7 [8:9], P2, K8, P2, K7 [8:9], P3, K1, P3, K7, P5, K9 [11:13] sts.
11th row Work 28 [30:32] sts as given for 3rd row, P6 [7:8], Cr3R, P8, Cr3L, P6 [7:8], patt to end as given for 3rd row.
12th row Work 28 [30:32] sts as given for 4th row, K6 [7:8] P2, K10, P2, K6 [7:8], patt to end as given for 4th row.
13th row Work 28 [30:32] sts as given for 5th row, P6 [7:8], Cr3L, P8, Cr3R, P6 [7:8], patt to end as given for 5th row.
14th row As 10th.
15th row Work 28 [30:32] sts as given for 3rd row, P7 [8:9], Cr3L, P6, Cr3R, P7 [8:9], patt to end as given for 3rd row.
16th row As 8th.
17th row Work 28 [30:32] sts as given for 5th row, P8 [9:10], Cr3L, P4, Cr3R, P8 [9:10], patt to end as given for 5th row.
18th row As 6th.
19th row Work 28 [30:32] sts as given for 3rd row, P9 [10:11], Cr3L, P2, Cr3R, P9 [10:11], patt to end as given for 3rd row.
20th row As 4th.
21st row Work 28 [30:32] sts as given for 5th row, P10 [11:12], Cr3L, Cr3R, P10 [11:12], patt to end as given for 5th row.
22nd row As 2nd.
Rows 3-22 form patt. Cont in patt until work measures 8½ [9:9½]in from beg, ending with a WS row.
Shape armholes
Keeping patt correct, cast off 2 [3:4] sts at beg of next 2 rows and 2 sts at beg of next 6 rows. 66 [70:74] sts. Cont without shaping until armholes measure 3½ [4:4½]in from beg, ending with a WS row.
Shape shoulders
Bind off 7 sts at beg of next 4 rows and 7 [8:9] sts at beg of next 2 rows. Sl rem 24 [26:28] sts on holder.

Right front
Using No.2 needles cast on 55 [57:61] sts. Work 1¼in rib as given for back, ending with a 2nd row and inc one st at beg of last row on 28in size only. 55 [58:61] sts.
Next row Rib 8 sts and sl these sts on holder for front band, change to No.4 needles, P8 [9:10] sts, K4, P9, K3, P1, K3, P5, (Tw2R) twice, K1, P9 [11:13] sts. 47 [50:53] sts.
2nd row K9 [11:13] sts, P5, K5, P3, K1, P3, K9, C4P, K8 [9:10] sts.
3rd row P7 [8:9] sts, Cr3R, Cr3L, P8, sl 1, K2, P1, K2, sl 1, P5, K1, (Tw2R) twice, P9 [11:13] sts.
4th row K9 [11:13] sts, P5, K5. sl 1, P2, K1, P2, sl 1, K8, P2, K2, P2, K7 [8:9] sts.
5th row P6 [7:8] sts, Cr3R, P2, Cr3L, P7, C3F, P1, C3B, P5, (Tw2R) twice, K1, P9 [11:13] sts.
Cont in patt as established until work measures same as back to underarm, ending with a RS row.
Shape armhole
At arm edge, bind off 2 [3:4] sts once and 2 sts every other row 3 times. 39 [41:43] sts. Cont without shaping until armhole measures 2 [2½:3] in from beg, ending with a RS row.
Shape neck
Next row Patt 33 [34:35] sts, turn and sl rem 6 [7:8] sts on holder.
At arm edge, every other row bind off 4 sts once, 3 sts once and 2 sts once. Dec one st at neck edge every other row 3 times, ending with a RS row.
Shape shoulder
At arm edge, bind off 7 sts every other row twice and 7 [8:9] sts once.

Left front
Using No.2 needles cast on 55 [57:61] sts. Work ¾in rib as given for back, ending with a WS row.
Next row (buttonhole row) Rib to last 6 sts, bind off 3 sts, rib to end.
Next row Rib to end, casting on 3 sts above those bound off on previous row.
Cont in rib until work measures 1¼in from beg, ending with a 2nd row and inc one st at end of last row on 28in size only. 55 [58:61] sts.
Change to No.4 needles.
Next row P9 [11:13] sts, K1, (Tw2L) twice, P5, K3, P1, K3, P9, K4, P8 [9:10] sts, turn and sl rem 8 sts on holder for front band.
47 [50:53] sts.
Next row K8 [9:10] sts, C4P, K9, P3, K1, P3, K5, P5, K9 [11:13] sts.
Complete to correspond to right front, reversing all shaping.

Sleeves
Using No.2 needles cast on 41 [45:49] sts. Work 1¼in rib as given for back, ending with a 2nd row and inc on st in center of last row. 42 [46:50] sts. Change to No.4 needles.
1st row P1 [2:3] sts, K3, P1, K3, P11 [12:13], K4, P11 [12:13], K3, P1, K3, P1 [2:3] sts
2nd row K1 [2:3] sts, P3, K1, P3, K11 [12:13], C4P, K11 [12:13], P3, K1, P3, K1 [2:3] sts.
3rd row P1 [2:3] sts, sl 1, K2, P1, K2, sl 1, P10 [11:12], Cr3R, Cr3L, P10 [11:12], sl 1, K2, P1, K2, sl 1, P1 [2:3] sts.
Cont in patt as established, inc one st at each end of every 6th row until there are 62 [68:74] sts. Cont without shaping until sleeve measures 9½ [10½:11½]in from beg, ending with a WS row.
Shape saddle cap
Bind off 2 sts at beg of next 2 [4:6] rows and one st at beg of next 4 [6:8] rows. 54 sts.
*Bind off 2 sts at beg of next 2 rows, dec 1st at beg of next 2 rows; repeat from * 3 times. 36 sts. Bind off 2 sts at beg of next 10 rows. 16 sts. Cont on these sts for length of shoulder, ending with a WS row. Slip sts on holder.

Right front band
Using No.2 needles and with WS of work facing, attach yarn to sts of right front, inc in first st, rib to end. Cont in rib until band fits along front edge, when slightly stretched, ending with a WS row. Slip sts on holder. Mark positions for 6 buttons on right front, first to come in ribbing and last to come on neckband, with 4 more evenly spaced between.

Left front band
Work as given for right front band, working buttonholes as on left front when markers are reached.

Neckband
Sew saddle caps of sleeves to front and back shoulders. Using No.2 needles and with RS of work facing, rib across 8 sts of right front band, K next st tog with first st of front neck, K rem 5 [6:7] sts of front neck, pick up and K 13 sts up side of neck, K across sts of right sleeve, back neck and left sleeve K2 tog at each seam and at center back, pick up and K13 sts down other side of neck, K5 [6:7] front neck sts, K next st tog with first st of left front band, rib to end. 107 [111:115] sts. Work 9 rows rib, working buttonholes as before on 4th and 5th rows. Bind off in rib.

Finishing
Press each piece under a damp cloth with a warm iron. Set in sleeves. Join side and sleeve seams. Sew on front bands. Press seams. Sew on buttons.

Man's cardigan back
Using No.2 needles cast on 117 [123:129] sts. Work 1½in rib as given for back of boy's cardigan,

ending with a 2nd row. Change to No.4 needles.
1st row P14 [16:18] sts, (Tw2L) twice, K1, P7, K3, P1, K3, P12, K4, P19 [21:23], K4, P12, K3, P1, K3, P7, K1, (Tw2R) twice, P14 [16:18] sts.
2nd row K14 [16:18] sts, P5, K7, P3, K1, P3, K12, C4P, K19 [21:23], C4P, K12, P3, K1, P3, K7, P5, K14 [16:18] sts.
3rd row P14 [16:18] sts, K1, (Tw2L) twice, P7, sl 1, K2, P1, K2, sl 1, P11, Cr3R, Cr3L, P17 [19:21], Cr3R, Cr3L, P11, sl 1, K2, P1, K2, sl 1, P7, (Tw2R) twice, K1, P14 [16:18] sts.
4th row K14 [16:18] sts, P5, K7, sl 1, P2, K1, P2, sl 1, K11, P2, K2, P2, K17 [19:21], P2, K2, P2, K11, sl 1, P2, K1, P2, sl 1, K7, P5, K14 [16:18] sts.
5th row P14 [16:18] sts, (Tw2L) twice, K1, P7, C3F, P1, C3B, P10, Cr3R, P2, Cr3L, P15 [17:19], Cr3R, P2, Cr3L, P10, C3F, P1, C3B, P7, K1, (Tw2R) twice, P14 [16:18] sts.
6th row K14 [16:18] sts, P5, K7, P3, K1, P3, K10, P2, K4, P2, K15 [17:19], P2, K4, P2, K10, P3, K1, P3, K7, P5, K14 [16:18] sts.
7th row Work 33 [35:37] sts as given for 3rd row, P9, Cr3R, P4, Cr3L, P13 [15:17], Cr3R, P4, Cr3L, P9, patt to end as given for 3rd row.
8th row Work 33 [35:37] sts as given for 4th row, K9, P2, K6, P2, K13 [15:17] P2, K6, P2, K9, patt to end as given for 4th row.
9th row Work 33 [35:37] sts as given for 5th row, P8, Cr3R, P6, Cr3L, P11 [13:15], Cr3R, P6, Cr3L, P8, patt to end as given for 5th row.
10th row Work 33 [35:37] sts as given for 6th row, K8, P2, K8, P2, K11 [13:15], P2, K8, P2, K8, patt to end as given for 6th row.
11th row Work 33 [35:37] sts as given for 3rd row, P7, Cr3R, P8, Cr3L, P9 [11:13], Cr3R, P8, Cr3L, P7, patt to end as given for 3rd row.
12th row Work 33 [34:37] sts as given for 4th row, K7, P2, K10, P2, K9 [11:13], P2, K10, P2, K7, patt to end as given for 4th row.
13th row Work 33 [35:37] sts as given for 5th row, P7, Cr3L, P8, Cr3R, P9 [11:13], Cr3L, P8, Cr3R, P7, patt to end as given for 5th row.
14th row As 10th.
15th row Work 33 [35:37] sts as given for 3rd row, P8, Cr3L, P6, Cr3R, P11 [13:15], Cr3L, P6, Cr3R, P8, patt to end as given for 3rd row.
16th row As 8th.
17th row Work 33 [35:37] sts as given for 5th row, P9, Cr3L, P4, Cr3R, P13 [15:17], Cr3L, P4, Cr3R, P9, patt to end as given for 5th row.
18th row As 6th.
19th row Work 33 [35:37] sts as given for 3rd row, P10, Cr3L, P2, Cr3R, P15 [17:19], Cr3L, P2, Cr3R, P10, patt to end as given for 3rd row.
20th row As 4th.
21st row Work 33 [35:37] sts as given for 5th row, P11, Cr3L, Cr3R, P17 [19:21] Cr3L, Cr3R, P11, patt to end as given for 5th row.
22nd row As 2nd.
Rows 3-22 form patt. Cont in patt until work measures 15½ [16:16½]in from beg, ending with a WS row.
Shape armholes
Bind off 3 sts at beg of next 2 rows.
****Next row** K2 sts, sl 1, K1, psso, patt to last 4 sts, K2 tog, K2 sts.
Next row P3 sts, patt to last 3 sts, P3. **
Rep last 2 rows until 39 [41:43] sts rem, ending with a WS row. Slip sts on holder.

Right front
Using No.2 needles cast on 69 [73:75] sts. Work 1½in rib as given for back, ending with a 2nd row and inc one st at beg of last row on 38 and 42in sizes only. 70[73:76] sts.
Next row Rib 12 sts and slip these sts on holder for front band, change to No.4 needles, P9 [10:11] sts, K4, P12, K3, P1, K3, P7, K1, (Tw2R) twice, P14 (16:18) sts. 58 [61:64] sts.
Next row K14 [16:18] sts, P5, K7, P3, K1, P3, K12, C4P, K9 [10:11] sts.
Next row P8 [9:11] sts, Cr3R, Cr3L, P11, sl 1, K2, P1, K2, sl 1, P7, (Tw2R) twice, K1, P14 [16:18] sts.
Next row K14 [16:18] sts, P5, K7, sl 1, P2, K1, P2, sl 1, K11, P2, K2, P2, K8 [9:10] sts.
Next row P7 [8:9] sts, Cr3R, P2, Cr3L, P10, C3F, P1, C3B, P7, K1, (Tw2R) twice, P14 [16:18] sts.
Cont in patt as established until work measures same as back to underarm, ending with a RS row.
Shape armhole
Bind off 3 sts at beg of next row.
Next row Patt to last 4 sts, K2 tog, K2 sts.
Next row P3 sts, patt to end.
Rep last 2 rows until 31 [32:33] sts rem, ending with a RS row.
Shape neck
Next row Patt 23 sts, turn and slip rem 8 [9:10] sts on holder.
Cont dec at armhole edge on next and every other row, *at the same tine* bind off at neck edge 3 sts once, 2 sts every other row twice and one st 4 times, ending with a WS row. 5 sts.
Next row K1, K2 tog, K2 sts.
Next row P4 sts.
Next row K2 tog, K2 sts.
Bind off.

Left front
Using No.2 needles cast on 69 [73:75] sts.
Work ¾in rib as given for back, ending with a 2nd row.
Next row (buttonhole row) Rib to last 8 sts, bind off 3 sts, rib to end.
Next row Rib to end, casting on 3 sts above those bound off on previous row.
Cont in rib until work measures 1½in from beg, ending with a 2nd row and inc one st at end of last row on 38 and 42in sizes only. 70 [73:76] sts. Change to No.4 needles.
Next row P14 [16:18] sts, (Tw2L) twice, K1, P7, K3, P1, K3, P12, K4, P9 [10:11] sts, turn and slip rem 12 sts on holder for front band. 58 [61:64] sts.
Next row K9 [10:11] sts, C4P, K12, P3, K1, P3, K7, P5, K14, [16:18] sts.
Complete to correspond to right front, reversing all shaping.

Sleeves
Using No.2 needles cast on 55 [59:63] sts.
Work 2¼in rib as given for back, ending with a 2nd row and inc one st in center of last row. 56 [60:64] sts.
Change to No.4 needles.
1st row (Tw2L) 0 [1:2] times, P7, K3, P1, K3, P12, K4, P12, K3, P1, K3, P7, (Tw2R) 0 [1:2] times.
2nd row P0 [2:4] sts, K7, P3, K1, P3, K12, C4P, K12, P3, K1, P3, K7, P0 [2:4] sts.
Cont in patt as established, inc one st at each end of every 8th row, working first 5 [3:1] of inc sts into patt panel of 5 sts then rem sts into reversed st st, until there are 86 [90:94] sts. Cont without shaping until sleeve measures 18 [18½:19]in from beg, ending with a WS row.
Shape cap
Bind off 3 sts at beg of next 2 rows. 80 [84:88] sts. Rep from ** to ** as given for back until 8 sts rem, ending with a WS row. Slip sts on holder.
Right front band
Using No.2 needles and with WS of work facing, attach yarn to 12 sts on holder, inc in first st, rib to end.
Cont in rib until band fits along front edge to neck when slightly stretched, ending with a WS row. Slip sts on holder.
Mark positions for 7 buttons on right front, first to come in lower edge and last to be in neck band, with 5 more evenly spaced between.

Left front band
Work as given for right front band working buttonholes as before as markers are reached.

Neckband
Join raglan seams. Using No.2 needles and with RS of work facing, rib across 12 sts of right front band, K next st tog with first st of front neck, K rem 7 [8:9] sts of front neck, pick up and K 18 sts up side of neck, K across sts of right sleeve, back neck and left sleeve K2 tog at each seam, pick up and K18 sts down other side of neck, K7 [8:9] front neck sts, K next st tog with first st of front band, rib to end. 129 [133:137] sts. Work 2in rib, working buttonhole as before after 1in. Bind off in rib.

Finishing
Press each piece under a damp cloth with a warm iron. Join side and sleeve seams. Sew on front bands. Press seams. Sew on buttons.

52 *Cardigan in arrowhead pattern*

Sizes
To fit 36 [38:40:42]in chest
The figures in brackets [] refer to the 38, 40 and 42in sizes respectively
Length to shoulder, 25 [26:27:28]in
Sleeve seam, 17½ [18:18½:19]in
Gauge
6 sts and 8 rows to 1in over patt worked on No.4 knitting needles
Materials
13 [14:15:16] balls Unger Les Bouquets in main color, A
1 ball of contrasting color, B
2 balls of contrasting color, C
No.3 knitting needles
No.4 knitting needles
One 22 [22:24:24]in open end zipper

Back
Using No.3 needles and A, cast on 121 [127:133:139] sts.
1st row K1, *P1, K1, rep from * to end.
2nd row P1, *K1, P1, rep from * to end.
Rep these 2 rows once more, then 1st row once. Attach C. P 1 row, then rib 3 rows. Attach A. P 1 row, then rib 1 row. Attach B. P 1 row, then rib 3 rows. Break off B. With A, P 1 row, then rib 1 row. With C, P 1 row, then rib 3 rows. Break off C. With A, P 1 row, then rib 3 rows. ** Change to No.4 needles. P 1 row. Commence patt.
1st row K1 [0:3:2] sts, *P1, K3, rep from * to last 4 [3:2:1] sts, P1, K3 [2:1:0].
2nd row P3 [2:1:0] sts, K1, *P3, K1, rep from * to last 1 [0:3:2] sts, P1 [0:3:2].
3rd row K2 [K5:K2, P1, K5:K1, P1, K3, P1, K5] sts, *P1, K3, P1, K5, rep from * to last 9 [2:5:8] sts, P1, K3, P1, K4 [P1, K1:P1, K3, P1:P1, K3, P1, K3].
Cont in patt working from chart, beg and ending rows as established, until work measures 16½ [17:17½:18]in from beg, ending with a WS row.
Shape armholes
Keeping patt correct, bind off 5 sts at beg of next 2 rows, 3 sts at beg of next 2 rows and 2 sts at beg of next 2 [2:4:4] rows. 101 [107:109:115] sts. Dec one st at each end every other row 4 [6:6:8] times 93 [95:97:99] sts. Cont without shaping until armholes measure 8½ [9:9½:10]in from beg, ending with a WS row.
Shape shoulders
Bind off 6 sts at beg of next 8

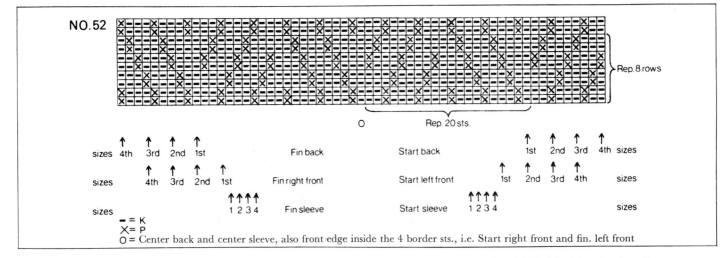

NO.52

Rep. 8 rows

O   Rep. 20 sts.

sizes   4th   3rd   2nd   1st   Fin back   Start back   1st   2nd   3rd   4th   sizes

sizes   4th   3rd   2nd   1st   Fin right front   Start left front   1st   2nd   3rd   4th   sizes

sizes   1 2 3 4   Fin sleeve   Start sleeve   1 2 3 4   sizes

— = K
X = P
O = Center back and center sleeve, also front edge inside the 4 border sts., i.e. Start right front and fin. left front

rows and 6 [7:7:8] sts at beg of next 2 rows. Bind off rem 33 [33:35:35] sts.

Right front

Using No.3 needles and A, cast on 61 [65:67: 71] sts.
1st row K3 sts, *P1, K1, rep from * to end.
2nd row *P1, K1, rep from * to last 3 sts, P1, K2.
Keeping 2 sts at front edge in garter st, work as given for back to **. Change to No.4 needles.
Next row Inc 1 [0:1:0] st, P to last 4 sts, K1, P1, K2. 62 [65:68:71] sts. Commence patt.
1st row K3 sts, P1, K1, *P1, K3, rep from * to last 1 [0:3:2] sts, P1 [0:P1, K2:P1, K1].
Keeping 4 sts at front edge as established, cont in patt working from chart until front measures same as back to underarm, ending at armhole edge.
Shape armhole
Keeping patt correct, bind off 5 sts every other row once; 3 sts once and 2 sts 1 [1:2:2] times. Dec one st at armhole edge every other row 4 [6:6:8] times. 48 [49:50:51] sts. Cont without shaping until armhole measures 6 [6½:7:7½]in from beg, ending at center front edge.
Shape neck
At next edge, bind off 6 [6:7:7] sts once, 3 sts once and 2 sts every other row twice. Dec one st at neck edge every other row 5 times. 30 [31:31:32] sts. Cont without shaping until armhole measures same as back to shoulder, ending at armhole edge.
Shape shoulder
Bind off 6 sts every other row 4 times and 6 [7:7:8] sts once.

Left front

Using No.3 needles and A, cast on 61 [65:67: 71] sts.
1st row *K1, P1, rep from * to last 3 sts, K3.
2nd row K2, P1, *K1, P1, rep from * to end.
Keeping 2 sts at front edge in garter st work as given for back to **, inc one st at end of last row on 36 and 40in sizes only. 62 [65:68:71] sts. Change to No.4 needles.
Next row K2, P1, K1, P to end.
Complete to correspond to right front, reversing all shaping and noting that 1st patt row is as foll:
1st row K2 [1:0:3] sts, *P1, K3, rep from * to end.

Sleeves

Using No.3 needles and A, cast on 67 [69:71: 73] sts. Work as given for back to **. Change to No.4 needles. P 1 row. Commence patt.
1st row K2 [3:0:1] sts, *P1, K3, rep from * to last 1 [2:3:4] sts, P1, K0 [1:2:3].
This row establishes patt. Cont in patt working from chart and inc one st at each end of 3rd and every foll 8th row until there are 93[95:99:101] sts, working extra sts into patt. Cont without

shaping until sleeve measures 17½ [18:18½:19]in from beg, ending with a WS row.
Shape cap
Bind off 5 sts at beg of next 2 rows. Dec one st at each end every other row 13 [14:14:15] times. 57 [57:61:61] sts. Bind off 2 sts at beg of next 12 [12:14:14] rows and 3 sts at beg of next 4 rows. Bind off rem 21 sts.

Collar

Using No.3 needles and A, cast on 117 [121: 125:129] sts. Work 1in K1, P1 rib as given for back, ending with a 2nd row.
Next row Rib to last 9 sts, turn, sl 1, rib to last 9 sts, turn.
Next row Sl 1, rib to last 13 sts, turn, sl 1, rib to last 13 sts, turn.
Cont in this way working 4 sts less on every row until 33 sts rem unworked at each end.
Next row (RS) Rib to end.
Work 4 more row rib. Attach B. K 1 row, then rib 3 rows. With A, K 1 row, then rib 1 row. Attach C. K 1 row, then rib 3 rows. Break off C. With A, K 1 row, then rib 1 row. With B, K 1 row, then rib 3 rows. Break off B. With A, K 1 row, then rib 5 rows. Bind off in rib.

Finishing

Press each piece under a damp cloth with a warm iron. Join shoulder, side and sleeve seams. Sew in sleeves. Sew on collar. Sew in zipper. Press seams.

see chart above

53 Family pullovers in cables and seed stitch

Sizes
To fit 24 [26:28:30:32:34:36:38:40:42:44]in bust/chest
The figures in brackets [] refer to the 26, 28, 30, 32, 34, 36, 38, 40, 42 and 44in sizes respectively
Length to shoulder, 16 [18:20:22:24:24½:25: 25½:27:27½:28]in
Sleeve seam, 12[13½:15:16:17:17½:17½:18:18: 18½:18½]in
Gauge
5 sts and 7 rows to 1in over st st worked on No.8 knitting needles
Materials
Bernat Berella Germantown
4 [5:5:6:7:7:8:8:9:9:10] skeins
No.6 knitting needles
No.8 knitting needles

Set of 4 No.4 double-pointed needles
One cable needle
Note
Abbreviations are given in patt of Pullover A

Pullover A back
Using No.6 needles cast on 73 [79:85:91:97:103: 109:115:121:127:133] sts.
1st row K1, *P1, K1, rep from * to end.
2nd row P1, *K1, P1, rep from * to end.
Rep these 2 rows for 1½ [1½:1½:1½:2:2:2:2:2½: 2½:2½]in, ending with a 2nd row and inc one st in center of last row. 74 [80:86:92:98:104:110:116: 122:128:134] sts. Change to No.8 needles. Commence patt.
1st row K24 [27:30:33:36:39:42:45:48:51:54] sts, P2, K3, P2, K12, P2, K3, P2, K to end.
2nd and every other row P24 [27:30:33:36:39: 42:45:48:51:54] sts, K2, P3, K2, P12, K2, P3, K2, P to end.
3rd row as 1st.
5th row K24 [27:30:33:36:39:42:45:48:51:54] sts, P2, sl next st onto cable needle and hold at front of work, K2 sts then K1 from cable needle— called C3F —, P2, sl next 3 sts onto cable needle and hold at back of work, K3 then K3 from cable needle, sl next 3 sts onto cable needle and hold at front of work, K3 then K3 from cable needle – called C12 –, P2, sl next 2 sts onto cable needle and hold at back of work, K1 then K2 from cable needle – called C3B –, P2, K to end.
7th row As 1st.
9th row As 1st.
11th row K24 [27:30:33:36:39:42:45:48:51: 54] sts, P2, C3F, P2, K12, P2, C3B, P2, K to end.
12th row As 2nd.
These 12 rows form patt. Cont in patt until work measures 10½ [12:13½:15:16½:16½:16½:16½:17½: 17½:17½]in from beg, ending with a WS row.
Shape armholes
Bind off 4 [4:4:4:5:5:5:5:6:6:6] sts at beg of next 2 rows; 3 sts at beg of next 2 rows and 2 sts at beg of next 2[2:2:4:4:4:6:6:6:8:8] rows. Dec one st at each end of every other row 2 [3:4:3:3:4:3:4: 4:3:4] times. 52 [56:60:64:68:72:76:80:84:88:92] sts. Cont without shaping until armholes measure 4½ [5:5½:6:6¼:6¾:7¼:7¾:8:8½:9]in from beg, ending with a WS row.
Shape shoulders
Bind off 5 [5:6:6:7:7:6:6:7:7:7] sts at beg of next 4 [4:4:4:4:6:6:6:6:6] rows and 4 [6:5:7:6:8:5:7: 5:7:8] sts at beg of next 2 rows. Sl rem 24 [24:26:26:28:28:30:30:32:32:34] sts on holder.

Pullover A front
Work as given for back until armholes measure 4 [4:4:4:6:6:6:6:8:8:8] rows less than back, ending with a WS row.
Shape neck
Next row Patt 16 [18:19:21:23:25:26:28:30:

32:33] sts, turn and sl rem sts on holder.
Work 3 [3:3:3:5:5:5:5:7:7:7] rows on these sts, dec one st at neck edge on first and every other row.

Shape shoulder
At arm edge, bind off 5 [5:6:6:7:7:6:6:7:7:7] sts every other row 2 [2:2:2:2:2:3:3:3:3:3] times and 4 [6:5:7:6:8:5:7:5:7:8] sts once.
With RS of work facing, skip first 20 [20:22:22: 22:22:24:24:24:24:26] sts and leave for center neck, attach yarn to rem sts, K2 tog, patt to end. Complete to correspond to first side, reversing shaping.

Pullover A sleeves
Using No.6 needles cast on 39 [41:43:45:47:49: 51:53:55:57:59] sts. Work 1½ [1½:1½:1½:2:2:2: 2½:2½:2½]in rib as given for back, ending with a 2nd row and inc one st in center of last row. 40 [42:44:46:48:50:52:54:56:58:60] sts. Change to No.8 needles.
1st row K14 [15:16:17:18:19:20:21:22:23:24] sts, P2, K3, P2, K3, P2, K to end.
2nd and every other row P14 [15:16:17:18:19: 20:21:22:23:24] sts, K2, P3, K2, P3, K2, P to end.
3rd row As 1st.
5th row K14 [15:16:17:18:19:20:21:22:23:24] sts, P2, C3B, P2, C3F, P2, K to end.
6th row As 2nd.
These 6 rows form patt. Cont in patt, inc one st at each end of 6th [6th:8th:8th:8th:8th:8th: 8th:8th:8th:8th] row until there are 60 [62:64: 66:70:72:74:76:80:82:84] sts. Cont without shaping until sleeve measures 12 [13½:15:16:17: 17½:17½:18:18:18½:18½]in from beg, ending with a WS row.

Shape saddle cap
Bind off 4 [4:4:4:5:5:5:5:6:6:6] sts at beg of next 2 rows. Dec one st at each end of next and every other row until 28 [28:32:32:34:34:38:38:40:40: 40] sts rem, ending with a WS row.
Bind off 2 sts at beg of next 6 [6:8:8:8:8:10:10: 10:10:10] rows. Cont on rem 16 [16:16:16:18: 18:18:18:20:20:20] sts for length of shoulder, ending with a WS row. Slip sts on holder.

Pullover A neckband
Sew saddle caps of sleeves to front and back shoulders. Using 4 No.4 double-pointed needles and with RS of work facing, K across all sts on holders, K2 tog at each back seam and pick up and K3 [3:3:3:4:4:4:4:5:5:5] sts at each side of front neck. 80 [80:84:84:92:92:96:96:104:104: 108] sts. Work in rounds of K1, P1 rib for 5[5:5: 6:6:6:7:7:7:8:8]in. Bind off loosely in rib.

Finishing
Press each piece under a damp cloth with a warm iron. Join side, sleeve and underarm seams. Press seams.

Pullover B back
Using No.6 needles cast on 74 [80:86:92:98: 104:110:116:122:128:134] sts. Beg with a K row work 6 [6:6:6:8:8:8:8:10:10:10] rows st st.
Next row P all sts to form hemline.
Change to No.8 needles. P 1 row. Commence patt.
1st row K2 [5:8:8:11:14:14:17:20:20:23] sts, *P2, K3, P2, K12, P2, K3, P2, *, K18 [18:18: 24:24:24:30:30:30:36:36] sts, rep from * to *, K to end.
2nd and every other row P2 [5:8:8:11:14:14: 17:20:20:23] sts, *K2, P3, K2, P12, K2, P3, K2, *, P18 [18:18:24:24:24:30:30:30:36:36] sts, rep from * to *, P to end.
3rd row As 1st.
5th row K2 [5:8:8:11:14:14:17:20:20:23] sts, *P2, C3F, P2, C12, P2, C3B, P2, *, K18 [18:18: 24:24:24:30:30:30:36:36]sts, rep from * to *, K to end.
Keeping 2 panels of 26 sts in patt as on Pullover

A, complete as given for pullover A.

Pullover B front
Keeping patt correct as given for pullover B back, work as given for pullover A front.

Pullover B sleeves
Using No.6 needles cast on 39[41:43:45:47:49: 51:53:55:57:59] sts. Work 1½[1½:1½:1½:2:2: 2:2:2½:2½:2½]in rib as given for pullover A, ending with a 2nd row and inc one st in center of last row. 40[42:44:46:48:50:52:54:56:58:60] sts. Change to No.8 needles.
1st row K12[13:14:15:16:17:18:19:20:21:22] sts, P2, K12, P2, K to end.
2nd and every other row P12 [13:14:15:16:17: 18:19:20:21:22] sts, K2, P12, K2, P to end.
3rd row As 1st.
5th row K12[13:14:15:16:17:18:19:20:21:22] sts, P2, C12, P2, K to end.
Cont in patt as established, working C12 on every 12th row and complete as given for pullover A sleeves.

Pullover B neckband
Work as given for pullover A neckband.

Finishing
Press and make as given for pullover A. Fold hemline in half to WS and sl st down.

Pullover C back
Using No.6 needles cast on 73[79:85:91:97: 102:109:115:121:127:133] sts. Work 1½[1½:1½: 1½:2:2:2:2:2½:2½:2½]in rib as given for pullover A back, ending with a 2nd row and inc one st in center of last row. 74[80:86:92:98:104:110:116: 122:128:134] sts. Change to No.8 needles.
1st row K0[1:0:0:1:0:0:1:0:0:1] st, (P1, K1) 2 [3:5:5:5:7:7:8:9:10] times, *P2, K2 [2:2:2: 3:3:3:3:4:4:4], P2, K12, P2, K2 [2:2:2:3:3:3:3: 4:4:4], P2, *, (sl next 2 sts onto cable needle and hold at back of work, K1 then P2 from cable needle – called C3B –, sl next st onto cable needle and hold at front of work, P2 then K1 from cable needle – called C3F –) 3 [3:3:4:4:4: 5:5:5:6:6] times, rep from * to *, (K1, P1) 2 [3:5:5:5:7:7:8:9:9:10] times, K0[1:0:0:1:0:0: 1:0:0:1] st.
2nd row P0 [1:0:0:1:0:0:1:0:0:1] st, (K1, P1) 2[3:5:5:5:7:7:8:9:9:10] times, *K2, P2[2:2:2: 3:3:3:3:4:4:4], K2, P12, K2, P2[2:2:2:3:3:3:3: 4:4:4], K2, *, (P1, K4, P1) 3[3:3:4:4:4:5:5:5: 6:6] times, rep from * to *, (P1, K1) 2 [3:5:5:5: 7:7:8:9:9:10] times, P0 [1:0:0:1:0:0:1:0:0:1].
3rd row P0 [1:0:0:1:0:0:1:0:0:1] st, (K1, P1) 2[3:5:5:5:7:7:8:9:9:10] times, *P2, K2 [2:2:2: 3:3:3:3:4:4:4], P2, K12, P2, K2 [2:2:2:3:3:3:3: 4:4:4], P2, *, (K1, P4, K1) 3 [3:3:4:4:4:5:5:5: 6:6] times, rep from * to *, (P1, K1) 2 [3:5:5:5: 7:7:8:9:9:10] times, P0 [1:0:0:1:0:0:1:0:0:1],
4th row K0 [1:0:0:1:0:0:1:0:0:1] st, (P1, K1) 2 [3:5:5:5:7:7:8:9:9:10] times, *K2, P2 [2:2:2: 3:3:3:3:4:4:4], K2, P12, K2, P2:2:2:3:3:3:3:3: 4:4:4], K2, *, (P1, K4, P1) 3 [3:3:4:4:4:5:5:5:5: 6:6] times, rep from * to *, (K1, P1) 2[3:5:5:5: 7:7:8:9:9:10] times, K0 [1:0:0:1:0:0:1:0:0:1].
5th row Work 4 [7:10:10:10:11:14:14:17:18:18:21] sts as given for 1st row, *P2, K2 [2:2:2:3:3:3: 3:4:4:4], P2, C12, P2, K2 [2:2:2:3:3:3:3:3:4:4:4], P2, *, (K1, P1) 3 [3:3:4:4:4:5:5:5:6:6] times, rep from * to *, patt to end as given for 1st row.
6th row As 2nd.
7th row Work 28 [31:34:34:37:40:40:43:46:46: 49] sts as given for 3rd row, (C3F, C3B) 3 [3:3: 4:4:4:5:5:5:6:6] times, patt to end as given for 3rd row.
8th row Work 28 [31:34:34:37:40:40:43:46:46: 49] sts as given for 4th row, (K2, P2, K2) 3 [3:3: 4:4:4:5:5:5:6:6] times, patt to end as given for 4th row.
9th row Work 28 [31:34:34:37:40:40:43:46:46:

49 [sts as given for 1st row, (P2, K2, P2) 3 [3: 3:4:4:4:5:5:5:6:6] times, patt to end as given for 1st row.
10th row Work 28 [31:34:34:37:40:40:43:46:4:6 49] sts as given for 2nd row, (K2, P2, K2) 3 [3: 3:4:4:4:5:5:5:6:6] times, patt to end as given for 2nd row.
11th row Work 28 [31:34:34:37:40:40:43:46:46: 49] sts as given for 3rd row, (P2, K2, P2) 3[3:3: 4:4:4:5:5:5:6:6] times, patt to end as given for 3rd row.
12th row As 8th.
These 12 rows form patt. Keeping patt correct throughout, complete as given for Pullover A back.

Pullover C front
Keeping patt correct as given for pullover C back, work as given for pullover A front.

Pullover C sleeves
Using No.6 needles cast on and work in rib as given for pullover A sleeves. Change to No.8 needles.
1st row K0 [1:0:1:1:0:1:0:0:1:0] st, (P1, K1) 4 [4:5:5:5:6:6:7:7:7:8] times, P2, K2 [2:2:2:3: 3:3:3:4:4:4], P2, K12, P2, K2 [2:2:2:3:3:3:3 4:4:4], P2, (K1, P1) 4 [4:5:5:5:6:6:7:7:7:8] times. K0 [1:0:1:1:0:1:0:0:1:0].
2nd row P0 [1:0:1:1:0:1:0:0:1:0] st, (K1, P1) 4 [4:5:5:5:6:6:7:7:7:8] times, K2, P2 [2:2:2:3: 3:3:3:4:4:4], K2, P12, K2, P2 [2:2:2:3:3:3:3: 4:4:4], K2, (P1, K1) 4 [4:5:5:5:6:6:7:7:7:8] times, P0 [1:0:1:1:0:1:0:0:1:0].
3rd row P0 [1:0:1:1:0:1:0:0:1:0] st, (K1, P1) 4 [4:5:5:5:6:6:7:7:7:8] times, patt 24 [24:24: 24:26:26:26:26:28:28:28] sts as given for 1st row, (P1, K1) 4 [4:5:5:5:6:6:7:7:7:8] times, P0 [1:0:1:1:0:1:0:0:1:0].
4th row K0 [1:0:1:1:0:1:0:0:1:0] st, (P1, K1) 4 [4:5:5:5:6:6:7:7:7:8] times, patt 24 [24: 24:24:26:26:26:28:28:28] sts as given for 2nd row, (K1, P1) 4[4:5:5:5:6:6:7:7:7:8] times, K0 [1:0:1:1:0:1:0:0:1:0].
Cont in patt as established, working C12 on next and every 12th row. Complete as given for pullover A sleeves.

Pullover C neckband
Work as given for jersey A neckband.

Finishing
As given for pullover A.

Bulky Aran cardigan

Sizes
To fit 34 [36:38:40:42:44]in chest
The figures in brackets [] refer to the 36, 38, 40, 42 and 44in sizes respectively
Length to top of shoulder, 24½ [25:25½:26:26½: 27]in
Sleeve seam, 18½ [18½:19½:19½:20½:20½]in

Gauge
9 sts and 12 rows to 2in over st st worked on No.8 knitting needles

Materials
10[11:12:12:12:13] 2oz balls Bear Brand or Fleisher or Botany Shamrock
No.6 knitting needles
No.8 knitting needles
Cable needle. 5 buttons

Back
Using No.6 needles cast on 84 [88:92:98:102: 106] sts. Work 11 rows K1, P1 rib.
Next row (inc row) Rib 3 [5:7:11:13:15] sts, *inc in next st, rib 1, rep from * to last 5 [7:9:

11:13:15] sts, inc in next st, rib to end. 123 [127:131:141:145] sts.
Change to No.8 needles. Commence patt.
1st row P1 [3:5:2:4:6] sts, * make a sl loop in a short length of contrasting yarn and place on needle and on the foll rows sl this marker from one needle to another until patt is established – called sl marker –, K9, (P1 [1:1:2:2:2], K2, P4, K2) 4 times, P1 [1:1:2:2:2], K9, sl marker, *, P1 [1:1:2:2:2], K9, P1 [1:1:2:2:2], rep from * to * once more, P1 [3:5:2:4:6] sts.
2nd row K1 [3:5:2:4:6] sts, *P9, (K1 [1:1:2:2:2], P2, K4, P2) 4 times, K1 [1:1:2:2:2], P9, *, K1 [1:1:2:2:2], P9, K1 [1:1:2:2:2], rep from * to * once more, K1 [3:5:2:4:6] sts.
3rd row P1 [3:5:2:4:6] sts, *sl next 2 sts onto cable needle and hold at back of work, K2 sts then K2 sts from cable needle – called C4B –, K1, sl next 2 sts onto cable needle and hold at front of work, K2 sts then K2 sts from cable needle – called C4F, –, (P1 [1:1:2:2:2], sl next 2 sts onto cable needle and hold at front of work, P2 sts then K2 sts from cable needle – called T4F, –, sl next 2 sts onto cable needle and hold at back of work, K2 sts then P2 sts from cable needle – called T4B –,) 4 times, P1 [1:1:2:2:2], C4B, K1, C4F, *, P1 [1:1:2:2:2], C4B, K1, C4F, P1 [1:1:2:2:2], rep from * to * once more, P1 [3:5:2:4:6] sts.
4th row K1 [3:5:2:4:6] sts, *P9, K3 [3:3:4:4:4], (P4, K5 [5:5:6:6:6]) 3 times, P4, K3 [3:3:4:4:4], P9, *, K1 [1:1:2:2:2], P9, K1 [1:1:2:2:2], rep from * to * once more, K1 [3:5:2:4:6] sts.
5th row P1 [3:5:2:4:6] sts, *K9, P3 [3:3:4:4:4], (K4, P5 [5:5:6:6:6]) 3 times, K4, P3 [3:3:4:4:4], K9, *, K1 [1:1:2:2:2], K9, P1 [1:1:2:2:2], rep from * to * once more, P1 [3:5:2:4:6] sts.
6th row As 4th.
7th row P1 [3:5:2:4:6] sts, *C4B, K1, C4F, (P1 [1:1:2:2:2], T4B, T4F) 4 times, P1 [1:1:2:2: 2], C4B, K1, C4F, *, P1 [1:1:2:2:2], C4B, K1, C4F, P1 [1:1:2:2:2], rep from * to * once more, P1 [3:5:2:4:6] sts.
8th row As 2nd.
These 8 rows form patt. Cont in patt until work measures 15in from beg, ending with a WS row.
Shape raglan armholes
**Bind off 3 [2:1:3:2:1] sts at beg of next 2 rows.
3rd row K2 sts, sl 1, K1, psso, patt to last 4 sts, K2 tog, K2 sts.
4th row P3 sts, patt to last 3 sts, P3 sts. **
Rep last 2 rows until 101 [103:105:107:109:111] sts rem, ending with a WS row.
*** **Next row** K2 sts, sl 1, K2 tog, psso, patt to last 5 sts, K3 tog, K2 sts.

Next row P3 sts, patt to last 3 sts, P3sts
Next row K2 sts, sl 1, K1, psso, patt to last 4 sts, K2 tog, K2 sts.
Next row P3 sts, patt to last 3 sts, P3 sts. ***
Rep last 4 rows until 35 [37:39:41:43:45] sts rem, ending with a RS row.
Next row P3 [4:5:3:4:5] sts, *P2 tog, P1, rep from * to last 5 [6:7:5:6:7] sts, P2 tog, P to end. Bind off rem 25 [27:29:29:31:33] sts.

Left front
Using No.8 needles cast on 25 [25:25:29:29:29] sts for pocket lining. Beg with a K row work 19 [19:27:27:27:27] rows st st.
Next row P1, *inc in next st, P1, rep from * to last 2 [2:2:4:4:4] sts, inc in next st, P to end. 37 [37:37:42:42:42] sts.
Next row P3 [3:3:4:4:4] sts, (K4, P5 [5:5:6:6: 6]) 3 times, K4, P3 [3:3:4:4:4] sts.
Next row K3 [3:3:4:4:4] sts, (P4, K5 [5:5:6:6: 6]) 3 times, P4, K3 [3:3:4:4:4] sts.
Next row (P1 [1:1:2:2:2] sts, T4B, T4F) 4 times, P1 [1:1:2:2:2] sts.
Next row (K1 [1:1:2:2:2] sts, P2, K4, P2) 4 times, K1 [1:1:2:2:2] sts.
Next row (P1 [1:1:2:2:2] sts, K2, P4, K2) 4

times, P1 [1:1:2:2:2] sts.
Slip sts on holder.
Using No.6 needles cast on 42 [44:46:48:50:52] sts. Work 11 rows K1, P1 rib. ****
Next row (inc row) Rib 3 [5:7:11:13:15] sts, *inc in next st, rib 1, rep from * to last 9 [9:9: 7:7:7] sts, inc in next st, rib to end. 58[60:62: 64:66:68] sts.
Change to No.8 needles. Commence patt.
1st row P1 [3:5:2:4:6] sts, sl marker, work from * to * as given for 1st row of back, sl marker, P2. This row establishes patt. Cont in patt as given for back until 16 [16:24:24:24:24] rows have been worked, ending with an 8th patt row.
Place pocket
1st row Patt 11 [13:15:13:15:17] sts, (K2 tog, P1, P2 tog, P1, K2 tog, P1 [1:1:2:2:2]) 4 times, patt to end. 46[48:50:52:54:56] sts.
2nd row Patt 11 sts, beg with K1 work 25 [25:25:30:30:30] sts in K1, P1 rib, patt to end.
3rd row Patt 10 [12:14:11:13:15] sts, work across next 25 [25:25:30:30:30] sts in rib as established, patt to end.
Rep 2nd and 3rd rows twice more, then 2nd row once.
Next row Patt 10 [12:14:11:13:15] sts, bind off next 25 [25:25:30:30:30] sts, patt to end.
Next row Patt 11 sts, work in patt across 37 [37:37:42:42:42] sts of pocket lining, patt to end. 58 [60:62:64:66:68] sts.
Cont in patt until work measures same as back to underarm, ending with a WS row.
Shape raglan armhole
Next row At arm edge, bind off 3 [2:1:3:2:1] sts, patt to end.
Next row Patt to last 3 sts, P3.
Shape front
Next row K2 sts, sl 1, K1, psso, patt to last 2 sts, K2 tog.
Keeping 3 sts at raglan edge in st st cont to dec one st at raglan edge on every other row, *at the same time* dec one st at neck edge on every 4th row until 43 sts rem, ending with a WS row.
Next row K2 sts, sl 1, K2 tog, psso, patt to last 2 sts, K2 tog.
Next row Patt to last 3 sts, P3.
Next row K2 sts, sl 1, K1, psso, patt to end.
Next row Patt to last 3 sts, P3.
Rep last 4 rows until 8 sts rem. Keeping neck edge straight, cont to dec at raglan edge until 5 sts rem, ending with a WS row.
Next row K2 sts, K2 tog, P1.
Next row Patt to last 3 sts, P3.
Next row K3 tog, P1.
Next row P2 sts.
Next row K2 tog. Fasten off.

Right front
Work as given for left front to ****.
Next row (inc row) Rib 9]9:9:7:7:7] sts, *inc in next st, rib 1, rep from * to last 3 [5:7:11:13: 15] sts, inc in next st, rib to end. 58 [60:62:64: 66:68] sts.
Change to No.8 needles. Commence patt.
1st row P2 sts, sl marker, work from * to * as given for 1st row of back, sl marker, P1 [3:5:2: 4:6] sts.
Cont in patt as given for back until 16 [16:24: 24:24:24] rows have been worked, ending with an 8th patt row.
Place pocket
1st row Patt 12 [12:12:13:13:13] sts, (K2 tog, P1, P2 tog, P1, K2 tog, P1 [1:1:2:2:2]) 4 times, patt to end. 46 [48:50:52:54:56] sts.
2nd row Patt 10 [12:14:11:13:15] sts, beg with a K st work 25 [24:25:30:30:30] sts in K1, P1 rib, patt to end.
3rd row Patt 11 sts, work across next 25 [25:25: 30:30:30] sts in rib as established, patt to end.
Rep 2nd and 3rd rows twice more, then 2nd row once.
Next row Patt 11 sts, bind off next 25 [25:25: 30:30:30] sts in rib, patt to end.

Next row Patt 10 [12:14:11:13:15] sts, work in patt across 37 [37:37:42:42:42] pocket lining sts, patt to end. 58 [60:62:64:66:68] sts.
Complete to correspond to left front, reversing all shapings and shaping front as foll:
Next row K2 tog, patt to last 4 sts, K2 tog, K2 sts.
Sleeves
Using No.6 needles cast on 40 [42:44:48:50:52] sts. Work 11 rows K1, P1 rib.
Next row (inc row) Rib 3 [5:5:7:7:9] sts, *inc in next st, rib 1, rep from * to last 5[5:7:7:9:9] sts, inc in next st, rib to end. 57 [59:61:66:68:70] sts.
Change to No.8 needles. Commence patt.
1st row P1 [2:3:3:4:5] sts, sl marker, work from * to * as given for 1st row of back, sl marker, P1 [2:3:3:4:5] sts.
This row establishes patt. Cont in patt as given for back, inc one st at each end of 3rd and every foll 6th [6th:6th:8th:8th:8th] row until there are 83 [85:87:90:92:94] sts, working increased sts into reversed st st. Cont without shaping until sleeve measures 18½ [18½:19½:19½:20½:20½]in from beg, ending with a WS row.
Shape raglan cap
Work as given for back from ** to **, then rep last 2 rows until 41 [41:41:22:22:22] sts rem, ending with a WS row. Work as given for back from *** to ***. Rep last 4 rows until 9 [9:9:10: 10:10] sts rem, ending with a WS row.
Bind off.
Front band
Using No.6 needles cast on 10 sts. Work in K1, P1 rib until band, when slightly stretched, fits up right front, around neck and down left front to beg of front shaping. Mark positions for 5 buttons on right front, first to come ½in above cast on edge and last to come ½in below front shaping with 3 more evenly spaced between. Cont in rib, working buttonholes as markers are reached, as foll:
Next row (buttonhole row) Rib 4 sts, bind off 2 sts, rib to end.
Next row Rib to end, casting on 2 sts above those bound off on previous row.
Cont in rib until band fits down left front to lower edge. Bind off in rib.

Finishing
Press each piece lightly on WS under a damp cloth with a warm iron. Join raglan seams. Join side and sleeve seams. Sew front band in place. Sew pocket linings down. Press seams. Sew on buttons.

55 Checkered cardigan with shawl collar

Sizes
To fit 38 [40:42:44:46]in chest
The figures in brackets [] refer to the 40, 42, 44 and 46in sizes respectively
Length to shoulder, 24 [24¼:24½:24¾:25]in, adjustable
Sleeve seam, 17½ [18:18:18½:18½:19]in, adjustable
Gauge
10½ sts and 14 rows to 2in over patt worked on No.6 knitting needles
Materials
4 [5:5:5:5] paks Bear Brand or Fleisher or Botany Twin-Pak
Knitting Worsted in main color, A
3 [3:3:3:3] paks of contrasting color, B
No.4 knitting needles
No.6 knitting needles
7 buttons

Note

Always carry color not in use across back of work

Back

Using No.4 needles and A, cast on 101 [107:113: 119:125] sts.

1st row K1, *P1, K1, rep from * to end.

2nd row P1, *K1, P1, rep from * to end.

Rep these 2 rows until work measures 2in from beg, ending with a 2nd row. Change to No.6 needles. Commence patt.

1st row Attach B, K0 [K3B: K2B, 1A, 3B: K2A, 3B, 1A, 3B: K0], *K5A, 3B, 1A, 3B, rep from * to last 5 [8:11:14:5] sts, K5A, K0 [K3B: K3B, 1A, 2B: K3B, 1A, 3B, 2A: K0].

2nd row P0 [P3B: P2B, 1A, 3B: P2A, 3B, 1A, 3B: P0], *P5A, 3B, 1A, 3B, rep from * to last 5 [8:11:14:5] sts, P5A, P0 [P3B: P3B, 1A, 2B: P3B, 1A, 3B, 2A: P0].

Rep 1st and 2nd rows twice more.

7th row K0 [K3A: K2A, 1B, 3A: K2B, 3A, 1B, 3A: K0], *K5B, 3A, 1B, 3A, rep from * to last 5 [8:11:14:5] sts, K5B, K0 [K3A: K3A, 1B, 2A: K3A, 1B, 3A, 2B: K0].

8th row P0 [P3A: P2A, 1B, 3A: P2B, 3A, 1B, 3A: P0], *P5B, 3A, 1B, 3A, rep from * to last 5 [8:11:14:5] sts, P5B, P0 [P3A: P3A, 1B, 2A: P3A, 1B, 3A, 2B: P0].

Rep 7th and 8th rows once more.

11th row As 1st.

12th row As 2nd.

13th row As 7th.

14th row As 8th.

15th row As 7th.

16th row As 8th.

These 16 rows form patt and are rep throughout. Cont in patt until work measures 16in from beg, or desired length to underarm ending with a WS row.

Shape armholes

Keeping patt correct, bind off 6 [6:7:8:8] sts at beg of next 2 rows. Dec one st at each end of every other row 7 [8:8:8:9] times. 75 [79:93:87: 91] sts. Cont without shaping until armholes measure 8 [8¼:8½:8¾:9]in from beg, ending with a WS row.

Shape shoulders

Bind off 6 sts at beg of next 6 rows and 6 [7:8:9:10] sts at beg of next 2 rows. Bind off rem 27 [29:31:33:35] sts.

Left front

Using No.4 needles and A, cast on 26 sts for pocket lining. Beg with a K row work 32 rows st st, dec one st at each end of last row. Slip sts on holder.

Using No.4 needles and A, cast on 51 [57:57:63: 63] sts. Work 2in K1, P1 rib as given for back. Change to No.6 needles. Commence patt. **

1st row Attach B, K0 [K1A, 3B, 5A: K1B, 5A: K3A: K0], *K3B, 1A, 3B, 5A, rep from * to last 3 [0:3:0:3] sts, K3B [K0:K3B:K0:K3B].

2nd row P3B [P0: P3B: P0: P3B], *P5A, 3B, 1A, 3B, rep from * to last 0 [9:6:3:0] sts, P0 [P5A, 3B, 1A: P5A, 1B: P3A: P0].

These 2 rows form patt. Cont in patt until 24 rows have been worked.

Place pocket

Next row Patt 12 sts, sl next 24 sts onto holder, with RS of work facing cont in patt across pocket lining sts, patt to end.

Cont in patt until work measures same as back to underarm, ending at armhole edge.

Shape armhole and front edge

Next row Bind off 6 [6:7:8:8] sts, patt to last 2 sts, dec one st.

Dec one st at armhole edge every other row 7 [8:8:8:9] times, *at the same time* cont to dec one st at front edge on every foll 3rd row, until 24 [25:26:27:28] sts rem.

Cont without shaping until armhole measures same as back to shoulder, ending at armhole edge.

Shape shoulder

Bind off at arm edge every other row 6 sts 3 times and 6 [7:8:9:10] sts once.

Right front

Work as given for left front to **.

1st row Attach B, K3B [K0: K3B: K0: K3B], *K5A, 3B, 1A, 3B, rep from * to last 0 [9:6:3:0] sts, K0 [K5A, 3B, 1A: K5A, 1B: K3A: K0].

2nd row P0 [P1A, 3B, 5A: P1B, 5A: P3A: P0], *P3B, 1A, 3B, 5A, rep from * to last 3 [0:3:0:3] sts, P3B [P0: P3B: P0: P3B].

Cont as given for left front until 24 rows have been worked.

Place pocket

Next row Patt 15 [21:21:27:27] sts, sl next 24 sts onto holder, with RS of pocket lining sts facing, cont in patt across sts on holder, patt to end.

Complete to correspond to left front, reversing all shapings.

Sleeves

Using No.4 needles and A, cast on 53 [53:59:59: 59] sts.

Work 2½in K1, P1 rib as given for back. Change to No.6 needles. Commence patt.

1st row Attach B, K5A [K5A: K3B, 5A: K3B, 5A: K3B, 5A], *K3B, 1A, 3B, 5A, rep from * to last 0 [0:3:3:3] sts, K0 [K0: K3B: K3B: K3B].

2nd row P0 [P0: P3B: P3B: P3B], *P5A, 3B, 1A, 3B, rep from * to last 5 [5:8:8:8] sts, P5A [P5A: P5A, 3B: P5A, 3B: P5A, 3B].

These 2 rows form patt. Cont in patt, inc one st at each end of 3rd and every foll 6th row until there are 77 [79:81:83:85] sts, and working increased sts into patt when possible. Cont without shaping until sleeve measures 17½ [18:18½:18½: 19]in from beg, or desired length to underarm, ending with a WS row.

Shape cap

Bind off 6 [6:7:8:8] sts at beg of next 2 rows. Dec one st at each end of next and every other row until 35 sts rem. Bind off 2 sts at beg of next 6 rows and 3 sts at beg of next 4 rows. Bind off rem 11 sts.

Right shawl collar and button band

Join shoulder seams. Using No.4 needles and A, cast on 11 sts.

Work in K1, P1 rib as given for back until band measures 19in from beg, or desired length of front edge to beg of front shaping, ending with a 2nd row.

Shape collar

Next row (RS) Rib to last st, inc one st.

Next row Rib to end.

Rep last 2 rows until there are 40 sts. Cont without shaping until collar fits up front neck to shoulder, ending at outer edge.

Shape curve

Next row Rib 30 sts, turn.

Next row Sl 1, rib to end.

Next row Rib 20 sts, turn.

Next row Sl 1, rib to end.

Next row Rib 10 sts, turn.

Next row Sl 1, rib to end. **

Cont in rib across all sts for 1¼in more, ending at outer edge. Rep from ** to ** once more.

Cont in rib across all sts until collar fits to center back neck, ending at inner edge. Bind off 10 sts at beg of next and every other row 3 times. Mark positions for 7 buttons on right front band, first to come ½in above cast on edge and last to come ¾in below collar shaping, with 5 more evenly spaced between.

Left shawl collar and buttonhole band

Work as given for right half, reversing shaping and working buttonholes as markers are reached, as foll:

Next row (RS) Rib 4 sts, bind off 3 sts, rib to end.

Next row Rib to end, casting on 3 sts above those bound off on previous row.

Finishing

Press each piece under a damp cloth with a warm iron. Join side and sleeve seams. Sew in sleeves. Join right and left shawl collar at center back. Sew on bands and collar to front ddges, having collar seam at center back neck.

Pocket tops Using No.4 needles, A, and with RS of work facing, attach yarn to 24 sts on holder, and work in K1, P1 rib to end. Work 5 more rows rib. Bind off loosely in rib.

Sew down pocket linings and pocket tops. Press all seams. Sew on buttons.

Textured sleeveless vest for man or woman

Sizes

To fit 32 [34:36:38:40:42:44]in bust/chest
The figures in brackets [] refer to the 34, 36, 38, 40, 42 and 44in sizes respectively
Length to shoulder, 22 [22½:23:23½:24:24½: 25]in

Gauge

7 sts and 12 rows to 1in over patt worked on No.4 knitting needles

Materials

7 [8:8:9:10:10:11] skeins Bear Brand or Fleisher or Botany Win Sport
No.3 knitting needles
No.4 knitting needles
6 buttons

Back

Using No.3 needles cast on 94 [100:104:110: 116:122:126] sts. Work 2in K1, P1 rib, ending with a RS row.

Next row Rib 11 [11:10:10:13:13:12] sts, *inc in next st, rib 2 sts, rep from * to last 11 [11:10: 10:13:13:12] sts, inc in next st, rib to end. 119 [127:133:141:147:155:161] sts.

Change to No.4 needles. Commence patt.

1st row (RS) K to end.

2nd row K to end.

3rd row K1, *sl 1 p-wise, K1, rep from * to end.

4th row K1, *ytf, sl 1 p-wise, ytb, K1, rep from * to end.

These 4 rows form patt. Cont in patt until work measures 13½ [13½:14:14:14½:14½:15]in from beg, ending with a WS row.

Shape armholes

Keeping patt correct, bind off 4[4:5:5:5:6:6] sts at beg of next 2 rows. Dec one st at each end of next and every other row until 91 [95:101:107: 111:115:119] sts rem. Cont without shaping until armholes measure 8 [8½:8½:9:9:9½:9½]in from beg, ending with a WS row.

Shape shoulders

Bind off 7 [7:8:8:7:9:10] sts at beg of next 6 [2:6:2:2:4:4] rows and 8 [8:9:9:10:10:10] sts at beg of next 2 [6:2:6:6:4:4] rows. Bind off rem 33 [33:35:37:37:39:39] sts.

Left front

Using No.3 needles cast on 46 [50:52:56:58:60: 62] sts. Work 2in K1, P1 rib, ending with a RS row.

Next row Rib 5 [7:5:6:8:6:4] sts, *inc in next st, rib 2 sts, rep from * to last 5 [7:5:7:8:6:4] sts, inc in next st, rib to end. 59 [63:67:71:73: 77:81] sts.

Change to No.4 needles. Work in patt as given for back until front measures same as back to underarm, ending with a WS row.

Shape armhole and neck edge

Next row Bind off 4 [4:5:5:5:6:6] sts, patt to last 2 sts, work 2 tog.

109

Keeping patt correct, dec one st at armhole edge on every other row *at the same time* dec one st at neck edge on every foll 6th [6th:5th:5th:6th: 6th:5th] row until 41 [42:46:49:50:52:53] sts rem. Keeping armhole edge straight, cont to dec at neck edge only as before until 29 [31:33:35: 37:38:40] sts rem. Cont without shaping until armhole measures same as back to shoulder, ending at armhole edge.

Shape shoulder
Bind off 7 [7:8:8:7:9:10] sts every other row 3 [1:3:1:1:2:2] times and 8 [8:9:9:10:10:10] sts every other row 1 [3:1:3:3:2:2] times.

Right front
Work as given for left front reversing all shapings.

Front band
Using No.3 needles cast on 11 sts.
1st row K1, *P1, K1, rep from * to end.
2nd row P1, *K1, P1, rep from * to end.
Rep these 2 rows for ½in.
Next row (buttonhole row) Rib 4 sts, bind off 3 sts, rib to end.
Next row Rib to end, casting on 3 sts above those bound off on previous row.
Cont in rib, working 5 more buttonholes in this way at intervals of 2¼ [2¼:2½:2½:2½:2½:2½]in measured from base of previous buttonhole. Cont until band is long enough, when slightly stretched, to fit up left front, across back neck and down right front. Bind off in rib.

Armhole edging
Join shoulder seams. Using No.3 needles and with RS of work facing, pick up and K100 [104: 104:108:108:112:112] sts evenly around armhole edge.
Next row P to end.
Beg with a K row work 4 rows st st.
Next row P all sts to mark fold line.
Beg with a P row work 7 rows st st. Bind off loosely.

Finishing
Press each piece under a damp cloth with a warm iron for wool, omitting ribbing. Join side seams. Fold armhole edges in half to WS and sl st down. Sew on front bands, placing buttonholes on right front for woman and left front for man. Sew on buttons.

Cardigans for mother and daughter

Sizes
To fit 24 [27:30:33:36]in chest/bust
The figures in brackets [] refer to the 27, 30, 33 and 36in sizes respectively
Length to shoulder, 14 [16:18:20:22]in
Sleeve seam, 11 [13:15:17:17½]in
Gauge
7½ sts to 1in and 32 rows to 3in over patt worked on No.3 needles

Materials
6[7:9:10:12] skeins Dawn Wintuk Baby Yarn
No.2 knitting needles
No.3 knitting needles
4[4:5:6:6] buttons

Back
Using No.2 needles cast on 93[105:117:129: 141] sts.
1st row K1, *P1, K1, rep from * to end.
2nd row P1, *K1, P1, rep from * to end.
Rep these 2 rows 3 times more, then row 1 once

more. Change to No.3 needles.
Commence patt.
1st row (WS) K3 sts, *P3, K3, rep from * to end.
2nd row P3 sts, *K3, P3, rep from * to end.
3rd row As 1st.
4th row K 3rd st in front of first 2 sts, then K first and 2nd sts and sl all 3 sts off needle tog – called Cr3 –, *K3, Cr3, rep from * to end.
5th row As 2nd.
6th row As 1st.
7th row As 2nd.
8th row K3 sts, *Cr3, K3, rep from * to end.
These 8 rows form patt. Cont in patt until work measures 9 [10½:12:13:14]in from beg, ending with a WS row.
Shape armholes
Bind off 4[5:5:6:6] sts at beg of next 2 rows and 2 sts at beg of next 2[2:4:4:6] rows. 81[91:99: 109:117] sts. Dec one st at each end every other row 2[3:3:4:4] times. 75[83:91:99:107] sts. Cont without shaping until armholes measure 5[5½:6:7:8]in from beg, ending with a WS row.
Shape shoulders
Bind off 6[6:5:6:6] sts at beg of next 6[6:8:8:8] rows and 5[7:7:5:7] sts at beg of next 2 rows. Slip rem 29[33:37:41:45] sts on holder.

Left front
Using No.2 needles cast on 61[67:73:85:91] sts.
1st row *K1, P1, rep from * to last 19[19:19: 25:25] sts, K9[9:9:12:12] sts, sl 1, K to end.
2nd row P19[19:19:25:25] sts, *K1, P1, rep from * to end.
Rep these 2 rows 3 times more, then first of them again. Change to No.3 needles.
Commence patt.
1st row (WS) P19[19:19:25:25] sts, *P3, K3, rep from * to end.
2nd row *K3, P3, rep from * to last 19[19:19: 25:25] sts, K9[9:9:12:12] sts, sl 1, K to end.
3rd row As 1st.
4th row *Cr3, K3, rep from * to last 19[19:19: 25:25] sts, K9[9:9:12:12] sts, sl 1, K to end.
5th row P19[19:19:25:25] sts, *K3, P3, rep from * to end.
6th row *K3, P3, rep from * to last 19[19:19: 25:25] sts, K9[9:9:12:12] sts, sl 1, K to end.
7th row As 5th.
8th row *K3, Cr3, rep from * to last 19[19:19: 25:25] sts, K9[9:9:12:12] sts, sl 1, K to end.
These 8 rows form patt. Cont in patt until work measures same as back to underarm, ending at armhole edge with a WS row.
Shape armhole
At arm edge, bind off 4[5:5:6:6] sts once and 2 sts every other row at beg of next 1[1:2:2:3] rows. 55[60:64:75:79] sts. Dec one st at armhole edge every other row 3[4:4:5:5] times. 52[56:60: 70:74] sts. Cont without shaping until armhole measures 3½[4:4½:5:6]in from beg, ending at front edge.
Shape neck
Bind off at neck edge every other row 19[19: 19:25:25] sts once, 4[4:5:5:6] sts once, 2[3:3: 3:4] sts once and 2 sts every other row at neck edge 1[1:1:2:2] times. Dec one st at neck edge every other row 2[3:4:4:4] times. Cont without shaping until armhole measures same as back to shoulder, ending at armhole edge.
Shape shoulder
At neck edge, bind off 6[6:5:6:6] sts every other row 3[3:4:4:4] times and 5[7:7:5:7] sts once.
Right front
Mark positions for buttons on left front edge, first on last row of welt and last ½in below neck edge, with rem equally spaced between.
Using No.2 needles cast on 61[67:73:85:91] sts.
1st row K9[9:9:12:12] sts, sl 1, K9[9:9:12:12] sts, *P1, K1, rep from * to end.
2nd row *P1, K1, rep from * to last 19[19:19: 25:25] sts, P to end.

Rep these 2 rows 3 times more.
Next row (buttonhole row) K3[3:3:5:5] sts, bind off 3 sts, K3[3:3:4:4] sts, sl 1, K3[3:3:4:4] sts, bind off 3 sts, K3[3:3:5:5] sts, *P1, K1, rep from * to end.
Change to No.3 needles.
Next row *K3, P3, rep from * to last 19[19:19: 25:25] sts, P, to end casting on 3 sts above those bound-off on previous row.
Complete to correspond to left front, reversing all shapings and working buttonholes as before as markers are reached.

Sleeves
Using No.2 needles cast on 45[45:51:51:57] sts. Work 9 rows rib as given for back. Change to No.3 needles. Cont in patt as given for back, inc one st at each end of every 8th row until there are 61[61:67:67:73] sts, then at each end of every foll 6th row until there are 71[77:83: 89:95] sts, working increased sts into patt when possible. Cont without shaping until sleeve measures 11[13:15:17:17½]in from beg, ending with a WS row.
Shape cap
Bind off 4[5:5:6:6] sts at beg of next 2 rows. Dec one st at each end every other row until 45[47:51:53:57] sts rem, ending with a WS row. Bind off 2 sts every other row 8[8:10:10:12] times, 3 sts every other row 4 times and 4 sts every other row twice. Bind off rem 9[11:11: 13:13] sts.

Neckband
Join shoulder seams. Using No.2 needles and with RS of work facing, attach yarn at beg of patt at right front neck edge, pick up and K 25[27:29:31:33] sts up right front neck, K across back neck sts, pick up and K 25[27:29: 31:33] sts down left front neck to beg of patt. Beg with a P row work 5[5:5:9:9] rows st st.
Next row (picot row) K1, *ytf, K2 tog, rep from * to end. Beg with a P row work 6[6:6:10: 10] rows st st. Bind off.

Finishing
Press each piece under a damp cloth with a warm iron. Sew in sleeves. Join side and sleeve seams. Fold front bands in half to WS at sl st line and sl st down. Fold neckband in half to WS at picot row and sl st down. Button-hole st around double buttonholes. Sew on buttons.

Ribbed jumpsuit and matching hat

Sizes
To fit 22 [24]in chest
The figures in brackets [] refer to the 24in size only
Length to shoulder, 26½ [30½]in
Sleeve seam, 8 [9½]in
Gauge
6 sts and 8 rows to 1in over st st worked on No.5 needles.
Materials
6[7] balls Reynolds Classique
No.3 knitting needles
No.5 knitting needles
12 [14]in open-end zipper

Leg
Using No.3 needles cast on 62[66] sts.
1st row K2, *P2, K2, rep from * to end.
2nd row P2, *K2, P2, rep from * to end.
These 2 rows form patt. Cont in patt until work measures 1½in from beg. Change to No.5 needles. Cont in patt, inc one st at each end of

every 8th row until there are 82[90] sts. Cont without shaping until work measures 12 [15]in from beg, ending with a WS row.

Shape crotch

Bind off 4 sts at beg of next 2 rows; then 2 sts at beg of next 2[4] rows. Dec one st at each end of next row. 68[72] sts. Rib 1 row, ending with a WS row. Slip sts on holder.

Work a 2nd piece in same manner.

Join pieces for body

Next row K3 sts, rib 65[69] sts, with RS of first piece facing, rib 65[69] sts, K3 sts. 136[144] sts.

Next row K3 sts, rib to last 3 sts, K3 sts. Keeping 3 sts each end in garter st throughout, cont in rib until work measures 17 [20½]in from beg, ending with a WS row.

Shape seat

Next row K3 sts, rib 104[108] sts, turn.

Next row Rib 78 sts, turn.

Next row Rib 72 sts, turn.

Next row Rib 66 sts, turn.

Cont in this way, working 6 sts less on every row until there are 30 sts in center. Cont in rib across all sts until work measures 22 [25½]in from beg, ending with a WS row.

Divide for armholes

Next row Rib 31[33] sts, bind off 6 sts, rib to last 37[39] sts, bind off 6 sts, rib to end.

Complete left front first. Rib 1 row. Dec one st at arm edge every other row 3[4] times. 28[29] sts. Cont without shaping until armhole measures 3½ [4]in from beg, ending with a WS row.

Shape shoulder

Next row Bind off 14 sts, turn and slip rem 14[15] sts on holder for neck. Break off yarn. With WS of work facing, attach yarn to center 62[66] sts for back. Rib 1 row. Dec one st at each end every other row 3[4] times. 56[58] sts Cont without shaping until armholes measure 3½ [4]in from beg, ending with a WS row.

Shape shoulder

Next row Bind off 14 sts, rib to last 14 sts, bind off to end. Slip rem 28[30] sts on holder.

With WS of work facing, attach yarn to rem sts and work right front to correspond to left front, reversing shaping

Sleeves

Using No.3 needles cast on 46[50] sts. Beg first row with P2, work 2in K2, P2 rib. Change to No.5 needles. Cont in rib, inc one st at each end of next and every foll 4th[6th] row until there are 66[70] sts. Cont without shaping until sleeve measures 8 [9½]in from beg, ending with a WS row.

Shape cap

Bind off 3 sts at beg of next 2 rows; then 2 sts at beg of next 2 rows. Dec one st at each end of every other row until 20[22] sts rem. Cont without shaping on these 20[22] sts for length of shoulder to neck edge, ending with a WS row. Slip sts on holder.

Neckband

Join saddle tops of sleeves to front and back shoulders. Using No.3 needles and with RS of work facing, rib across all sts on holders. 96[104] sts. Keeping 3 sts at each end in garter st, cont in rib for 3in. Bind off loosely in rib.

Finishing

Press lightly. Sew in sleeves. Join sleeve seams. Fold neckband in half to WS and sl st down. Join front seam leaving 12 [14]in open for zipper. Sew in zipper. Join leg seams. Press seams lightly under a damp cloth with a warm iron.

Hat

Using No.3 needles cast on 102 sts. Work 3in K2, P2 rib. Change to No.5 needles. Cont in rib until work measures 7½in from beg, ending with a WS row.

Shape top

Next row Rib 8 sts, *sl 1, K2 tog, psso, K3 tog, rib 20 sts, (P3 tog) twice, *, rib 20 sts, rep from * to * once, rib 10 sts. 86 sts.

Work 5 rows rib without shaping.

Next row Rib 6 sts, * (P3 tog) twice, rib 16 sts, sl 1, K2 tog, psso, K3 tog, *, rib 16 sts, rep from * to *, rib 8 sts. 70 sts.

Work 5 rows rib without shaping.

Next row Rib 4 sts, *sl 1, K2 tog, psso, K3 tog, rib 12 sts, (P3 tog) twice, *, rib 12 sts, rep from * to *, rib 6 sts. 54 sts.

Work 3 rows rib without shaping.

Next row K2, *(P3 tog) twice, rib 8 sts, sl 1, K2 tog, psso, K3 tog, *, rib 8 sts, rep from * to *, P2, K2, 38 sts.

Work 3 rows rib without shaping.

Next row *Sl 1, K2 tog, psso, K3 tog, rib 4 sts, (P3 tog) twice, *, rib 4 sts, rep from * to *, K2. 22 sts.

Rib 1 row. Break off yarn, thread through rem sts, draw up and fasten off.

Finishing

Join seam. Make a pompon and sew to top. Press seam very lightly under a damp cloth with a warm iron.

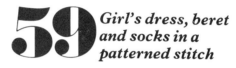

59 *Girl's dress, beret and socks in a patterned stitch*

Sizes

To fit 28 [31:34]in chest

The figures in brackets [] refer to the 31 and 34in sizes respectively

Jacket length to shoulder, 16½ [18:19½]in

Sleeve seam, 14 [15:16]in

Skirt length, 18 [19:20]in

Gauge

5½ sts and 7½ rows to 1in over st st worked on No.5 needles

Materials

10[11:13] balls Spinnerin Mona

No.3 knitting needles;

No.5 knitting needles

One cable needle

Five buttons

Waist length of elastic

Cardigan back

Using No.3 needles cast on 77[81:85] sts.

1st row K1, *P1, K1, rep from * to end.

2nd row P1, *K1, P1, rep from * to end.

Rep these 2 rows for 1in, ending with a 2nd row. Change to No.5 needles. Beg with a K row cont in st st until work measures 10½ [11½: 12½]in from beg, ending with a P row.

Shape armholes

Bind off 5[4:3] sts at beg of next 2 rows. Dec one st at each end every other row until 61[65:69] sts rem. Cont without shaping until armholes measure 6 [6½:7]in from beg, ending with a P row.

Shape shoulders

Bind off 6 sts at beg of next 4 rows; then 6[7:8] sts at beg of next 2 rows. Slip rem 25[27:29] sts on holder.

Cardigan left front

Using No.3 needles cast on 51[59:67] sts. Work 1in rib as given for back, ending with a 2nd row. Change to No.5 needles. Commence patt.

1st row (RS) P2, *K6, P2, rep from * to last 9 sts, turn and slip 9 sts on holder. 42[50:58] sts.

2nd row K2, *P2, P2 winding yarn twice round needle on each st, P2, K2, rep from * to end.

3rd row P2, *sl next 2 sts on cable needle and hold at back of work, K next st dropping extra loop, K2 from cable needle, sl next st on cable needle and hold at front of work dropping extra loop, K2 sts, K1 from cable needle – called C6 –, P2, rep from * to end.

4th row K2, *P6, K2, rep from * to end.

These 4 rows form patt. Cont in patt until work measures same as back to underarm, ending with a WS row.

Shape armhole

Bind off 5[6:8] sts at beg of next row. Work 1 row. Dec one st at arm edge, every other row until 34[40:45] sts rem. Cont without shaping until armhole measures 4 [4½:5]in from beg, ending at armhole edge.

Shape neck

Next row Patt 28[32:35] sts, turn and slip rem 6[8:10] sts on holder.

At neck edge bind off 3 sts; then 2 sts every other row twice. Dec one st at neck edge every other row 3 times, then cont without shaping until armhole measures same as back to shoulder, ending at armhole edge.

Shape shoulder

At arm edge bind off 6[7:8] sts every other row twice, then 6[8:9] sts once.

Cardigan right front

Work as given for left front, reversing all shaping.

Sleeves

Using No.3 needles cast on 41[45:49] sts. Work 2in rib as given for back, ending with a 2nd row and inc one st in center of last row. 42[46; 50] sts. Change to No.5 needles. Commence patt.

1st row K4[6:8] sts, P2, *K6, P2, rep from * 3 times more, K4[6:8] sts.

2nd row P4[6:8] sts, K2, *P2, P2 winding yarn twice round needle on each st, P2, K2, rep from * 3 times more, P4[6:8] sts.

3rd row K4[6:8] sts, P2, *C6, P2, rep from * 3 times more, K4[6:8] sts.

4th row P4[6:8] sts, K2, *P6, K2, rep from * 3 times more, P4[6:8] sts.

These 4 rows set patt. Cont in patt, inc one st at each end of next and every foll 8th row, working extra sts in st st, until there are 62[66: 70] sts. Cont without shaping until sleeve measures 14 [15:16]in from beg, ending with a WS row.

Shape cap

Bind off 5 sts at beg of next 2 rows. Dec one st at each end every other row until 40[42:44] sts rem. Bind off 2 sts at beg of next 8[8:10]; then 3 sts at beg of next 4 rows. Bind off rem 12[14:12] sts.

Left front band

Sl 9 sts on holder onto No.3 needle, with RS of work facing inc in loop before first st, rib to end. Cont in rib until band fits along front edge to neck edge, when slightly stretched, ending with a WS row. Slip sts on holder. Tack band in place and mark positions for 5 buttons, first in first row above welt and last on last RS row, with 3 more equally spaced between.

Right front band

Sl 9 sts on holder onto No.3 needle, with WS of work facing inc in loop before first st, rib to end.

Next row Rib 3 sts, bind off 3 sts, rib to end.

Next row Rib 4 sts, cast on 3 sts, rib to end.

Complete to correspond to left front band, work buttonholes as markers are reached.

Neckband

Join shoulder seams. Using No.3 needles and with RS of work facing, rib across sts of right

front band and right front neck working last st of band tog with first st of front neck, pick up and K 18 sts up side of neck, K across back neck sts, pick up and K 18 sts down other side of neck, work across left front neck and left front band sts, working 2 tog as before. 91[97:103] sts. Cont in rib for 1in. Bind off in rib.

Finishing
Press lightly. Sew in sleeves. Join side and sleeve seams. Sew on front bands. Sew on buttons.

Skirt back
Using No.3 needles cast on 89[97:105] sts. Work ½in rib as given for cardigan back, inc one st in st in center of last row. 90[98:106] sts. Change to No.5 needles. Cont in patt as given for cardigan left front until work measures 17[18:19]in from beg, or 1in less than desired length, ending with a WS row and dec one st in center of last row. Change to No.3 needles. Work 2in rib as given at beg. Bind off in rib.

Skirt front
Using No.3 needles cast on 97[105:113] sts. Work as given for skirt back.

Finishing
Press lightly. Join side seams. Fold ribbing at top in half to WS and sl st down. Thread elastic to measurement through waist.

Socks
Using No.3 needles cast on 55[59:63] sts. Work 1in rib as given for cardigan back, ending with a 2nd row and inc one st in center of last row. 56[60:64] sts.
Change to No.5 needles.
Next row K11[13:15] sts, P2, *K6, P2, rep from * 3 times more, K11[13:15] sts.
Next row P11[13:15]; *K2, P6; repeat from * 3 times, K2, P11 [13:15]. These 2 rows form the pattern. Cont in patt until work measures 4 [4½:5]in from beg, ending with a WS row.
Shape leg
Next row K1, K2 tog, patt to last 3 sts, sl 1, K1, psso, K1.
Cont dec in this way on every foll 6th row until 44[46:48] sts rem. Cont without shaping until work measures 12 [13:14]in from beg, ending with a WS row.
Divide for heel
Next row K10 sts, turn, sl next 24[26:28] sts on holder and leave for instep.
Next row P10 sts, then P across the 10 sts at other end of row.
Cont on these sts in st st for 2 [2¼:2½]in, ending with a P row.
Turn heel
Next row K12 sts, K2 tog, turn.
Next row P5 sts, P2 tog, turn.
Next row K6 sts, K2 tog, turn.
Cont to work one more st on every row until all sts are worked in, ending with a P row. 12 sts. Break off yarn.
With RS of work facing, attach yarn to beg of heel, pick up and K 10[11:12] sts down side of heel, K12 heel sts, then pick up and K 10[11:12] sts up other side of heel. 32[34:36] sts.
Next row P to end.
Next row K1, K2 tog, K to last 3 sts, sl 1, K1, psso, K1.
Rep last 2 rows 5 times more. Cont without shaping until work measures 5 [5½:6]in from where sts were picked up at heel, ending with a P row.
Shape toe
Next row K1, K2 tog, K to last 3 sts, sl 1, K1, psso, K1.
Next row P to end.
Rep last 2 rows 4[5:6] times more. Slip sts on holder to be woven together later.
Work instep
Sl instep sts onto No.5 needle, with RS of work facing attach yarn, K3[4:5] sts, patt 18 sts, K3[4:5] sts. Cont in patt as now set until instep measures same as under part of foot to toe, ending with a RS row.
Next row P3[4:5] sts, (K2 tog, P6) twice, K2 tog, P3[4:5] sts.
Shape toe
Work as given for under part of foot and P2 tog in center of last row. Weave sts together.
Finishing
Press lightly. Join back seam. Join side seams of foot.

Beret
Using No.3 needles cast on 101 sts. Work 1in rib as given for cardigan back, ending with a 2nd row.
Change to No.5 needles.
Next row K into front and back of every st. 202 sts.
Next row K2, *P6, K2, rep from * to end.
Cont in patt as given for cardigan front for 28 rows.
Next row P2 tog, *patt 6 sts, P2 tog, rep from * to end. 176 sts.
Work 7 more rows patt working P1 instead of P2 throughout.
Next row P1, *patt 5 sts, sl 1, K1, psso, rep from * to last 7 sts, patt 6 sts, P1. 152 sts.
Work 7 more rows patt without any P sts between. Change to No.3 needles.
Next row K2 tog, *P1, K1, rep from * to end. 151 sts.
Next row P1, *K1, P1, rep from * to end.
Next row Rib 14 sts, (sl 1, K2 tog, psso, rib 27 sts) 4 times, sl 1, K2 tog, psso, rib 14 sts. 141 sts.
Next row Rib to end.
Next row Rib 12 sts, (sl 1, K1, psso, K1, K2 tog, rib 23 sts) 4 times, sl 1, K1, psso, K1, K2 tog, rib 12 sts. 131 sts.
Next row Rib 12 sts, (P3, rib 23 sts) 4 times, P3, rib 12 sts.
Next row Rib 12 sts, (sl 1, K2 tog, psso, rib 23 sts) 4 times, sl 1, K2 tog, psso, rib 12 sts. 121 sts.
Next row Rib to end.
Cont to dec in this way every other row until 71 sts rem, ending with a RS row.
Next row Rib 6 sts, (P3 tog, rib 11 sts) 4 times, P3 tog, rib 6 sts.
Next row Rib 4 sts, (sl 1, K1, psso, K1, K2 tog, rib 7 sts) 4 times, sl 1, K1, psso, K1. K2 tog, rib 4 sts.
Next row Rib 4 sts, (P3 tog, rib 7 sts) 4 times, P3 tog, rib 4 sts. 41 sts.
Cont dec in this way on every row until 21 sts rem.
Next row K1, *K2 tog, rep from * to end. Break off yarn, thread through rem sts and fasten off.

Finishing
Press lightly. Join seam.

60 *One-piece dress with cabled bodice*

Sizes
To fit 22 [24:26:28]in chest
The figures in brackets [] refer to the 24, 26 and 28in sizes respectively
Length to shoulder, 13½ [14½:16½:19½]in
Sleeve seam, 1½ [1½:2:2]in
Gauge
6 sts and 8 rows to 1in over st st worked on No.4 needles

Materials
8[9:11:12] balls Reynolds Cascatelle
No.2 knitting needles
No.4 knitting needles
One cable needle
Set of 4 No.2 double-pointed needles

Back
Using No.2 needles cast on 100[106:120:130] sts. Beg with a K row work 1in st st, ending with a K row.
Next row K all sts tbl to form hemline.
Change to No.4 needles. Beg with a K row cont in st st until work measures 1½ [1½:2:2]in from hemline, ending with a P row.
Shape skirt
Next row K19[20:23:25] sts. K2 tog, K19[20:23:25] sts, sl 1, K1, psso, K16[18:20:22] sts, K2 tog, K19[20:23:25] sts, sl 1, K1, psso, K19 [20:23:25] sts.
Beg with a P row work 3[3:5:5] rows st st.
Next row K19[20:23:25] sts, K2 tog, K17[18:21:23] sts, sl 1, K1, psso, K16[18:20:22] sts, K2 tog, K17[18:21:23] sts, sl 1, K1, psso, K19 [20:23:25] sts.
Beg with a P row work 3[3:5:5] rows st st.
Cont dec in this way on next and every foll 4th [4th:6th:6th] row until 68[74:80:86] sts rem.
Cont without shaping until work measures 5½ [6½:8:9½]in from hemline, ending with a P row. Commence bodice patt.
1st row P2, *K4, P2, rep from * to end.
2nd row K2, *P4, K2, rep from * to end.
Rep these 2 rows once more.
5th row P2, *sl next 2 sts on cable needle and hold at front of work, K2 sts, then K2 from cable needle — called C4F —, P2, rep from * to end.
6th row As 2nd.
7th row As 1st.
8th row As 2nd.
These 8 rows form patt. Cont in patt until work measures 9 [9½:11:13½]in from hemline, ending with a WS row.

Shape armholes
Bind off 4 sts at beg of next 2 rows.
Next row K3 sts, K2 tog, patt to last 5 sts, sl 1, K1, psso, K3.
Next row P4 sts, patt to last 4 sts, P4.
Next row K4 sts, patt to last 4 sts, K4.
Next row P4 sts, patt to last 4 sts, P4.
Cont to dec in this way at each end of next and every foll 4th row until 46[50:56:60] sts rem.
Work 1[1:3:3] rows after last dec row.
Shape shoulders
Bind off 6[7:7:8] sts at beg of next 2 rows and 7[7:8:8] sts at beg of next 2 rows. Slip rem 20 [22:26:28] sts on holder.

Front
Work as given for back until 48[52:58:62] sts rem, then work 1 row after last dec row, ending with a WS row.
Shape neck
Next row Patt 16[17:18:19] sts, turn and slip rem sts on holder.
Next row Dec one st, patt to end.
Next row K3 sts, K2 tog, patt to end.
Next row Dec one st, patt to end.
Work 0[0:2:2] more rows without shaping.
Shape shoulder
At arm edge bind off 6[7:7:8] sts once and 7[7:8:8] sts once. With RS of work facing, sl first 16[18:22:24] sts on holder and leave for center neck, attach yarn to rem sts and patt to end. Complete to correspond to first side, reversing all shapings.

Sleeves
Using No.2 needles cast on 46[50:50:54] sts.
1st row K2, *P2, K2, rep from * to end.

2nd row P2, *K2, P2, rep from * to end.
Rep these 2 rows 1[1:2:2] times more. Change to No.4 needles. Beg with a K row cont in st st, inc one st at each end of first row, then cont without shaping until sleeve measures 1½ [1½:2: 2]in from beg, ending with a P row. 48[52:52: 56] sts.

Shape cap
Bind off 4 sts at beg of next 2 rows. Dec one st each end of next and every foll 4th row as given for back until 38[42:38:42] sts rem. Work 3 rows without shaping after last dec row. Cont to dec in this way at each end of next and every other row until 16[16:18:18] sts rem. Cont on these sts without shaping for length of shoulder to neck edge, ending with a P row. Slip sts on holder.

Neckband
Sew saddle top of sleeves to back and front shoulders. Using set of 4 No.2 needles and with RS of work facing, K across all sts on holders dec one st at each back seam and pick up and K3[3:5:5] sts up each side of front neck. 72[76:92:96] sts. Join. Work in rounds of K2, P2 rib for 1½ [1½:2:2]in. Bind off loosely in rib.

Finishing
Press each piece under a dry cloth with a cool iron. Sew in sleeves. Join side and sleeve seams. Fold neckband in half to WS and sl st down. Turn hem to WS at lower edge and sl st down.

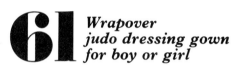

Wrapover judo dressing gown for boy or girl

Sizes
To fit 24 [26:28]in chest
The figures in brackets [] refer to the 26 and 28in sizes respectively
Length to shoulder, 20 [23:26]in
Sleeve seam, 9½ [11:12½]in

Gauge
7½ sts and 10 rows to 1in over patt worked on No.3 needles

Materials
6[7:7] balls Bear Brand or Fleisher Win-Sport in main color, A
2 balls of contrast color, B
No.2 knitting needles
No.3 knitting needles

Back
Using No.2 needles and A, cast on 120[127: 134] sts. Beg with a K row work ½in st st, ending with a K row.
Next row K all sts tbl to form hemline.
Change to No.3 needles. Commence patt.
1st row K to end.
2nd row K1, *P6,K1, rep from * to end.
These 2 rows form patt and are rep throughout. Cont in patt until work measures 1½ [2:2½]in from hemline, ending with a WS row. Dec one st at each end of next and every foll 10th[12th: 14th] row until 98[105:112] sts rem. Cont without shaping until work measures 14½ [17: 19½]in from hemline, ending with a WS row.

Shape armholes
Bind off 5 sts at beg of next 2 rows; then 2 sts at beg of next 6 rows. Dec 1 st at each end of every other row 3[4:5] times. 70[75:80] sts. Cont without shaping until armholes measure 5½ [6:6½]in from beg, ending with a WS row.

Shape shoulders
Bind off 4[5:5] sts at beg of next 4 rows, then 5[5:6] sts at beg of next 4 rows. Break off A and attach B. Change to No.2 needles. K 1 row dec one st in center of row on 24 and 28in

sizes only. 33[35:35] sts.
**Next row P1, *K1, P1, rep from * to end.
Next row K1, *P1, K1, rep from * to end.
Next row P1, *K1, P1, rep from * to end.
Next row (picot hem) K1, *ytf, K2 tog, rep from * to end.
Next row P1, *K1, P1, rep from * to end.
Next row K1, *P1, K1, rep from * to end.
Bind off loosely in rib. **

Left front
Using No.2 needles and A, cast on 78[85:92] sts. Beg with a K row work ½in st st, ending with a K row.
Next row K all sts tbl to form hemline.
Change to No.3 needles. Cont in patt as given for back until work measures 1½ [2:2½]in from hemline, ending with a WS row. Dec one st at beg of next and every foll 10th[12th:14th] row until 67[74:81] sts rem. Cont without shaping until work measures 20[24:28] rows less than back to underarm, ending with a WS row.

Shape front edge
Dec one st at front edge of every other row until 57[62:67] sts rem, ending with a WS row.

Shape armhole
Cont dec at front edge on every other row as before, *at the same time* bind off 5 sts at beg of next row, then 2 sts every other row 3 times, then dec one st at arm edge every other row 3[4:5] times. Cont to dec at front edge only on every other row until 18[20:22] sts rem. Cont without shaping until armhole measures same as back to shoulder, ending with a WS row.

Shape shoulder
Bind off 4[5:5] sts at beg of next 2 rows, then 5[5:6] sts at beg of next 2 rows.

Right front
Work as given for left front, reversing all shaping.

Sleeves
Using No.3 needles and A, cast on 59[61:63] sts.
1st row K to end.
2nd row P1[2:3] sts. K1, *P6, K1, rep from * to last 1[2:3] sts. P1[2:3].
These 2 rows set patt. Cont in patt, inc one st at each end of 13th and every foll 12th row until there are 71[75:79] sts. Cont without shaping until sleeve measures 9½ [11:12½]in from beg, or desired length to underarm, ending with a WS row.

Shape cap
Bind off 5 sts at beg of next 2 rows. Dec one st at each end of every other row 14[15:16] times. 33[35:37] sts. Bind off 2 sts at beg of next 6 rows, then 3 sts at beg of next 4 rows. Bind off rem 9[11:13] sts.

Sleeve edging
Using No.2 needles, B and with RS of work facing, pick up and K 53[55:57] sts around lower edge of sleeve. Work as given for back neck from ** to **

Front borders
Using No.2 needles, B and with RS of work facing, pick up and K 151[163:175] sts up right front edge beg at hemline. Work as given for back neck from ** to **. Work left front border in same way, beg at shoulder.

Finishing
Press each piece under a damp cloth with a warm iron. Join shoulder seams. Sew in sleeves. Join side and sleeve seams. Turn hem to WS at lower edge and sl st down. Turn front borders, back neck border and sleeve edges to WS at picot row and sl st down.
Press seams. Using B, make a thick cord sash to tie around waist.

Quick-to-knit plaid blanket

Size
Before doubling approximately 72in by 142in
Gauge
4 sts and 5 rows to 4in
Materials
Spinnerin Wintuk Sport
22 skeins main color A, gray
21 skeins first contrast B, black
6 skeins 2nd contrast C, gold
6 skeins 3rd contrast D, flame
One pair Bernat Aero Jackpin needles ½in
One No.K crochet hook
Note. 6 strands are used together throughout. Take both ends of each of 3 balls to obtain 6 threads.

Blanket
1st strip
Using 6 strands of B cast on 18 sts.
1st row *K1, P1, rep from * to end.
Work 6 rows st st beg with a K row.
Continue in st st working in stripes thus:
*2 rows A, 1 row B, 2 rows C, 1 row B, 2 rows A, 7 rows B, 7 rows A, 2 rows D, 1 row A, 2 rows C, 1 row A, 2 rows D, 7 rows A, 7 rows B, rep from *3 times then work 2 rows A, 1 row B, 2 rows C, 1 row B, 2 rows A and 6 rows B.
Last row Using B, *K1, P1, rep from * to end.
Bind off. Work 3 more strips in the same manner.

Finishing
Finish off all ends securely.
Sew strips together lengthwise.
Using No.K crochet hook and 6 strands of C work a chain the same length as the strip seam. Finish off ends. Work 2 more chains the same length. Pin chains in place along seam and from wrong side sew securely in place.
Using 6 strands of D crochet 10 chains the length of the strip.
Sew one chain on either side of gold chains. Sew rem 4 chains in place, one in the center of each strip.
Fold blanket in half and slip stitch cast-on and bound-off edges together.
Fringe
For each tassel use 6 strands of yarn 8in long. Place one tassel on each st or each row around sides matching colors.

Spherical lampshade

Size
To fit a round lampshade 22in diameter
Gauge
4 sts and 7 rows to 1in measured over st st
Materials
American Thread Puritan Bedspread Cotton, Art 40
23 balls
1 set of 4 No.4 double-pointed needles (10in)
Circular needle No.4 (29in)
Note. Yarn is used double throughout.

Lampshade (top section)
Using set of No.4 double-pointed needles. Cast on 70 sts. Divide on 3 needles.

Place marker thread before first st and join.
K 7 rounds.
K one more round dec 20 sts evenly. 50 sts.
1st patt round * P2, K1tbl, P2, yrn 7 times, rep from * to end of round. 10 bells.
2nd patt round * P2, K1tbl, P2, K into back of each of 7 loops to form 7 sts, rep from * to end.
3rd patt round * P2, K1tbl, P2, K5, K2 tog, rep from * to end.
4th patt round * P2, K1 tbl, P2, K4, K2 tog, rep from * to end.
5th patt round * P2, K1 tbl, P2, K3, K2 tog, rep from * to end.
6th patt round * P2, K1 tbl, P2, K2, K2 tog, rep from * to end.
7th patt round * P2, K1 tbl, P2, K1, K2 tog, rep from * to end.
8th patt round * P2, K1 tbl, P2, K2 tog, rep from * to end.
9th patt round * P1, P up 1, K1 tbl, P up 1, P1, yrn 7 times, rep from * to end. 20 bells.
Rep from 2nd – 8th patt rounds once.
Change to No.4 circular needle.
17th patt round As 9th patt round. 40 bells.
Rep 2nd – 8th patt rounds once.
25th patt round * P2, K1 tbl, P2, K1 tbl, P1, P2 tog, yrn 7 times, P2, K1 tbl, rep from * to end. 20 bells.
Work 2nd – 8th patt rows once noting that there are now 11 sts between bells.
33rd patt round As 9th patt round. 40 bells.
Rep 2nd – 8th patt rounds once.
41st patt round As 25th patt round. 20 bells.
Rep 2nd – 8th patt rounds once.
49th patt round As 9th patt round. 40 bells.
Rep 2nd – 8th patt rounds once.
57th patt round As 25th patt round. 20 bells.
Rep 2nd – 8th patt rounds once.
65th patt round As 9th patt round. 80 bells.
Rep 2nd – 8th patt rounds once.
73rd patt round * P2, K1 tbl, P2, K1 tbl, P1, P2 tog, yrn 7 times, P2, K1 tbl, P2, yrn 7 times, P2 tog, P1, K1 tbl, P2, yrn 7 times, P2 tog, K1 tbl, rep from * to end. 60 bells.
Rep 2nd – 8th rounds once.
81st patt round As 9th patt round. 80 bells.
Rep 2nd – 8th patt rounds once.
Thread sts onto a length of yarn longer than the circumference of the lampshade or bind off if preferred.
Work the bottom section in the same way.

Finishing
Pin the two sections on to the lampshade and weave or seam edges invisibly together.

Bunny pajama case

Size
10in high and 15in long without tail
Gauge
2 sts to 1in
Materials
Bernat Scandia
3 skeins
Bernat Aero Jackpin needles ½in
One 10in zipper
Scraps of black and white felt for eyes

Body
Using No.½in needles, cast on 8 sts.
1st row K.

2nd row Inc once in each of first 2 sts, K to end of row.
3rd row Inc in first st, K to end of row.
4th row K.
Rep 2nd – 4th rows twice more, then 2nd row once. K 12 rows.
23rd row K2 tog, K to end of row.
24th row K.
Rep 23rd and 24th rows twice more.
K 3 rows.
32nd row K to last st, inc.
33rd row Inc, K to end.
K 2 rows.
Rep 23rd and 24th rows twice then 23rd row once.
41st row K2 tog, K to last 2 sts, K2 tog.
42nd row K.
Rep 41st and 42nd rows 3 times more.
Bind off.
Work a second piece in the same way.

Ear
Using No.½in needles cast on 3 sts.
K 2 rows.
3rd row K to last st, inc.
K 2 rows.
6th row As 3rd row.
K 2 rows.
9th row As 3rd row.
K 8 rows.
18th row K2 tog, K to last 2 sts, K2 tog.
K 2 rows.
21st row As 18th row.
K one row.
Bind off
Make 2nd ear in the same way.

Finishing
Press all pieces on the wrong side under a damp cloth using a warm iron.
Place the two body pieces together and seam ½in from front edge leaving 1in open at back of head for ears and 10in open at bottom edge for zipper. Place ears from the right side into their spaces and secure.
Make a pompon from rem yarn for tail and sew on. Cut 2 white felt ovals 2in long and 1½in wide for eyes. Cut 2 black felt circles 1½in diameter. Sew black circle to white oval and sew in place. Cut white felt oval 2½in long and 2in wide for nose and sew in place.
Cut 2 white felt teeth 1½in deep and also some strips for whiskers Sew in place.

Hot water bottle cover

Size
11½in by 10in
Gauge
8 sts to 1in
Materials
Reynolds Gleneagles
1 skein purple
1 skein deep red
1 skein lilac
One pair No 6 needles
One No.F crochet hook
2 buttons
Note. Use yarn double throughout.

Back
Using No.6 needles and 2 strands of purple cast on 65 sts.
1st row (WS) P.

2nd row (K1, ytf, K4, sl1, K2tog, psso, K4, ytf, K1) 5 times.
Rep last 2 rows twice more
Break off yarn
leaving ends to darn in.
Attach 2 strands of deep red. Rep first and 2nd rows 3 times.
Break off yarn as before.
Attach 2 strands of lilac. Rep first and 2nd rows 3 times. Break off yarn as before.
These 18 rows form the patt and are rep throughout. Continue in patt until work measures 11½in ending with the last row of a color stripe.
Bind off purlwise.

Front
Work as given for back.

Finishing
Press pieces lightly under a damp cloth with a warm iron.
Using No.F crochet hook and 2 strands of purple work 1 row of sc around each edge of front and back.
With RS of front facing join front and back by working 1 row sc through both thicknesses from front edge down side and to within 1½in of center on lower edge. Break off yarn. Leave a 3in gap for base of bottle and attach yarn finishing lower edge and other side, then complete by working 1 row sc across top of front only making 2 button loops of ch3 each 1in in from either side. Fasten off.
Finish off ends and re-press.
Sew buttons to correspond with button loops.

Dog's sweater

Size
To fit 13½ [17¼:21¼]in chest
Length from neck to tail 11¾ [14½:17¼]in
Gauge
6 sts to 1in slightly stretched
Materials
Columbia-Minerva Wintuk Sports
2[2:2] skeins
One pair No.5 needles

Back
Using No.5 needles cast on 24 sts.
1st row (WS row) K1, *P2, K2, rep from * to last 3 sts, P2, K1.
2nd row (RS row) K3, * P2, K2, rep from * to last st, K1.
Rep 1st and 2nd rows twice more.
Next row K1, P2, inc by lifting thread before next st, rib to last 3 sts, inc by lifting thread before next st, P2, K1.
Next row K3, rib to last 3 sts, K3.
Rep last 2 rows until there are 56[72:88] sts, keeping 3 edge sts established and working inc sts into central ribs as they are made.
Work without shaping until 8¾[10¼:11¾]in from cast-on edge ending with a WS row.
Next row K2, S11, work 1, psso, rib to last 4 sts, K2 tog, K2.
Next row K1, P2, rib to last 3 sts, P2, K1.
Rep last 2 rows until 32[40:48] sts rem.
Work until 11¾[14½:17¼]in. Slip sts onto a holder.

Front
Using No.5 needles cast on 20[24:28] sts.

1st row (WS) K3, * P2, K2, rep from * to last st, K1.
2nd row (RS) K1, * P2, K2, rep from * to last 3 sts, P2, K1.
Rep 1st and 2nd rows until work measures 7¼[8¾:10¼]in from cast-on edge, ending with a WS row.

Collar
1st row With RS facing rib to last 2 sts, P2 tog, continue across sts for front from holder, K2 tog, rib to end. 50[62:74] sts.
Work in rib until collar measures 3¼[3½:4]in.
Bind off in rib.

Finishing
Sew collar seam. Continue seam below collar joining front and back for 1¼[1½:2¼]in.
Leave 3¼[3½:4]in unjoined for leg opening.
Seam remainder. Join other side of front and back in the same manner.

Initialled face cloth

Size
12in square
Gauge
7 sts to 1in
Materials
Coats & Clark's O.N.T. "Speed-Cro-Sheen"
1 ball in main color, A
1 ball in contrast color, B
One pair of No 3 needles

Face cloth
Using No 3 needles and B cast on 83 sts.
1st row K1, *P1, K1, rep from * to end.
2nd row P1, * K1, P1, rep from * to end.
Continue in rib for 2 rows more, dec 1 st at each end of both rows.
79 sts.
K 1 row Break off B leaving an end to darn in.
Attach A and P 1 row.
1st patt row P1, *K1, P1, rep from * to end.
2nd patt row K1, *P1, K1, rep from * to end.
3rd patt row As 2nd.
4th patt row As first.
These 4 rows form the patt.
Continue in patt until work measures 11½in from cast-on edge, ending with a 2nd patt row.
K 1 row.
Break off A as before.
Attach B.* P1 row.
Next row K1, * P1, K1, rep from * to end.
Work 3 rows more in rib inc 1 st at each end of next 2 rows only.
Bind off in rib. *

Side borders
Using B and with right side facing pick up and K 77 sts along side of center section. Work from * to * as for last border.
Rep along rem side.

Finishing
Finish off ends and sew corner border miters together.
Using one strand of B embroider the outline of initials in one corner. Using 2 strands of B fill in the space between outlines.
Press lightly under a damp cloth on the wrong side using a warm iron.

Ribbed square blanket

Size
About 30in by 40in or as required
Gauge
9 sts and 8 rows to 1in over patt worked on No.5 needles, unstretched
Materials
Spinnerin Wintuk Featherlon
5 skeins red, A
2 skeins pale pink, B; 2 skeins deep pink, C
No.5 knitting needles

Square
Using No.5 needles and A cast on 44 sts.
1st row K1, * K4, P2, rep from * to last st, K1.
2nd row K1, * K2, P4, rep from * to last st, K1.
Repeat first row until work measures 5in.
Bind off.
Work 23 squares more using A.
Work 12 squares more using B.
Work 12 squares more using C.

Finishing
Join squares together as shown in the diagram, alternating the direction of the rib.

See below for chart for assembling the ribbed squares.

Pompon trimmed blanket

Size
About 50in by 80in
Gauge
One square of 23 sts and 39 rows measures 5in
Materials
Reynolds Danksyarn
2 balls in each of 9 colors
No.6 knitting needles

Square
Using No.6 needles cast on 23 sts.
Work in garter st (every row knit) for 39 rows.
Bind off.

Finishing
Sew squares together on the wrong side.
Make pompons from leftover yarn and sew on corners of squares as shown in the illustration.

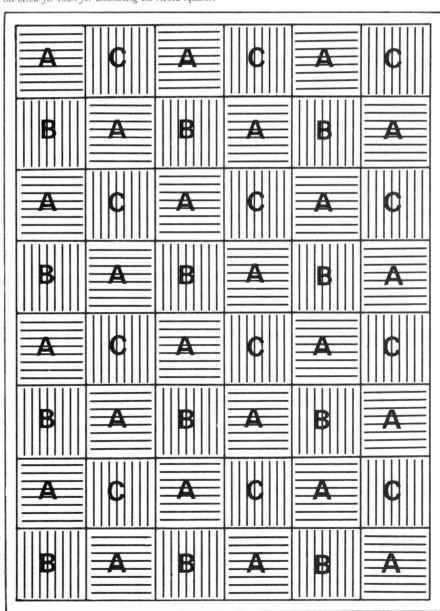

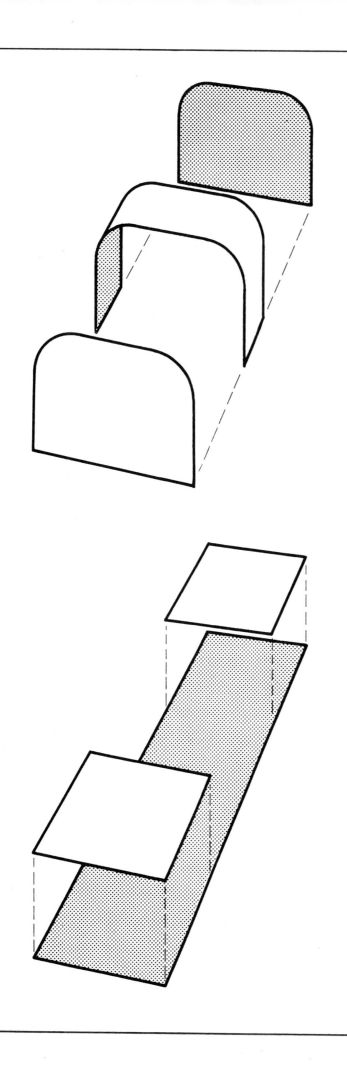

Toaster cover
and oven mitts

Size
Toaster cover: to fit a two slice toaster
Oven mitts: 30in long
Gauge
6½ sts and 8 rows to 2in measured over st st
Materials
Coats & Clark's O.N.T. "Speed-Cro-Sheen"
used double
For Toaster cover
4 balls scarlet, A
2 balls white, B
2 balls blue, C
For Oven mitts
6 balls scarlet, A
2 balls white, B
2 balls blue, C
2 pieces of padding 6½in square
For both
No.9 knitting needles
One No.J crochet hook
Note. Cotton is used 4 strands together
throughout
Toaster cover
Side pieces
Using No.9 needles and 4 strands of A cast on
33 sts K 4 rows
** 5th row K.
6th row P.
Continue in st st working patt thus:
1st patt row K1B, * 3A, 1B, rep from * to end
2nd patt row P1C, * 1B, 1A, 1B, 1C, rep
from * to end
3rd patt row K1A, * 1C, 1B, 1C, 1A, rep
from * to end
4th patt row P2A, * 1C, 3A, rep from * to
last 3 sts, 1C, 2A.
Using A K 1 row, P 1 row, K 1 row.******
8th patt row P7A, * 1B, 8A, rep from * once
more, 1B, 7A.
9th patt row K6A, * 1B, 1C, 1B, 6A, rep
from * once more, 1B, 1C, 1B, 6A.
10th patt row P5A, * 1B, 3C, 1B, 4A, rep
from * twice more, 1A.
11th patt row K4A, * 1B, 5C, 1B, 2A, rep
from * twice more, 2A.
Rep 10th, 9th and 8th rows once.
Using A K 1 row, P 1 row, K 1 row.
Rep 4th, 3rd, 2nd and first rows once.
Using A and dec one st at each end of every
row P 1 row, K 1 row, P 1 row, K 1 row.
Bind off rem sts loosely.
Work another piece in the same manner.
Center piece
Using 4 strands of A cast on 18 sts. Work in
garter st for 22in when slightly stretched.
Bind off.

Finishing
Press pieces lightly.
Using No.J crochet hook and 4 strands of B
work 1 row sc around center piece and side and
top edges on side pieces.
Pin center piece between side pieces and work
1 row sc using 4 strands of B through previous
row. Work 1 row more sc.

Oven mitts
Main part
Using No.9 needles and 4 strands of A cast on
21 sts. K 4 rows.
Work as side pieces of toaster cover from ** to
**.

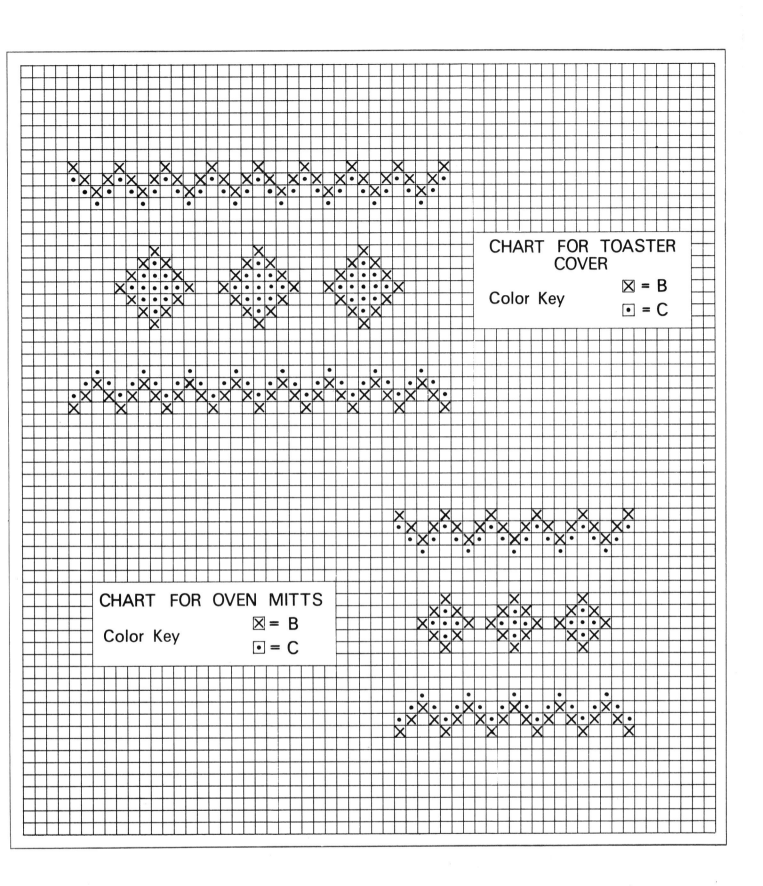

CHART FOR TOASTER COVER

Color Key

⊠ = B
⊡ = C

CHART FOR OVEN MITTS

Color Key

⊠ = B
⊡ = C

*** 8th patt row P4A, * 1B, 5A, rep from * once more, 1B, 4A.
9th patt row K3A, * 1B, 1C, 1B, 3A, rep from * once more, 1B, 1A.
10th patt row P2A, * 1B, 3C, 1B, 1A, rep from * twice more, 1A.
Rep 9th and 8th rows once.
Using A K 1 row, P 1 row, K 1 row.
Rep 4th, 3rd, 2nd and first rows once.
Continue using A only. *******

P 1 row, K 1 row, P 1 row.
Work in garter st for 25in when slightly stretched ending with a WS row.
Rep from ** to ** as for sides of toaster cover then from *** to *** as for other end.
P 1 row, K 5 rows.
Bind off knitwise.
Lining pieces
Using 4 strands of A cast on 19 sts.
Work 6in using st st. Bind off.

Finishing
Press lightly. Sew linings to WS of each end of garter st strips enclosing padding, so that they are covered by patterned section when folded back. Fold patterned sections into place. Using 4 strands of B work 1 row sc around all edges working through both thicknesses at ends.
Work 1 more round of sc.
Finish off.

72,73

Patchwork tea and coffee cozy

Size
To fit a teapot 6½in high
To fit a slender coffee pot 8in high
Gauge
5 sts and 7 rows to 1in
Materials
Reynolds Gleneagles
1 skein red
1 skein mango
1 skein gold
1 skein beige
One pair of No.6 needles
One No.F crochet hook
Note. Yarn is used double throughout.
When changing colors across rows twist colors
together to prevent holes. When changing
colors from previous row work st above to
correspond with sts on previous row, ie K the
P st and P the K st.

Tea cozy
Using No.6 needles and 2 strands of beige
cast on 44 sts.
Work from chart reading right side rows from
right to left and wrong side rows from left to
right. Bind off.
Work 2nd side in same manner.

Edging
Using No.F crochet hook and 2 strands of
beige work 1 row sc around outer edges
of each piece. Then work in sc through both
edges to join side and top leaving 3in spaces at
each side to correspond with spout and handle
and working topknot in center of top edge thus,
1sc into center sc (ch12, slip st to last sc)
3 times, then complete in sc.

Finishing
Press cozy on wrong side under a damp cloth
using a warm iron.

Coffee cozy
Work as given for tea cozy casting on 28 sts
instead of 44 sts. Work from coffee cozy chart.

*Read the charts from right to left for right side rows,
and from left to right for wrong side rows.*

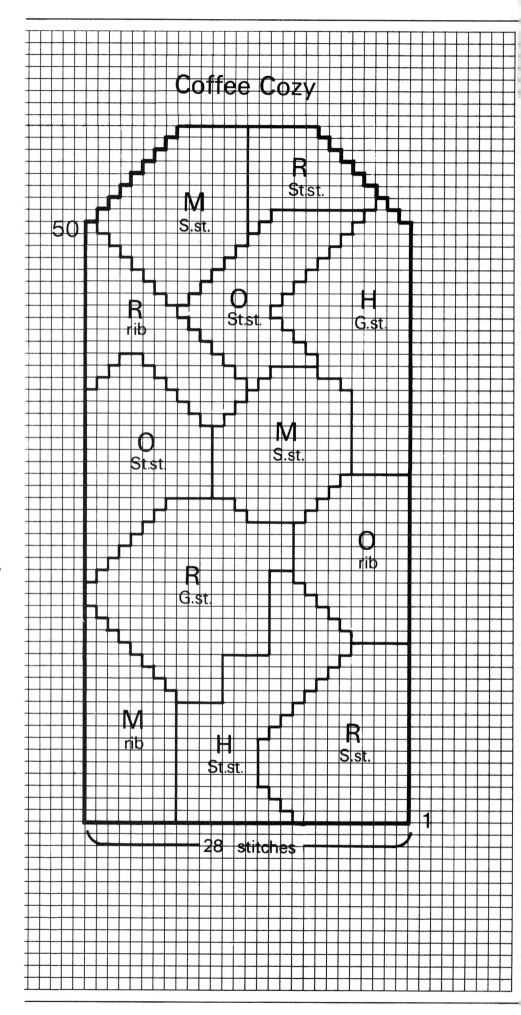

Coffee Cozy

Tea Cozy

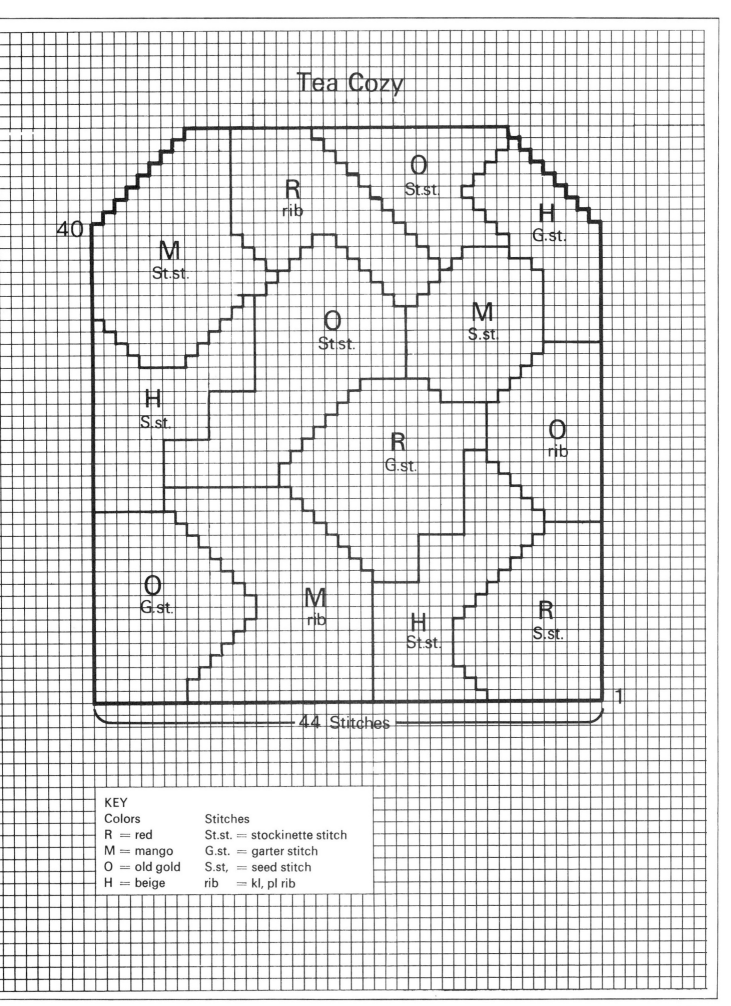

40

O
St.st.

R
rib

O
St.st.

H
G.st.

M
St.st.

M
S.st.

O
St.st.

H
S.st.

R
G.st.

O
rib

O
G.st.

M
rib

H
St.st.

R
S.st.

1

44 Stitches

KEY
Colors   Stitches
R = red   St.st. = stockinette stitch
M = mango   G.st. = garter stitch
O = old gold   S.st, = seed stitch
H = beige   rib   = kl, pl rib

74,75

Two floor pillows

Size
18in square by 3½in deep
Gauge
5½ sts to 1in
Materials
Spinnerin Wintuk Sport
Green cushion
2 skeins green, A
1 skein pink, B
1 skein blue, C
1 skein lemon, D
Blue cushion
2 skeins blue, A
1 skein pink, B
1 skein green, C
1 skein lemon, D
For both
One pair No.4 knitting needles
One foam form to fit

Green cushion
Using No.4 needles and B cast on 8 sts.
1st row K.
2nd and every other row K each st in the color in which it was worked on the previous row, keeping all threads on WS when working in more than one color.
3rd row K twice into each st.   16 sts.
5th row Keeping threads behind work on WS, *K2B, K up 1A, K2B, rep from * 3 times more.
7th row * (K1, K up 1, K1) B, (K up 1, K1, K up 1) A, (K1, K up 1, K1) B, rep from * 3 times more.
9th row * K3B, (K1, K up 1, K1, K up 1, K1) A, K3B, rep from * 3 times more.
11th row *K2B, 7A, 2B, rep from * 3 times more
13th row * K1B, (K2, K up 1, K5, K up 1, K2) A, K1B, rep from * 3 times more.
15th row Using C, K.
17th row Using C, K, inc 12 sts evenly across row.   64 sts.
19th row * K3A, (K1, K up 1, K1,) C, K3A, rep from * 7 times more.
21st row * K2A, 5C, 2A, rep from * 7 times more.
23rd row * K2A, (K3, K up 1, K2) C, K2A, rep from * 7 times more.
25th row * K3A, K4C, (K3, K up 1) A, rep from * 7 times more.
27th row * (K1, K up 1, K3) A, K2C, K5A, rep from * 7 times more.
29th row Using C, K.
31st row * (K6, K up 1) C, rep from * 15 times more.
33rd row * K3D, 9A, 2D, rep from * 7 times more.
35th row * K4D, (K4, K up 1, K3) A, K3D, rep from * 7 times more.
37th row * K5D, 6A, (K3, K up 1, K1) D, rep from * 7 times more.
39th row * K5D, (K3, K up 1, K3) A, K5D, rep from * 7 times more.
41st row * K4D, (K5, K up 1, K4) A, K4D, rep from * 7 times more.
43rd row * K3D, (K6, K up 1, K6) A, K3D, rep from * 7 times more.
45th row Using C, K.
47th row Using C, K, inc 24 sts evenly across row.   176 sts.

49th row * K2A, (K1, K up 1) C, 5A, 2C, 3A, 2C, 5A, (K1, K up 1) C, 1A, rep from * 7 times more.
51st row * K 3 times into next st B, 1A, 2C, 5A, 2C, 1A, K 4 times into next st D, 1A, 2C, 5A, 2C, 1A, rep from * 7 times more.
53rd row * (K3tog tbl, K1, K up 1) A, 2C, 5A, 2C, (K up 1, K1, K4 tog tbl, K1, K up 1) A, 2C, 5A, 2C, (K up 1, K1) A, rep from * 7 times more.
55th row * K1A, K3 times into next st B, 2A, 2C, 3A, 2C, 1A, K 4 times into next st D, 3A, K 4 times into next st D, 1A, 2C, 3A, 2C, 2A, K 3 times into next st B, rep from * 7 times more.
57th row * (K1, K3tog tbl, K2) A, 2C, 3A, 2C, (K1, K4tog tbl, K3, K4tog tbl, K1) A, 2C, 3A, 2C, (K2, K3tog tbl) A, rep from * 7 times more.
59th row * K 3 times into next st B, 2A, 2C, (K2, K up 1, K1) A, 2C, 1A, K 4 times into next st D, 2A, K 4 times into next st D, 2A, K 4 times into next st D, 1A, 2C, (K1, K up 1, K2) A, 2C, 2A, rep from * 7 times more.
61st row * (K3tog tbl, K1) A, 2C, 6A, 2C, (K4 tog tbl, K2, K4tog tbl, K2, K4 tog tbl) A, 2C, 6A, 2C, 1A, rep from * 7 times more.
63rd row * K3C, (K4, K up 1, K4) A, 2C, 2A, K 4 times into next st D, 2A, 2C, (K4, K up 1, K4) A, 2C, rep from * 7 times more.
65th row * K13A, 2C, (K1, K4tog tbl, K1) A, 2C, 12A, rep from * 7 times more.
67th row * K14A, 2C, 1A, 2C, 27A, 2C, 1A, 2C, (K13, K up 1) A, turn.
Work on these sts only to complete first quarter.
69th row (K2, K up 1, K13) A, 3C, 29A, 3C, (K13, K up 1, K2) A.
71st row (K2, K up 1, K15) A, 1C, 31A, 1C, (K15, K up 1, K2) A.
73rd row Using A, K2, K up 1, K to last 2 sts, K up 1, K2.
75th row (K2, K up 1, K9) A, K 4 times into next st D, (15A, K 4 times into next st D) 3 times, (K9, K up 1, K2) A.
77th row Using A, K2, K up 1, K to last st working clusters K4tog tbl as before, K up 1, K2.
79th row K2, K up 1, K to last 2 sts, K up 1, K2.
81st, 83rd and 85th rows As 79th row.
87th row (K2, K up 1) A, * 3C, 3A, rep from * 12 times more, 3C, (K up 1, K2) A.
89th row Using C, as 79th row.
91st row (K2, K up 1) A, * 3A, 3C, rep from * 12 times more, 3A, (K2, K up 1, K2) C.
93rd в **99th rows** Using A, as 79th row.
** K 32 rows without shaping for side, bind off or leave sts for weaving.
Attach yarn to next group of sts and work from 67th row in the same manner. Work other 2 sections to match. Do not bind off last section but work 198 rows on rem sts for under section. **

Blue cushion
Using No.4 needles and B cast on 8 sts.
1st row K.
2nd and every other row K each st in the color in which it was worked on the previous row, keeping all threads on WS when using 1 or more colors.
3rd row K twice into every st.   16 sts.
5th row * K1B, K up 1 A, K1B, rep from * 7 times more.
7th row * K1B, (K up 1, K1) A, 1B, rep from * 7 times more.
9th row * K1B, (K up 1, K2) A, 1B, rep from * 7 times more.
11th row * K1B, (K up 1, K3) A, 1B, rep from * 7 times more.
13th row * K1B, (K up 1, K4) A, 1B, rep from * 7 times more.

15th row * K1B, (K up 1, K5) A, 1B, rep from * 7 times more.
17 – 21st rows Using C, K.
23rd – 36th rows Using A, K, inc 16 sts evenly on 23rd, 27th and 31st rows.   112 sts.
37th row * K5A, 4C, 5A, rep from * 7 times more
39th row * (K2, K up 1, K1) A, 8C, (K1, K up 1, K2) A, rep from * 7 times more
41st row * K2A, 5C, (K1, K up 1, K1, K up 1) A, 5C, 2A, rep from * 7 times more
43rd row * K5C, 3A, (K1, K up 1, K1, K up 1) D, 3A, 5C, rep from * 7 times more.
45th row * 3C, 4A, 6D, 4A, 3C, rep from * 7 times more.
47th row * (K1, K up 1) C, 6A, 6D, 6A, (K up 1, K1) C, rep from * 7 times more.
49th row * (K1, K up 1, K7) A, 6D, 16A, 6D, (K7, K up 1, K1) A, turn and complete this section on these sts only.
15th row (K1, K up 1, K9) A, 4D, 18A, 4D, (K9, K up 1, K1) A.
53rd row (K2, K up 1, K10) A, 2D, 20A, 2D, (K10, K up 1, K2) A.
55th – 59th rows Using A, K2, K up 1, K to last 2 sts, K up 1, K2.
61st row (K2, K up 1) A, (5C, 7A) twice, (K2, K up 1, K2) C, (7A, 5C) twice, (K up 1, K2) A.
63rd row (K2, K up 1) A, 8C, (3A, 9C) 3 times, 3A, 8C, (K up 1, K2) A.
65th row (K2, K up 1) A, 4C, K 3 times into next st B, (11C, K 3 times into next st B) 4 times, 4C, (K up 1, K2) A.
67th row (K2, K up 1) A, 2C, (1A, 2C, 3B, 2C, 1A, 5C) 5 times, 2C, (K up 1, K2) A.
69th row (K2, K up 1) A, 1C, 2A, 2C, (K 3 times into next st B, K3 tog tbl C, K3 times into next st B, 2C, 2A, 1C, 2A, 2C) 5 times, (K up 1, K2) A.
71st row (K2, K up 1, K1) C, 3A, (2C, 3B, 1C, 3B, 2C, 5A) 5 times, 3A, (K1, K up 1, K2) C.
73rd row (K2, K up 1, K6) A, (1C, K3 tog tbl C, K 3 times into next st B, K3 tog tbl C, 1C, 7A) 5 times, (K6, K up 1, K2) A
75th row (K2, K up 1, K7) A, (2C, 3B, 2C, 7A) 5 times, (K up 1, K2) A.
77th row K1A, K 3 times into next st B, 9A, *(K1, K3 tog tbl, K1) C, 2A, (K 3 times into next st B, 1A) 3 times, 1A, rep from * 3 times more, (K1, K3 tog tbl, K1) C, 9A, K 3 times into next st B, 1A.
79th row (K1, K up 1) A, 3B, 9A, * 3C, 2A, (3B, 1A) 3 times, 1A, rep from * 3 times more, 3C, 9A, 3B, (K up 1, K1) A.
81st row K 3 times into next st B, (K1, K3tog tbl, K10) A, *1C, 3A, (K3 tog tbl, K1) A 3 times, 2A, rep rom * 3 times, 1C, (K10, K3 tog tbl, K2) A.
83rd row K3B, (K1, K up 1, K71, K up 1, K2) A.
85th row Using A, K3 tog tbl, K1, K up 1, K73, K up 1, K2.
87th, 89th and 91st rows Using A, K2, K up 1, K to last 2 sts, K up 1, K2.
93rd row (K2, K up 1) A, (3B, 3A) 13 times, 3B, (K up 1, K2) A.
95th row (K2, K up 1) A, (2B, 1A) 27 times, 2B, (K up 1, K2) A.
97th row (K2, K up 1, K2) B, (3A, 3B) 13 times, 3A, (K2, K up 1, K2) B.
99th, 101st, 103rd and 105th rows Using A, as 87th row.
Complete from ** to ** as given for green pillow, working other sections from 49th row.

Finishing
Press lightly. Seam top sections together. Seam or weave under side to edges, leaving last edge open. Slip foam pad in place. Sew or weave remaining edge.

Crash course in knitting

Everything a beginner needs to know and a comprehensive reference for the expert

Methods

There are two types of knitting—"flat" and "in the round". Flat knitting is worked backward and forward, using two needles. Round knitting is useful for items such as socks, gloves and certain types of sweaters and is worked with a set of four needles, pointed at both ends.

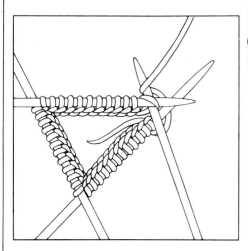

Alternatively, there are long flexible needles known as circular needles and these are used on larger items in the round to make them seamless. Circular needles can also be used for flat knitting working backward and forward in rows.

Needles

Needles are manufactured in varying sizes to combine with the different thicknesses of yarns to create different gauges. The range is wide, from very fine needles to those measuring one inch in diameter.

Gauge

This refers to the number of stitches and rows to the inch. Unless the same gauge is obtained as for the design of the original garment, then obviously it will not fit. It is always advisable before embarking on a project to work a gauge swatch of a minimum of four inches square. If there are too many stitches to the inch, change to a larger size of needle until the correct number is obtained.

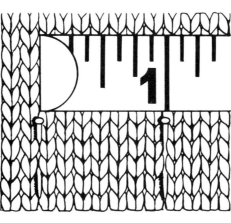

Conversely, if too few stitches are being made, adjust to a smaller needle until the correct gauge is acquired. Even half a stitch too many or too few, although seemingly little, amounts to nine stitches too many or too few on the back of a thirty-four inch sweater. This would mean the completed garment would be two inches too large or too small.

Substituting yarns

Each design has been worked out for the knitting yarn which is stated, but if you wish to substitute another, do so only if you are absolutely sure that the same gauge can be obtained. Not even two different sports yarns will knit to exactly the same gauge and the yardage on the different makes of the yarns will mean that you will need a different quantity.

Casting on

There are several methods of casting on, each with its own appropriate use. The following are the most often used.

Thumb method. This is worked using only one needle. It is an excellent way to begin most garments since it gives an elastic, hard-wearing edge. Make a slip loop in the yarn about three feet from the end. This length varies with the number of stitches required but one yard will cast on about one hundred stitches. Alternatively, take a guide from the width of the piece of knitting multiplied by three.

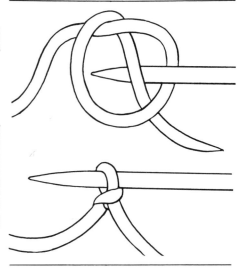

Slip the loop onto the needle, which should be held in the right hand.

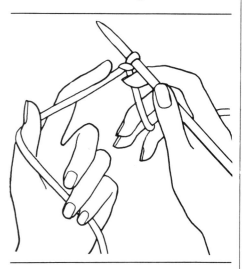

Working with the short length of yarn in the left hand, pass this around the left thumb.

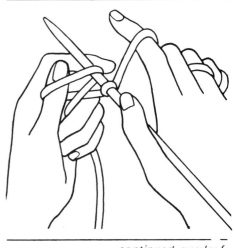

continued overleaf

Crash course in knitting

continued from previous page

Insert the point of the needle under the loop on the thumb and hook forward the long end of the yarn from the ball.

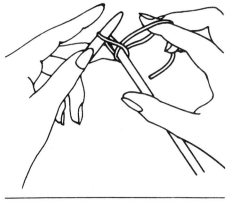

Wind the yarn under and over the needle and draw through the loop, leaving stitch on the needle.

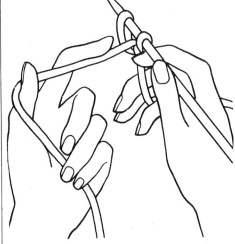

Tighten stitch on needle, noting that yarn is around the thumb ready for the next stitch.

Repeat actions 3 to 5 for the required number of stitches.

Two needle method. This method, sometimes known as the English cable version, is necessary when extra stitches are required during the knitting itself, for instance for a buttonhole or pocket although it can also be used at the beginning of a garment.

Make a slip loop in the yarn three inches from the end. It is not necessary to estimate the yarn required as the stitches are worked from the ball yarn. Slip the loop onto the left-hand knitting needle.

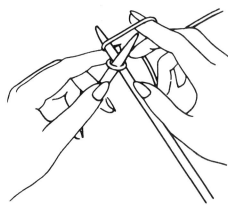

Insert right-hand needle into the loop holding yarn in the right hand and wind the yarn under and over the needle.

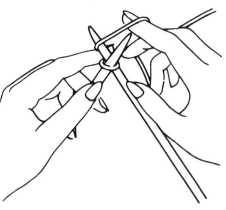

Draw the new loop through the first loop on left-hand needle thus forming a second loop. Pass newly made loop onto the left-hand needle.

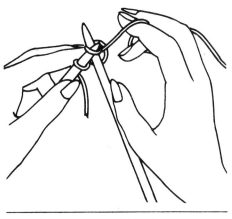

Place point of right-hand needle between two loops on the left-hand needle and wind yarn under and over the right-hand needle point and draw this new loop through between the two stitches on the left-hand needle. Slip this loop onto the left-hand needle.

Repeat action 3 between the last two stitches on the left-hand needle until the required number of stitches have been cast on.

Invisible method. This gives the flat hemmed effect of a machine knitted garment. It is a flexible, strong finish which can hold ribbon or elastic and is useful for designs which need casings.

Using a contrast yarn which is later removed, and the Thumb method, cast on half the number of stitches required, plus one. Now using the correct yarn, begin the ribbing.

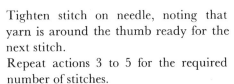

1st row K1, *ytf, K1, rep from * to end.
2nd row K1, *ytf, sl 1, ytb, K1, rep from * to end.
3rd row Sl 1, *ytb, K1, ytf, sl 1, rep from * to end.

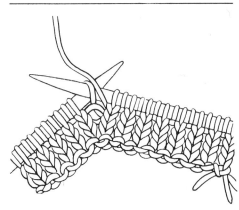

Repeat second and third rows once more.
6th row K1, *P1, K1, rep from * to end.
7th row P1, *K1, P1, rep from * to end.

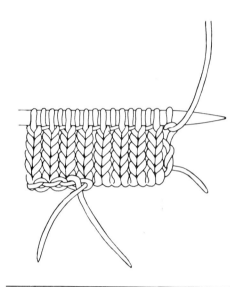

Continue in rib for the required depth. Rip contrasting yarn. The ribs should appear to run right around the edge.

Knit stitch

Take the needle with the cast-on stitches in the left hand, the other needle in the right hand. Insert the right-hand needle point through the first stitch on the left-hand needle from front to back.

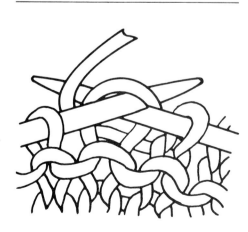

Keeping the yarn behind the needles, pass the yarn around the point of the right-hand needle so that it forms a loop.

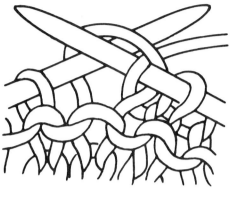

Draw this loop through the stitch on the left-hand needle, so forming a new loop on the right-hand needle.

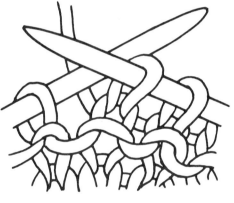

Allow the stitch on the left-hand needle to slip off.

Repeat this action until a loop has been drawn through each stitch on the left-hand needle and placed on the right-hand needle.

This completes one row. To work the next row, change the needle holding the stitches to the left hand and the free needle to the right hand. Repeat the same process as for the first row.

Purl stitch

Take the needle with the cast-on stitches in the left hand, the other needle in the right hand. Insert the right-hand needle point through the first stitch on the left-hand needle from back to front.

Keeping the yarn at the front of the needles, pass the yarn around the point of the right-hand needle to form a loop.

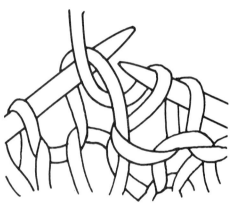

Draw this loop through the stitch on the left-hand needle, thus forming a new loop on the right-hand needle.

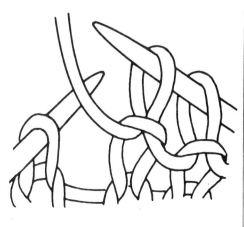

continued overleaf

Crash course in knitting

continued from previous page

Allow the stitch on the left-hand needle to slip off.

Repeat this action with each stitch along the row until all the stitches on the left-hand needle have been passed over to the right-hand needle. This completes one row. To work the next row, change the needle holding the stitches to the left hand and the free needle to the right hand. Repeat the process as for the first row.

Lifting dropped stitches

On stockinette stitch, insert a crochet hook into the dropped stitch with the knit side of the work facing. Lift the first thread above the stitch onto the hook tip and hold it in the hook curve as you slowly draw the hook back until the first stitch slips off the tip, leaving the lifted thread as the new stitch. Repeat this until all the threads have been lifted, then return the stitch to the needle.

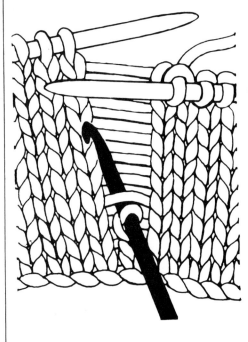

If the purl side is the right side, lift the stitch on the wrong or knit side.

Binding off

To bind off on a knit row, knit into each of the first two stitches. Then, *with the left-hand needle point, lift the first stitch over the second stitch, leaving only one stitch on the right-hand needle.

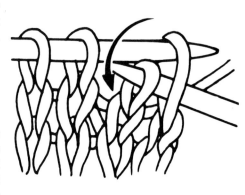

Knit the next stitch, repeat from * until one stitch remains. Cut the yarn and draw it through the last stitch, pulling tight.

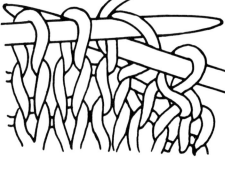

On a purl row, each stitch is purled before being bound off. To bind off on a patterned or ribbed row, each stitch is lifted over the next in the same way having first knitted the stitches as in the patterning.

Garter stitch

This consists of working every row in knit stitches. Because the wrong side of a knit row forms purl stitches, this gives a ridge of purl stitches on every second row on both sides of the work.

Stockinette stitch

By working a knit row alternately with a purl row, the ridges of the purl stitches form on the same side of the work and the right side gives a smooth fabric.

Ribbing

To form a ribbed pattern both knit and purl stitches are combined on the same row. This can be done by simple alternating of one knit, one purl stitch, or two knit, two purl stitches, although it can be worked in more unusual combinations repeated systematically. On the next row, the knit stitches become purl stitches and the purl stitches knit stitches.

The slipped stitch

The slipped stitch is so called because it is transferred from the left-hand needle to the right-hand needle without being worked. The yarn is carried either behind or in front of the stitch. It is used in several different ways—decreasing, making a fold for a pleat or facing, to form lacy patterns and to form a texture on the surface of the knitting.

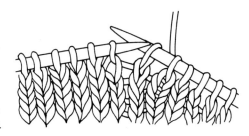

Slip stitch knitwise on a knit row.
Hold the yarn behind the work as if to knit the stitch. Insert the right-hand needle point into the stitch from front to back, as in the knit stitch, and slip it onto the right-hand needle.

Slip stitch purlwise on a knit row.
Hold the yarn behind the work as if to knit the stitch. Insert the right-hand needle point into the stitch from back to front, as in a purl stitch, and slip it onto the right-hand needle.

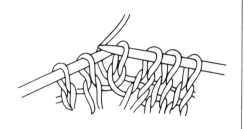

Instead, place the point of the right-hand needle into the back of the stitch and knit or purl into the stitch again. Slip both these stitches onto the right-hand needle, thus making two stitches out of one.

To increase between stitches on knit work. Using the right-hand needle, pick up the yarn which lies between the stitch just worked and the next one, and place it on the left-hand needle. Knit into the back of this loop. This twists and tightens the loops so that no hole is formed. Slip the loop off the left-hand needle.

To increase between stitches on purl work. Pick the loop up and purl into it from the back.

Multiple increase at the beginning of a row. Cast on the number of stitches required by the two needle method and work across the entire row in the usual manner.

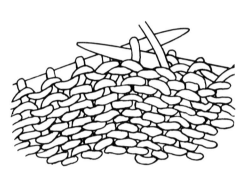

To increase invisibly. Insert the right-hand needle into the front of the stitch below that on the left-hand needle and knit a new stitch. If the increase is on purl work then purl the new stitch. The next stitch on the row being worked is then knitted or purled.

Slip stitch purlwise on a purl row.
Hold the yarn at the front of the work as if to purl the stitch. Insert the right-hand needle point from back to front as if to form a purl stitch, and slip it onto the right-hand needle.

It is important to remember that when decreasing by slipping a stitch on a knit row, the stitch must be slipped knitwise, otherwise it will become crossed. On a purl row, the stitch must be slipped purlwise. However, if the slipped stitch does not form a decrease, it must be slipped purlwise on a knit row to prevent it being crossed when purled on the following row.

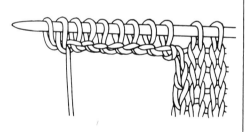

Multiple increase at the end of a row.
Reverse the work and cast on.

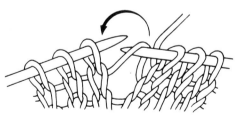

Increasing

The shape of the work is determined by increasing or decreasing. The simplest way is to knit twice into the same stitch. Knit or purl the stitch in the usual way but do not slip the stitch off the needle.

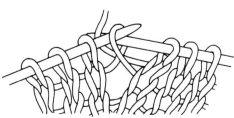

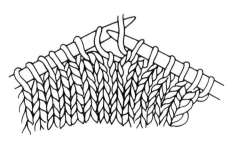

continued overleaf

Crash course in knitting

continued from previous page

Increasing between two knit stitches.
Bring the yarn forward as if to purl, then take it back over the right-hand needle ready to knit the next stitch.

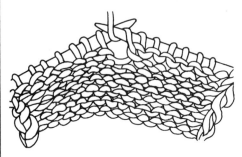

Increasing between two purl stitches.
A similar method can be used to the one previously given by taking the yarn over and around the needle before purling the next stitch.

To make a stitch between a purl and a knit stitch. This is particularly useful on ribbed work. The yarn is already in position to the front and the next stitch is knitted in the usual way, the yarn taken over the needle.

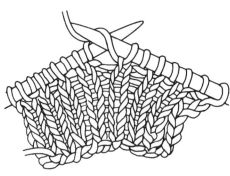

To make a stitch between a knit and a purl stitch. Bring the yarn forward and once around the needle before purling the next stitch.

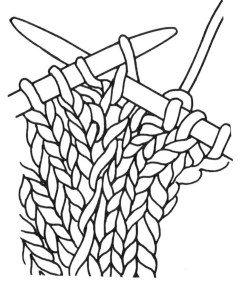

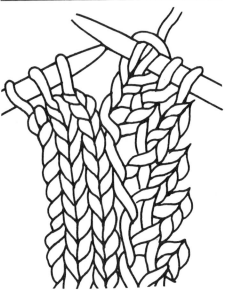

Decreasing
The simplest method of decreasing is to knit or purl two stitches together. This is sometimes worked into the back of the stitches.

Another method of decreasing is to slip one stitch, knit the next one and then slip the slipped stitch off the needle over the knitted one.

Multiple decreases. These are worked by binding off, maintaining the continuity of the pattern by knitting knit stitches and purling purl stitches before slipping one over the other.

Working with several colors

Stranding. The color that is not in use is taken across the back of the work while the color in use is being worked. It is important not to pull the yarn too tight or the work will pucker and there should be sufficient elasticity when the garment is worn. However, there should not be so much slackness that loops form.

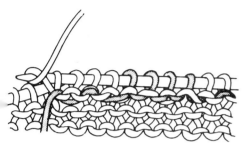

Weaving. This method takes more care but it is worth it for the professional finish it gives, especially if a color is out of use across a fairly large number of stitches. The principle is to weave the color not in use under the color being used. This is done by taking the color in use under the out-of-work strand before working the next stitch.

Marker threads

Sometimes it is necessary to mark a particular point in the work as a visual guide later. A short length of contrasting yarn is threaded through the stitch and tied in place so that it does not accidentally come out. Once it has served its purpose, simply pull it out.

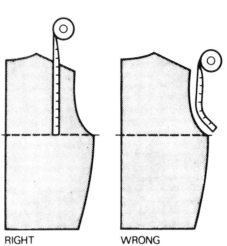

RIGHT   WRONG

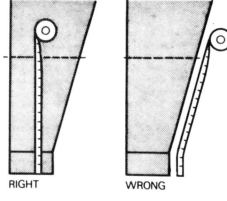

RIGHT   WRONG

Measuring

For accuracy, always lay knitting on a flat surface. Always use a rigid ruler and not a tape measure. Never measure around curves but measure, for example, the depth of an armhole on a straight line. In the same way, a sleeve should be measured up the center of the work and not along the shaped edge.

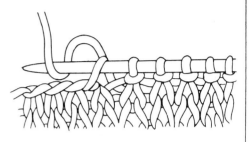

Picking up the stitches

As a general rule, when picking up stitches along a side edge, one stitch should be picked up for every two rows. However, whether the stitches are being picked up along the ends of the rows or along a bound-off edge, it will save time and aggravation to divide the length into eight by marking with pins. Spacing the number of stitches evenly then can be adjusted at this stage to prevent them having to be unraveled later. Insert the needle into the fabric edge, wrap the yarn around the needle and draw the loop through. This can be done with a crochet hook and then transferred to the knitting needle.

Finishing

The finishing of a garment is just as important as the working of it. First check whether the yarn can be pressed or not. Many man-made fibers stretch to an incredible degree and lose their texture when pressed.

Run in all ends of yarn securely. Place an ironing pad and pin evenly around the ments against those given in the directions once the pieces are pinned out, and stretch the knitting. Check the measurements against those given in the instructions once the pieces are pinned out and adjust if necessary.

For pressing, dip a piece of clean cotton cloth into warm water, and, when damp, place over the top of the work, but not over any ribbing. This has an elasticity which would be lost with pressing. With a warm iron press evenly but not heavily on the surface by pressing the iron down and lifting it up without moving along the surface.

continued overleaf

Crash course in knitting

continued from previous page

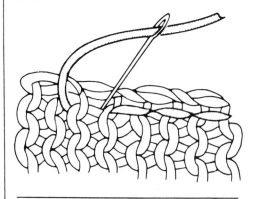

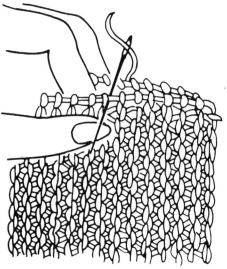

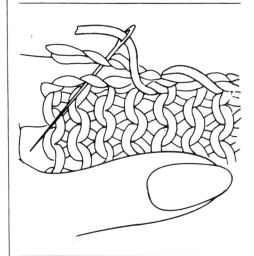

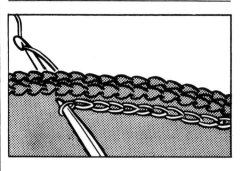

alt	alternate
beg	beginning
cm	centimetre
dec	decrease
grm(s)	gramme(s)
g st	garter stitch
in	inch(es)
inc	increase
K	knit
KB	knit into back of stitch
M1K	make one knitwise
M1P	make one purlwise
No.	number
P	purl
patt	pattern
PB	purl into back of stitch
psso	pass slip stitch over
rem	remaining
rep	repeat
RS	right side
sl 1	slip one knitwise
sl 1P	slip one purlwise
st(s)	stitch(es)
st st	stocking stitch
tbl	through back of loop(s)
tog	together
WS	wrong side
ytf	yarn to front
ytb	yarn to back
yon	yarn over needle
yrn	yarn around needle

Sew seams with a darning needle using either a back stitch seam or over-casting stitches. Alternatively, work a crocheted slip stitch along the seam line. For a flat seam, such as on ribbing, pass the threaded needle through the edge stitch on the right-hand side directly across to the edge stitch on the left-hand side and pull the yarn through. Turn the needle and work through the next stitch on the left-hand side directly across to the edge stitch on the right-hand side, again pulling the yarn through. Continue in this way.

An asterisk (*) shown in a pattern row denotes that the stitches shown after this sign must be repeated from that point. Square brackets [] denote instructions for larger sizes in the pattern. Round brackets denote that this section of the pattern is to be worked for all sizes.